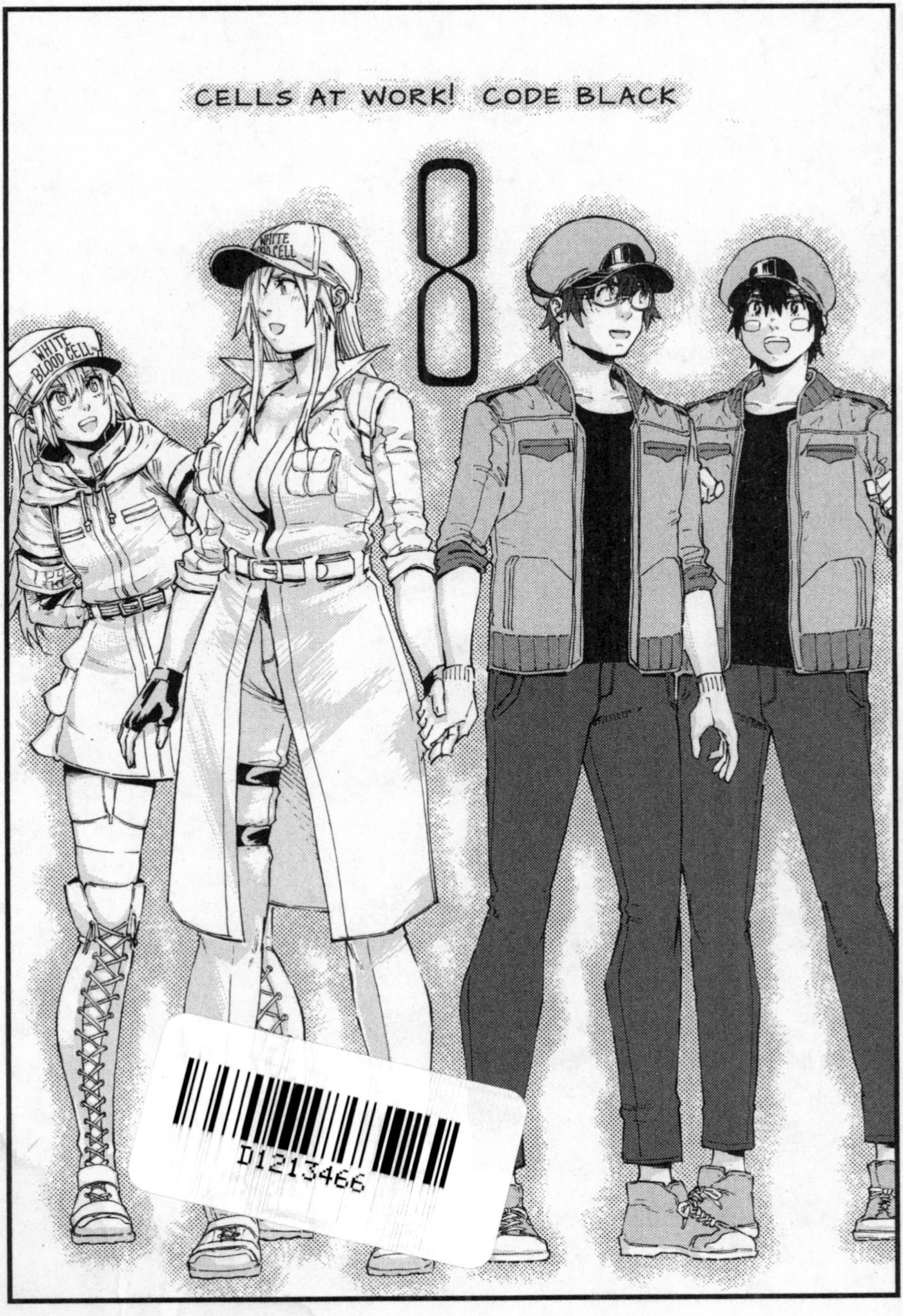
CELLS AT WORK! CODE BLACK
8
WHITE BLOOD CELL
WHITE BLOOD CELL

# Table of Contents

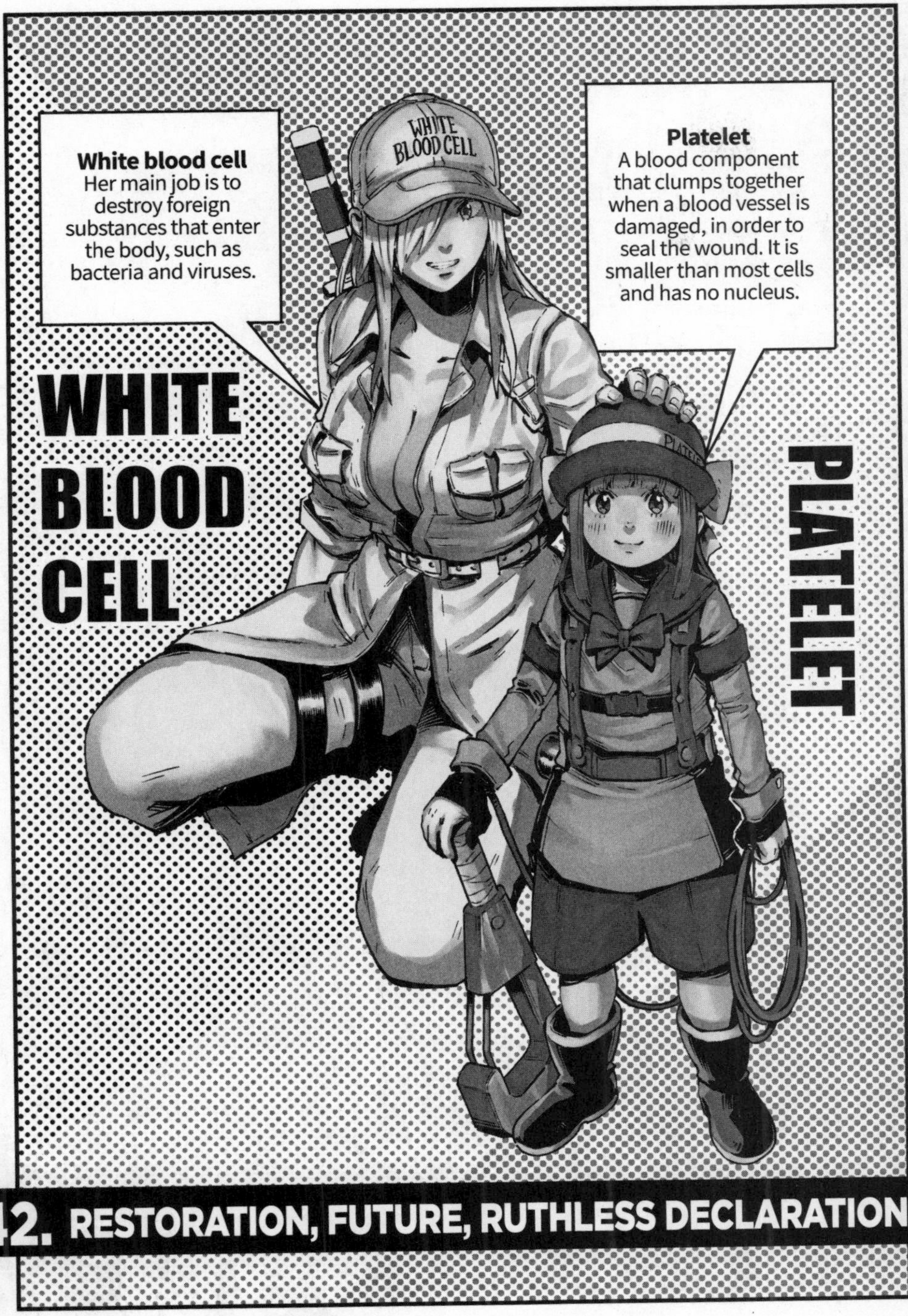
Platelet
A blood component that clumps together when a blood vessel is damaged, in order to seal the wound. It is smaller than most cells and has no nucleus.
PLATELET
WHITE BLOOD CELL
White blood cell
Her main job is to destroy foreign substances that enter the body, such as bacteria and viruses.
WHITE BLOOD CELL
42. RESTORATION, FUTURE, RUTHLESS DECLARATION

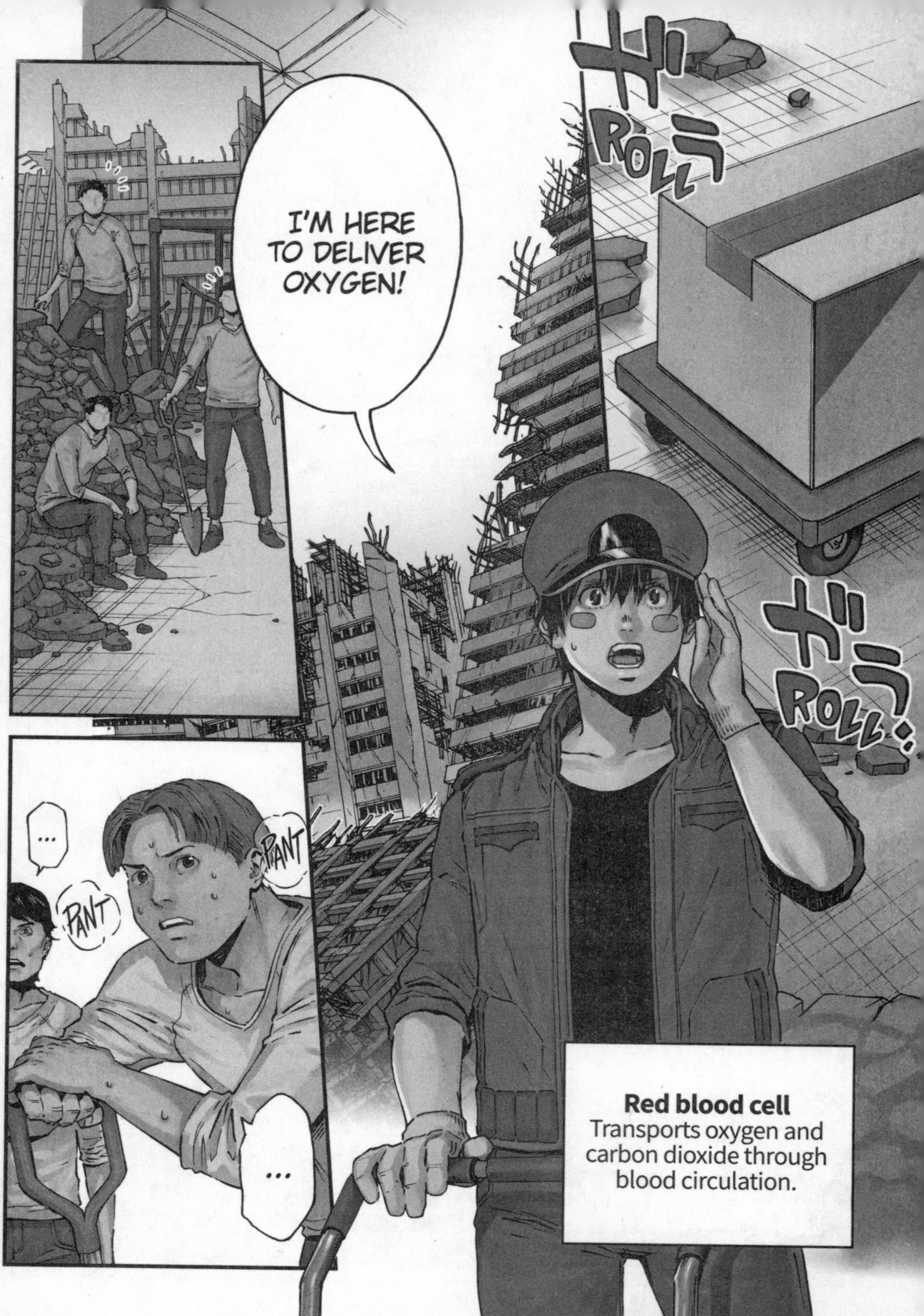
ROLL
I'M HERE TO DELIVER OXYGEN!
ROLL
Red blood cell
Transports oxygen and carbon dioxide through blood circulation.
PANT
...
PANT
...

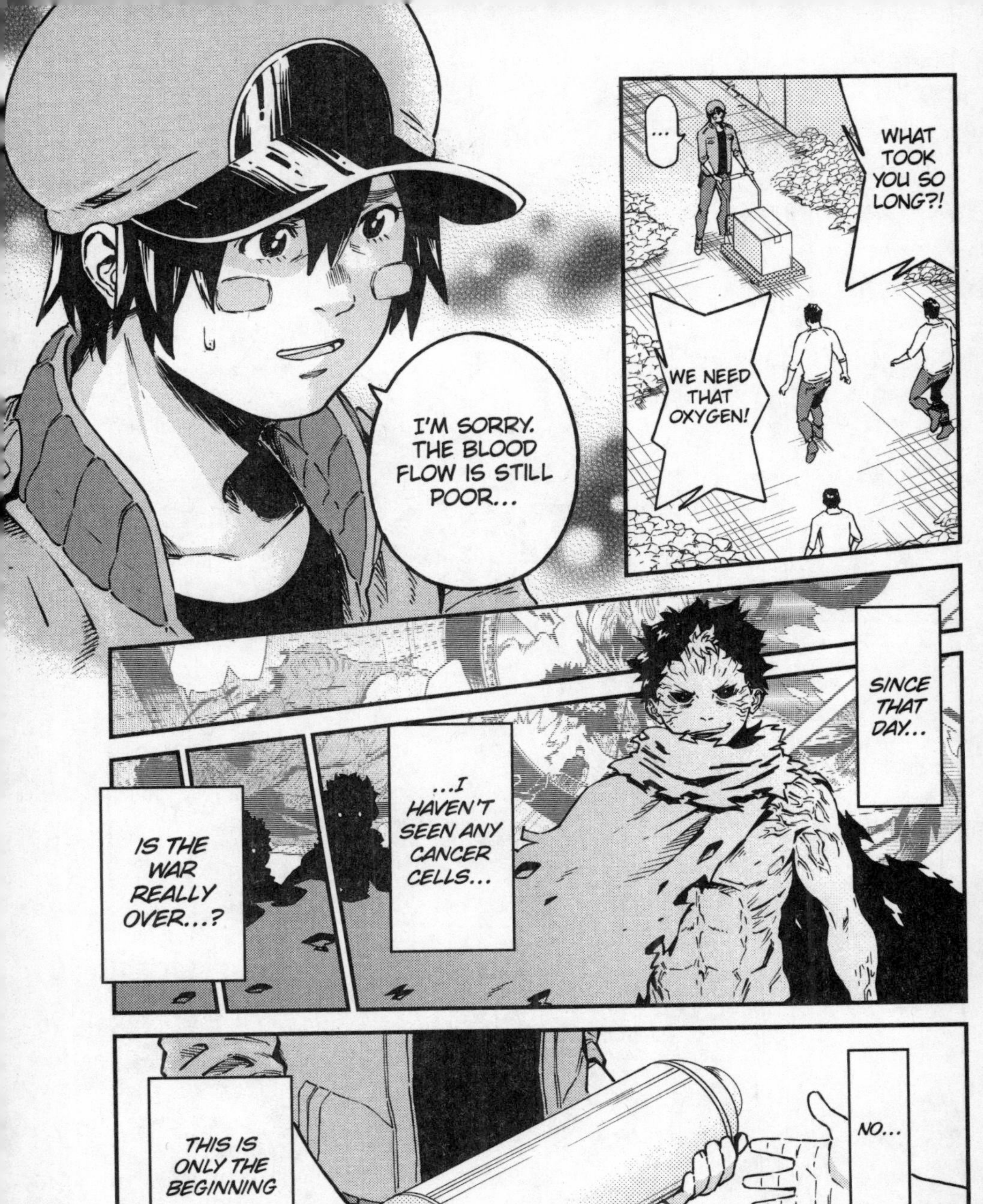
WHAT TOOK YOU SO LONG?!
...
WE NEED THAT OXYGEN!
I'M SORRY. THE BLOOD FLOW IS STILL POOR...
SINCE THAT DAY...
...I HAVEN'T SEEN ANY CANCER CELLS...
IS THE WAR REALLY OVER...?
NO...
THIS IS ONLY THE BEGINNING ...

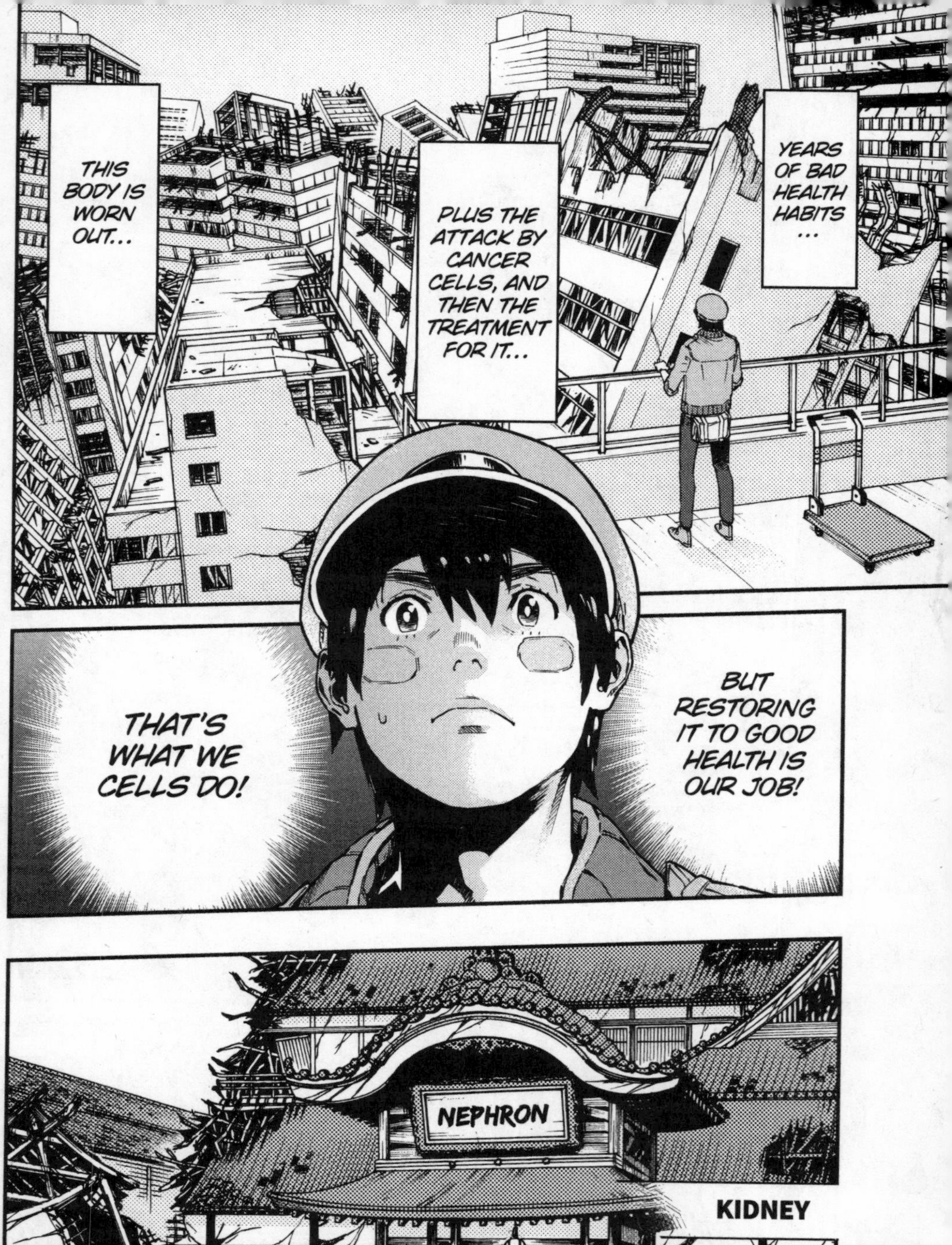
YEARS OF BAD HEALTH HABITS...
PLUS THE ATTACK BY CANCER CELLS, AND THEN THE TREATMENT FOR IT...
THIS BODY IS WORN OUT...
BUT RESTORING IT TO GOOD HEALTH IS OUR JOB!
THAT'S WHAT WE CELLS DO!
NEPHRON
KIDNEY

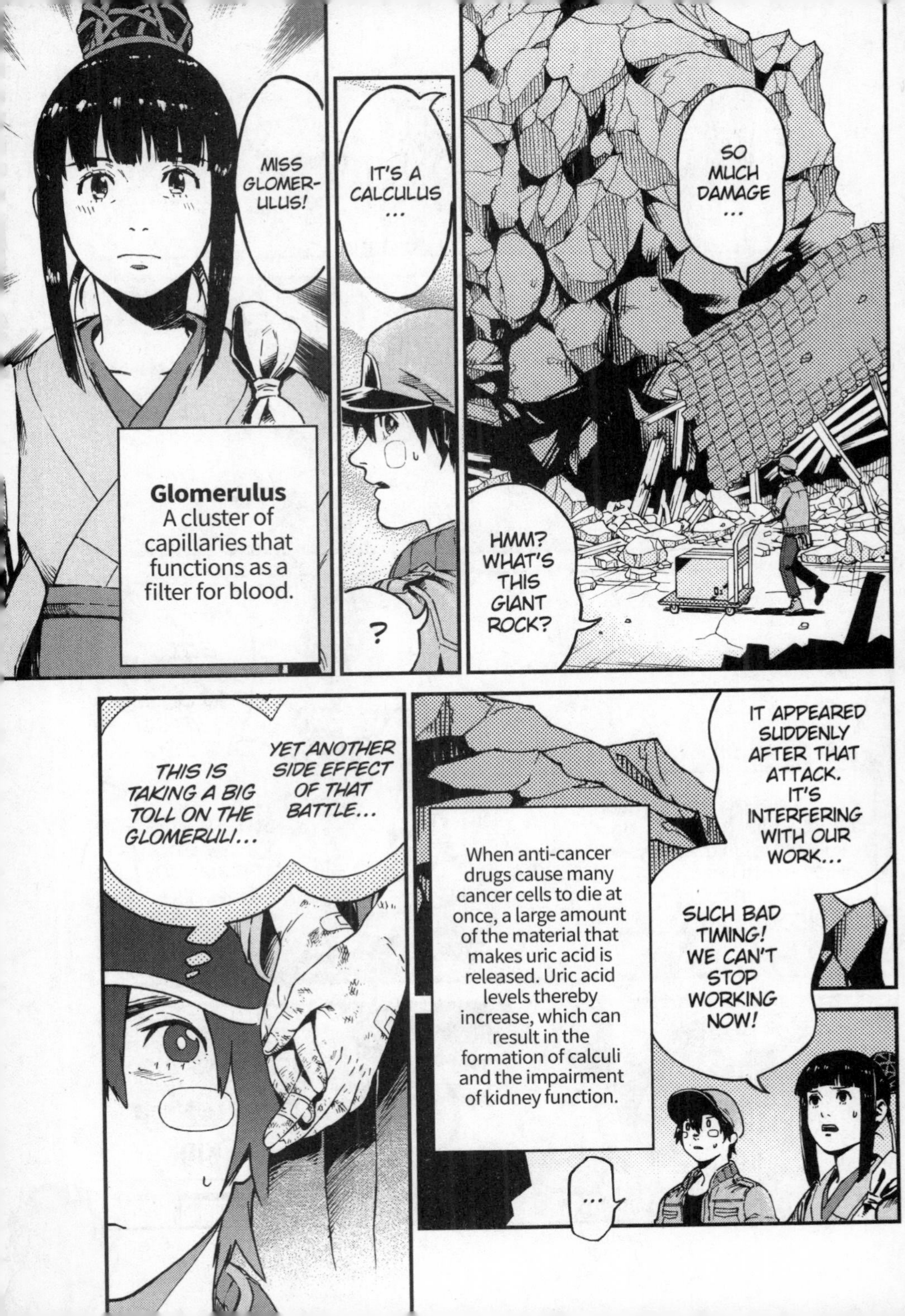
SO MUCH DAMAGE ...
HMM? WHAT'S THIS GIANT ROCK?
IT'S A CALCULUS ...
?
MISS GLOMER-ULUS!
Glomerulus
A cluster of capillaries that functions as a filter for blood.
IT APPEARED SUDDENLY AFTER THAT ATTACK. IT'S INTERFERING WITH OUR WORK...
SUCH BAD TIMING! WE CAN'T STOP WORKING NOW!
When anti-cancer drugs cause many cancer cells to die at once, a large amount of the material that makes uric acid is released. Uric acid levels thereby increase, which can result in the formation of calculi and the impairment of kidney function.
...
YET ANOTHER SIDE EFFECT OF THAT BATTLE...
THIS IS TAKING A BIG TOLL ON THE GLOMERULI...

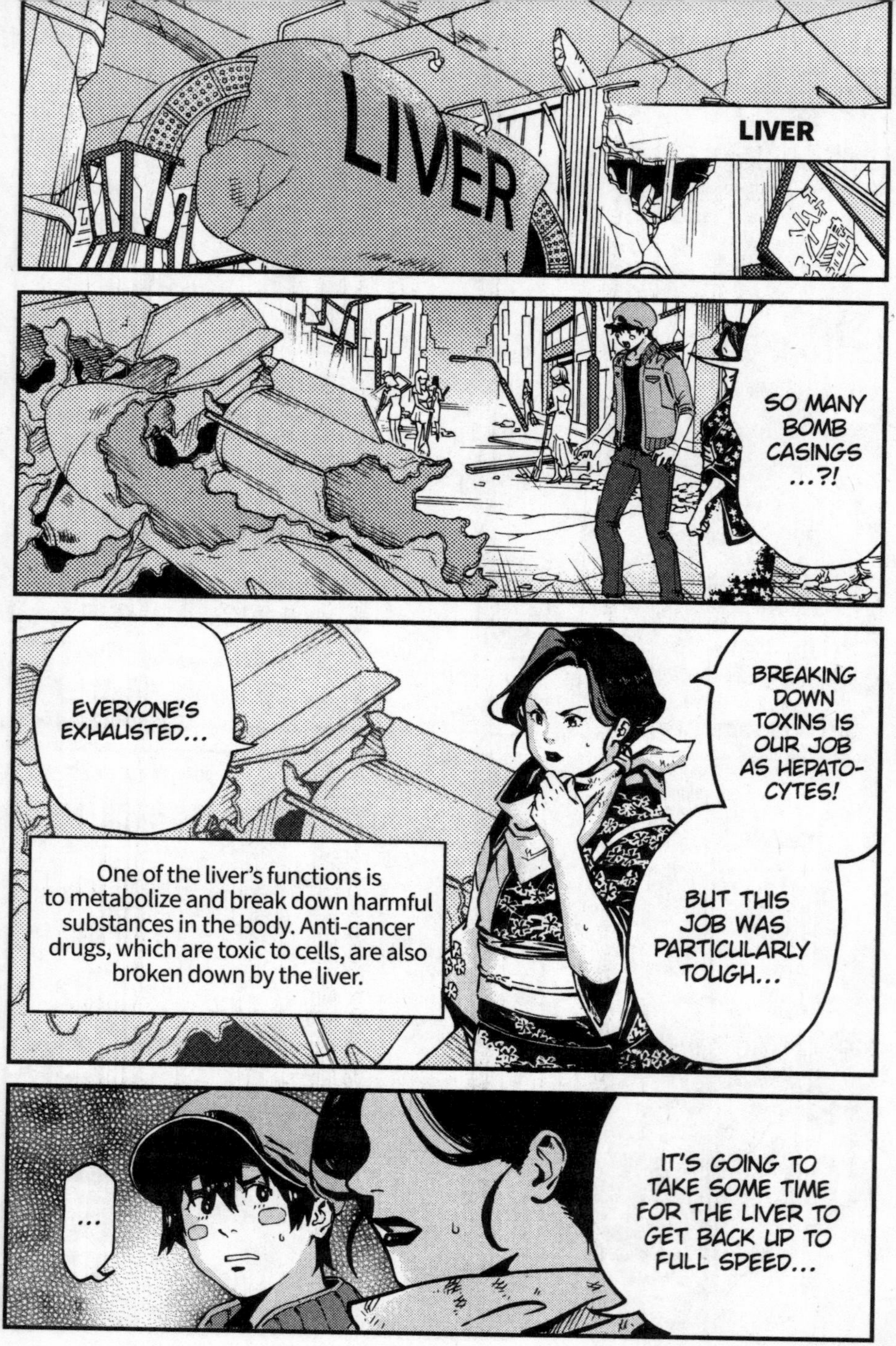
LIVER
LIVER
SO MANY BOMB CASINGS ...?!
BREAKING DOWN TOXINS IS OUR JOB AS HEPATO-CYTES!
EVERYONE'S EXHAUSTED...
BUT THIS JOB WAS PARTICULARLY TOUGH...
One of the liver's functions is to metabolize and break down harmful substances in the body. Anti-cancer drugs, which are toxic to cells, are also broken down by the liver.
IT'S GOING TO TAKE SOME TIME FOR THE LIVER TO GET BACK UP TO FULL SPEED...
...

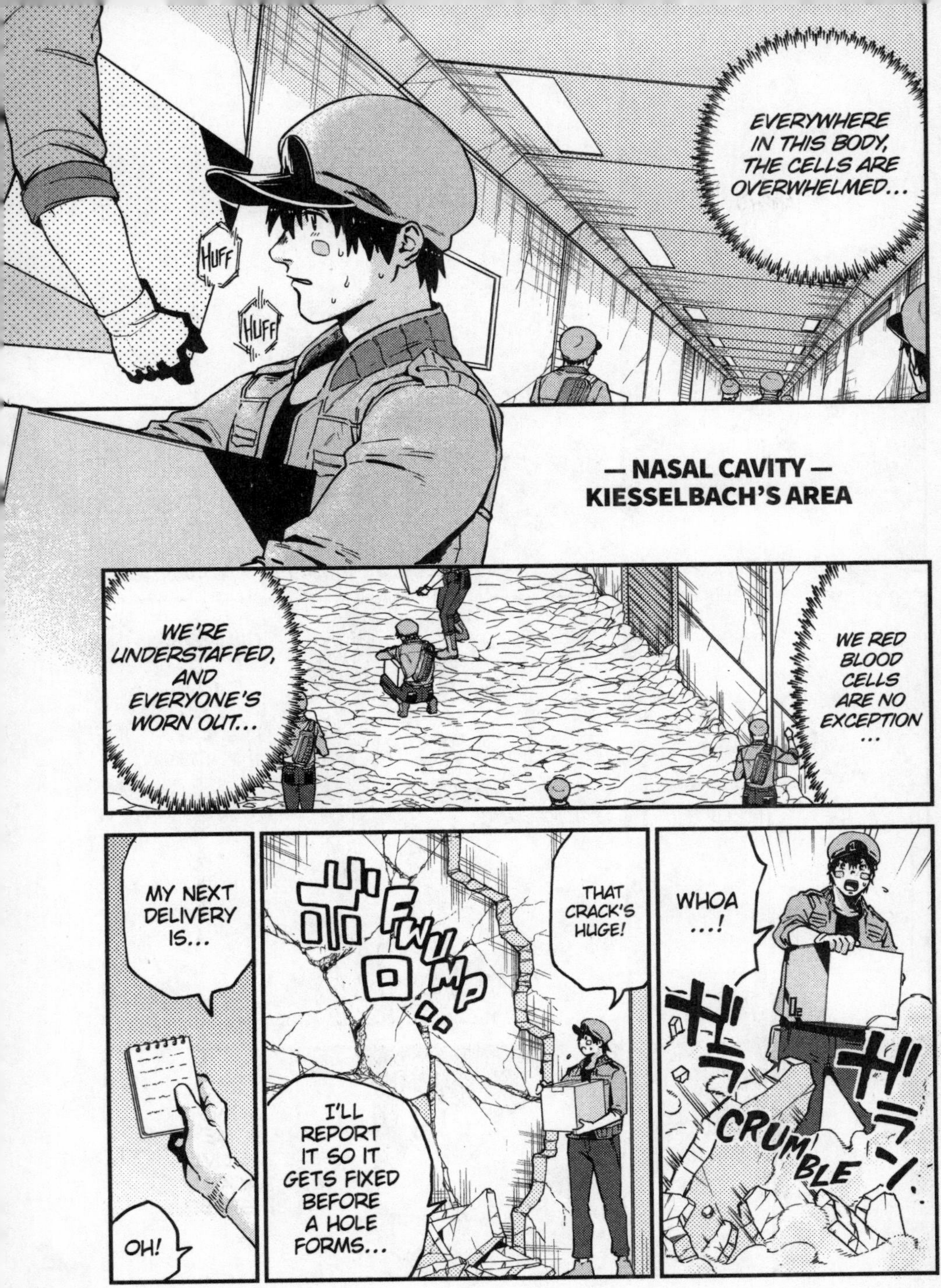
EVERYWHERE IN THIS BODY, THE CELLS ARE OVERWHELMED…
HUFF
HUFF
— NASAL CAVITY —
KIESSELBACH'S AREA
WE RED BLOOD CELLS ARE NO EXCEPTION …
WE'RE UNDERSTAFFED, AND EVERYONE'S WORN OUT…
WHOA …!
CRUMBLE
THAT CRACK'S HUGE!
FWUMP
I'LL REPORT IT SO IT GETS FIXED BEFORE A HOLE FORMS…
MY NEXT DELIVERY IS…
OH!

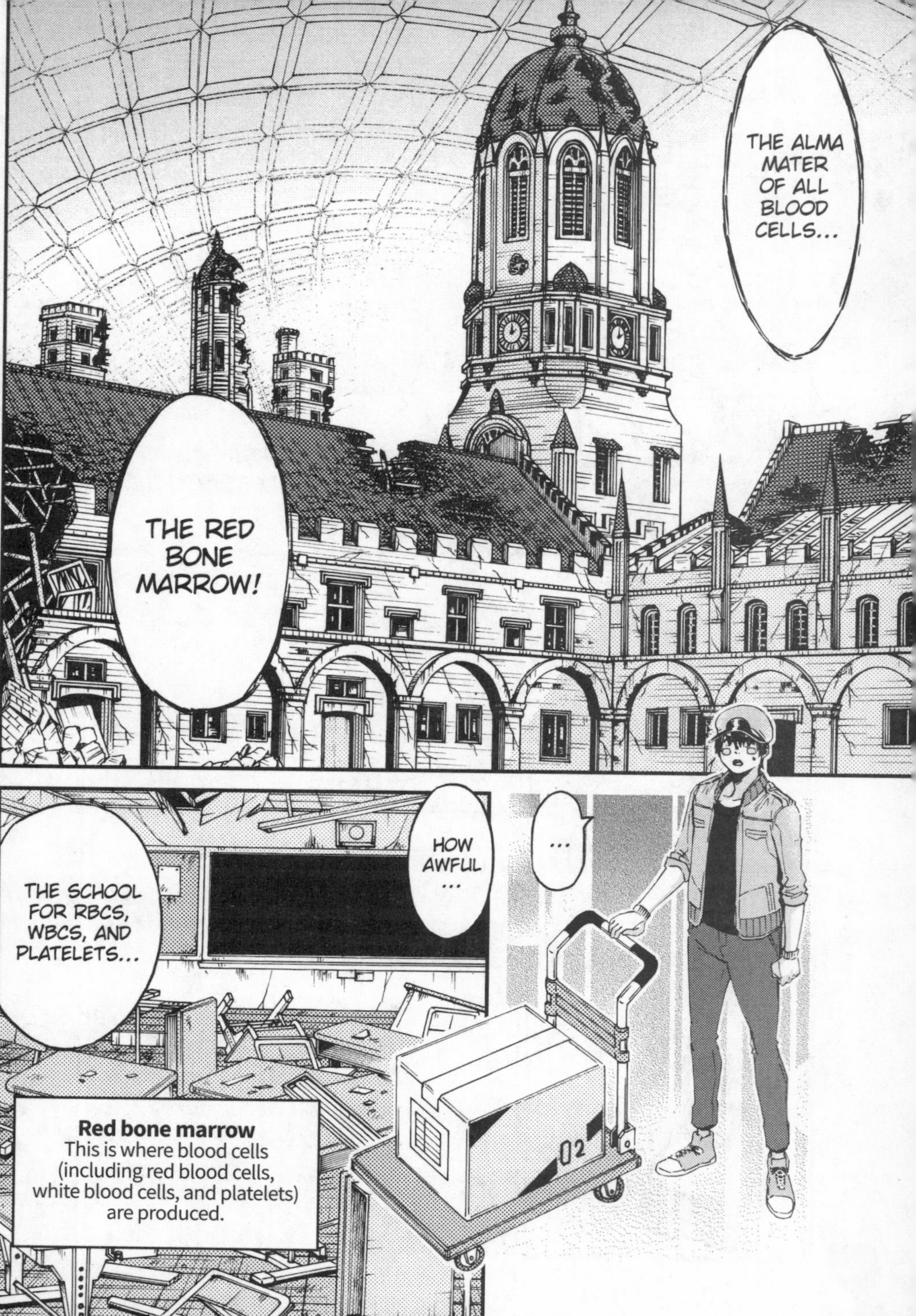
THE ALMA MATER OF ALL BLOOD CELLS...
THE RED BONE MARROW!
...
HOW AWFUL ...
THE SCHOOL FOR RBCS, WBCS, AND PLATELETS...
Red bone marrow
This is where blood cells (including red blood cells, white blood cells, and platelets) are produced.

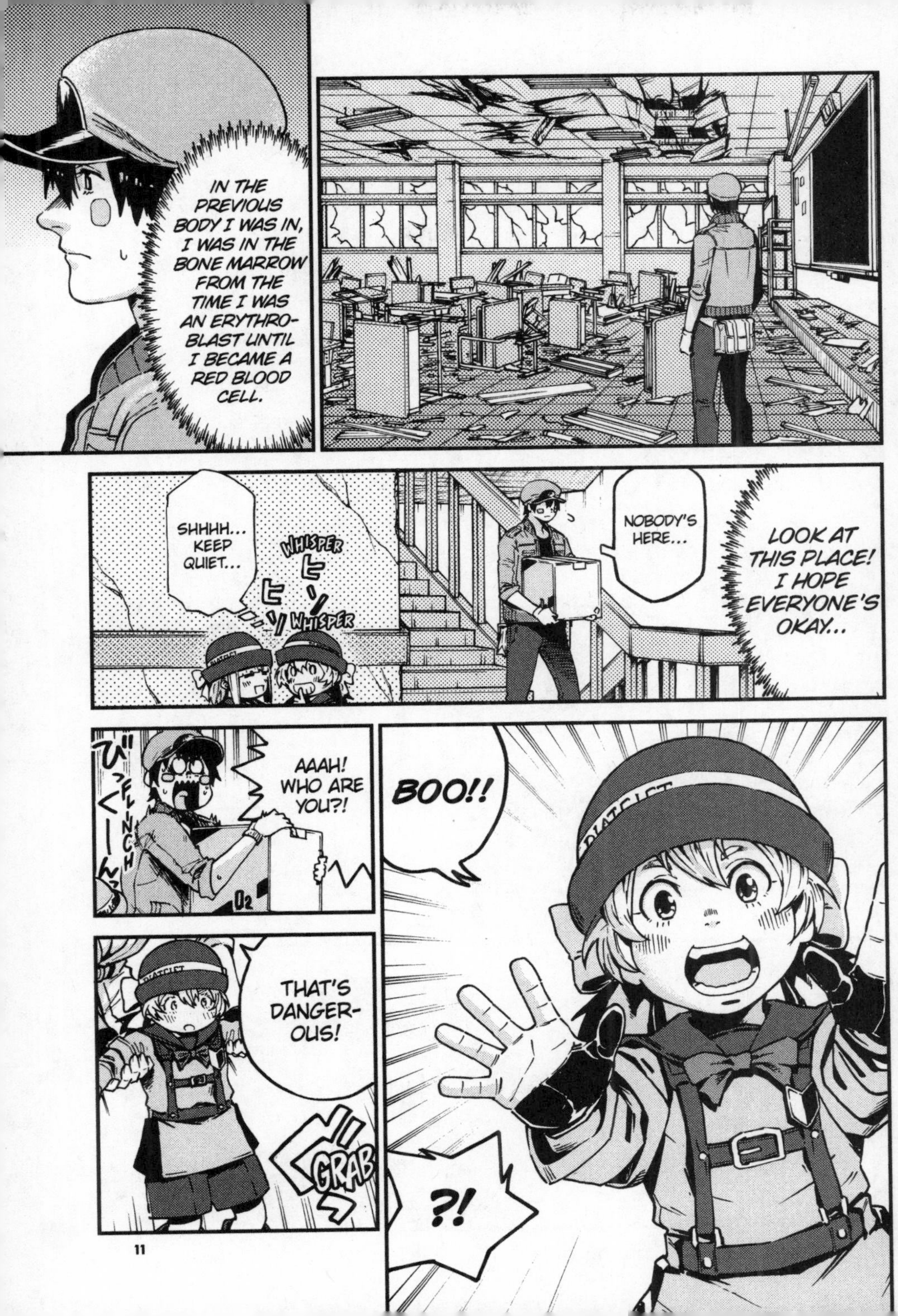
IN THE PREVIOUS BODY I WAS IN, I WAS IN THE BONE MARROW FROM THE TIME I WAS AN ERYTHRO-BLAST UNTIL I BECAME A RED BLOOD CELL.
LOOK AT THIS PLACE! I HOPE EVERYONE'S OKAY...
NOBODY'S HERE...
SHHHH... KEEP QUIET...
WHISPER
WHISPER
BOO!!
?!
AAAH! WHO ARE YOU?!
FLINCH
$O_2$
THAT'S DANGER-OUS!
GRAB

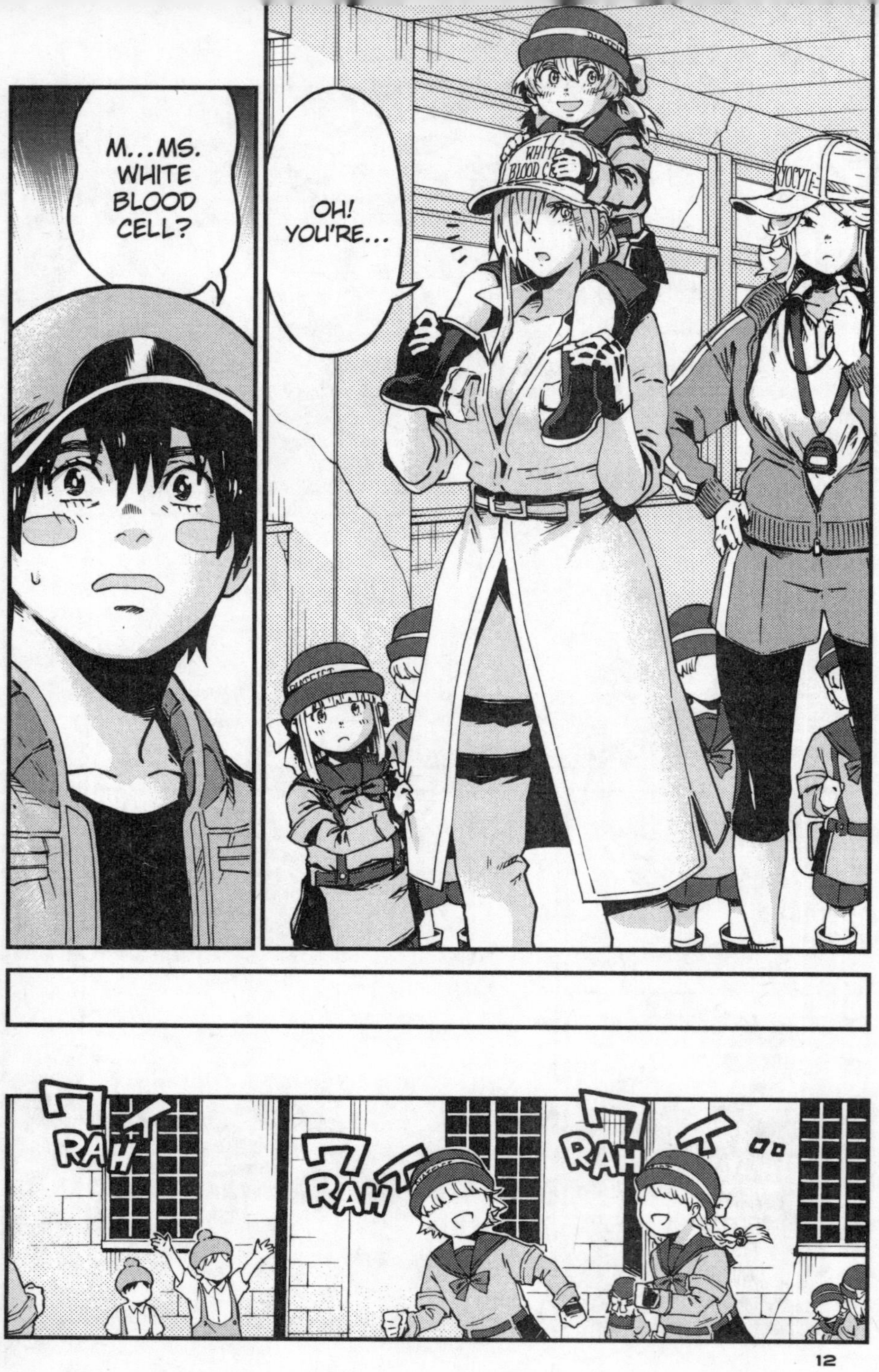
OH! YOU'RE...
M...MS. WHITE BLOOD CELL?
RAH
RAH
RAH

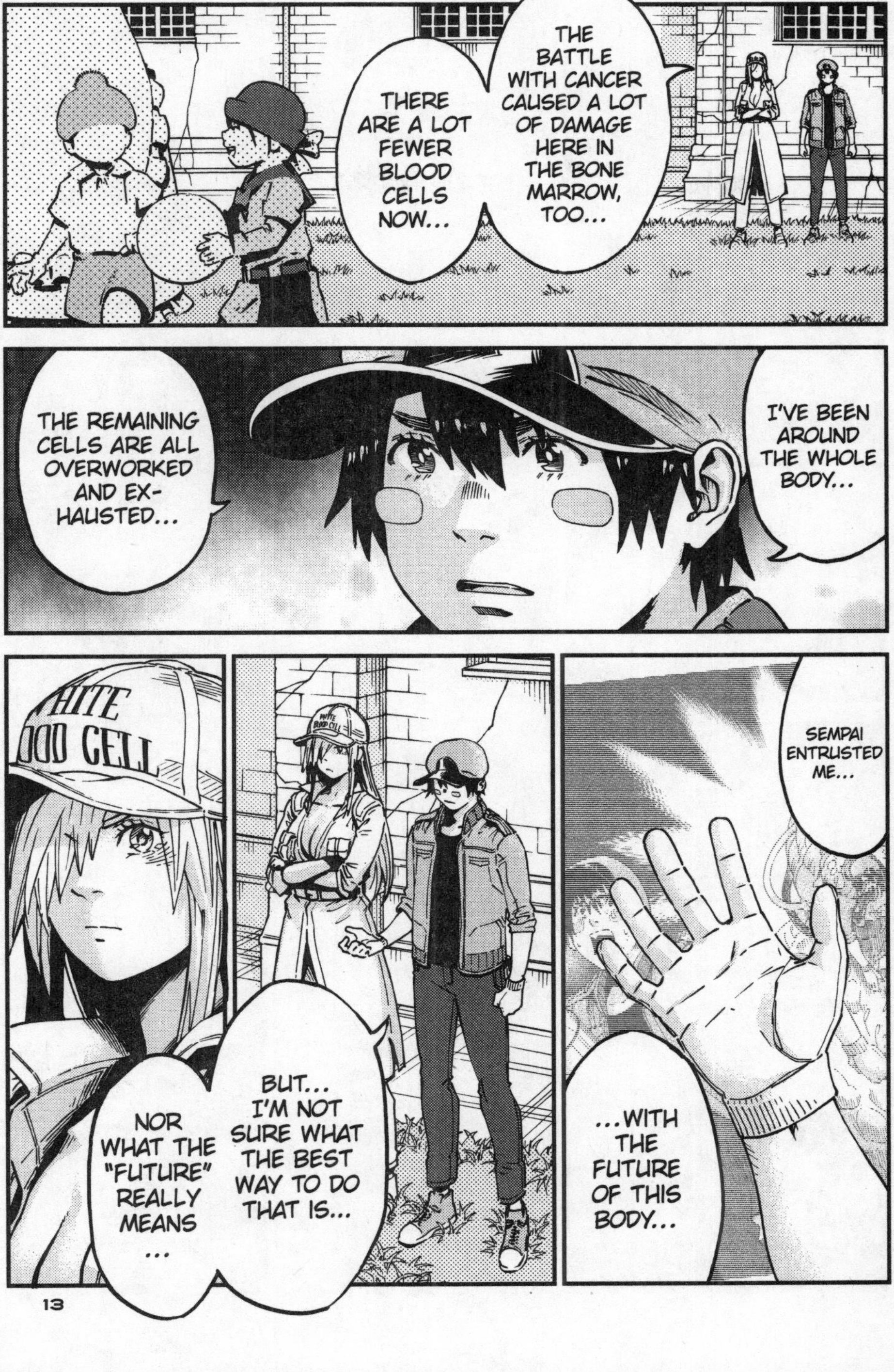
THE BATTLE WITH CANCER CAUSED A LOT OF DAMAGE HERE IN THE BONE MARROW, TOO...
THERE ARE A LOT FEWER BLOOD CELLS NOW...
I'VE BEEN AROUND THE WHOLE BODY...
THE REMAINING CELLS ARE ALL OVERWORKED AND EX-HAUSTED...
SEMPAI ENTRUSTED ME...
...WITH THE FUTURE OF THIS BODY...
BUT... I'M NOT SURE WHAT THE BEST WAY TO DO THAT IS...
NOR WHAT THE "FUTURE" REALLY MEANS ...

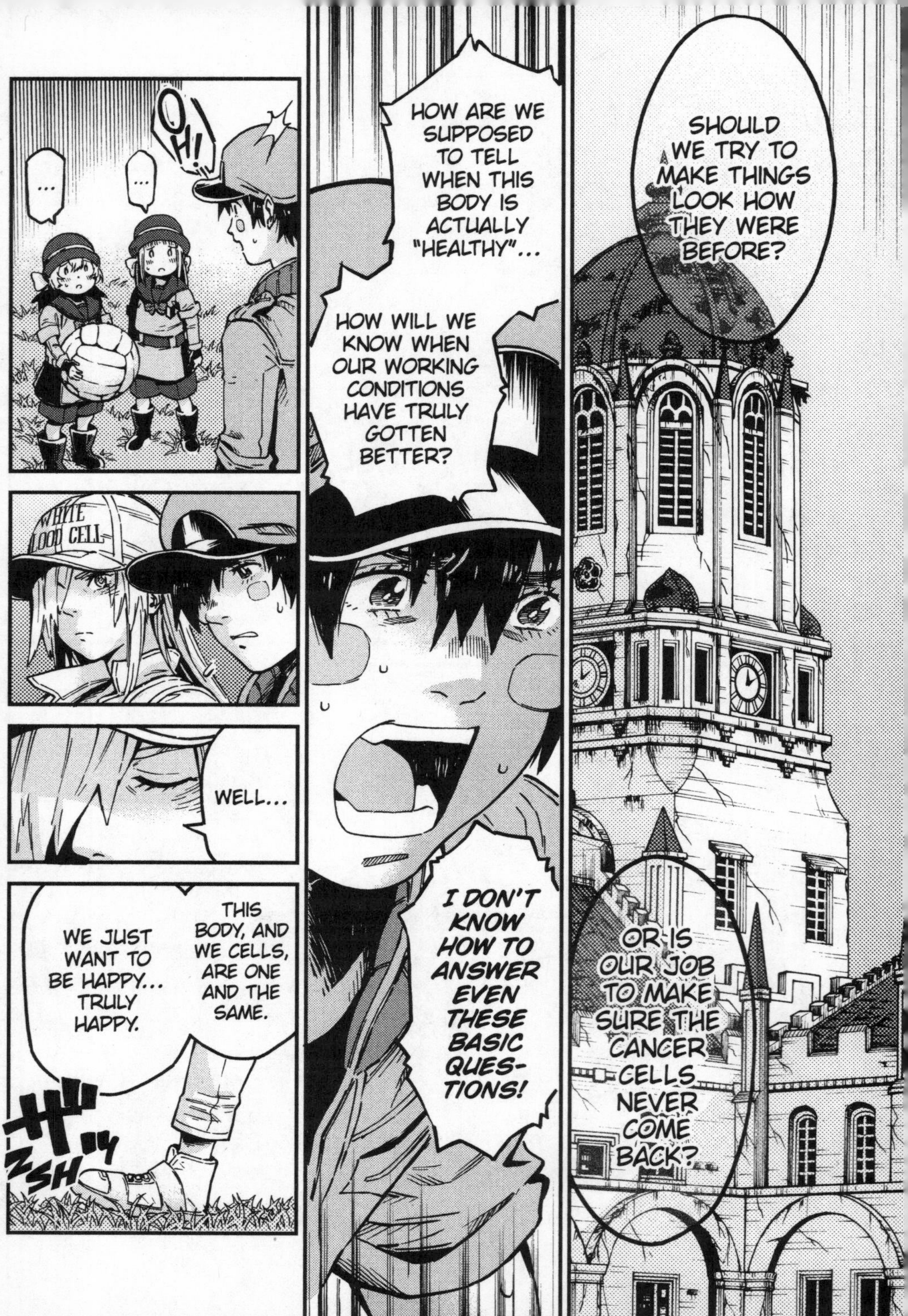
SHOULD WE TRY TO MAKE THINGS LOOK HOW THEY WERE BEFORE?
OR IS OUR JOB TO MAKE SURE THE CANCER CELLS NEVER COME BACK?
HOW ARE WE SUPPOSED TO TELL WHEN THIS BODY IS ACTUALLY "HEALTHY"...
HOW WILL WE KNOW WHEN OUR WORKING CONDITIONS HAVE TRULY GOTTEN BETTER?
I DON'T KNOW HOW TO ANSWER EVEN THESE BASIC QUES-TIONS!
OH!
...
...
WHITE BLOOD CELL
WELL...
THIS BODY, AND WE CELLS, ARE ONE AND THE SAME.
WE JUST WANT TO BE HAPPY... TRULY HAPPY.
ZSH

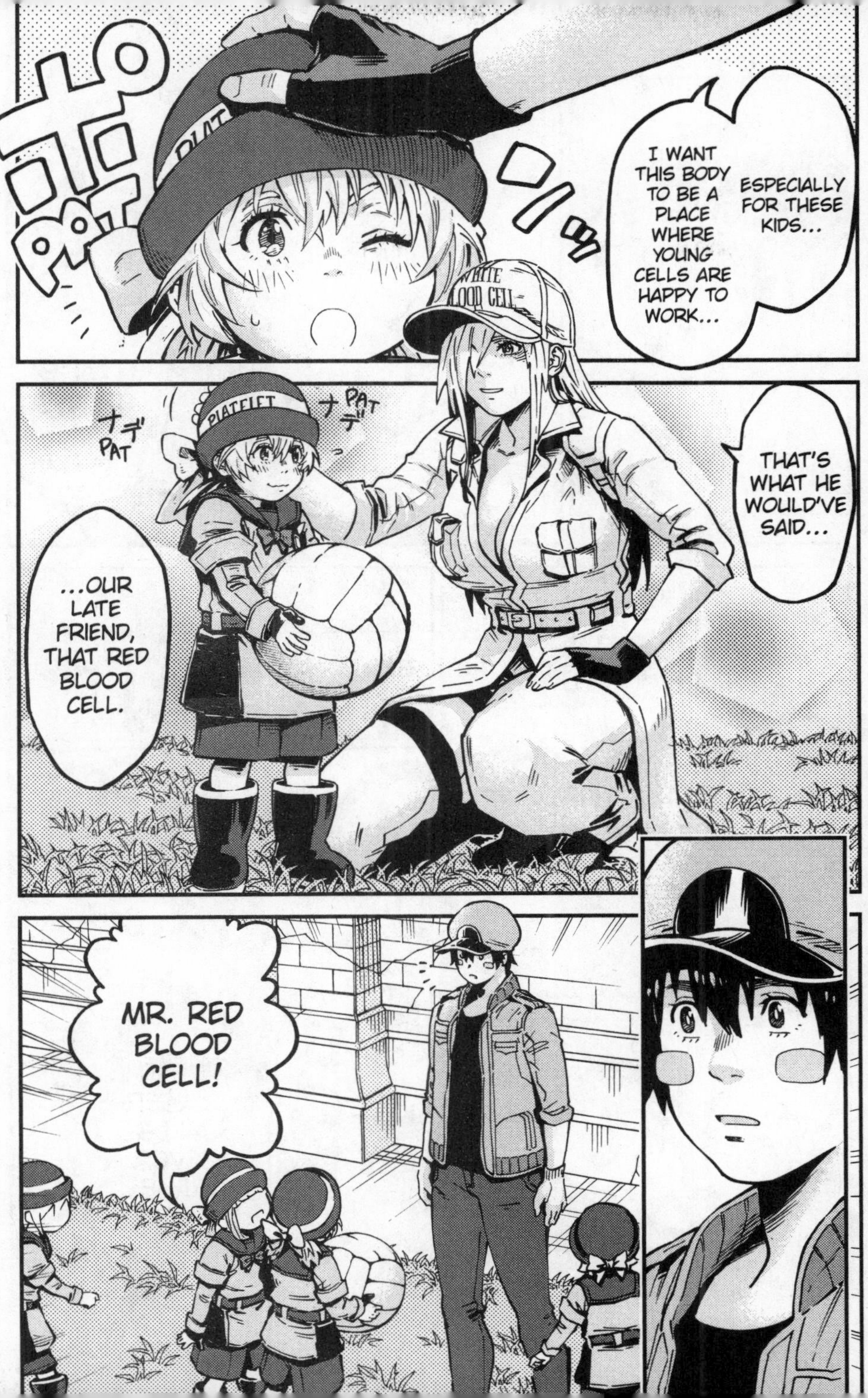
PAT
WHITE BLOOD CELL
I WANT THIS BODY TO BE A PLACE WHERE YOUNG CELLS ARE HAPPY TO WORK...
ESPECIALLY FOR THESE KIDS...
THAT'S WHAT HE WOULD'VE SAID...
ナデ PAT
ナデ PAT
PLATELET
...OUR LATE FRIEND, THAT RED BLOOD CELL.
MR. RED BLOOD CELL!

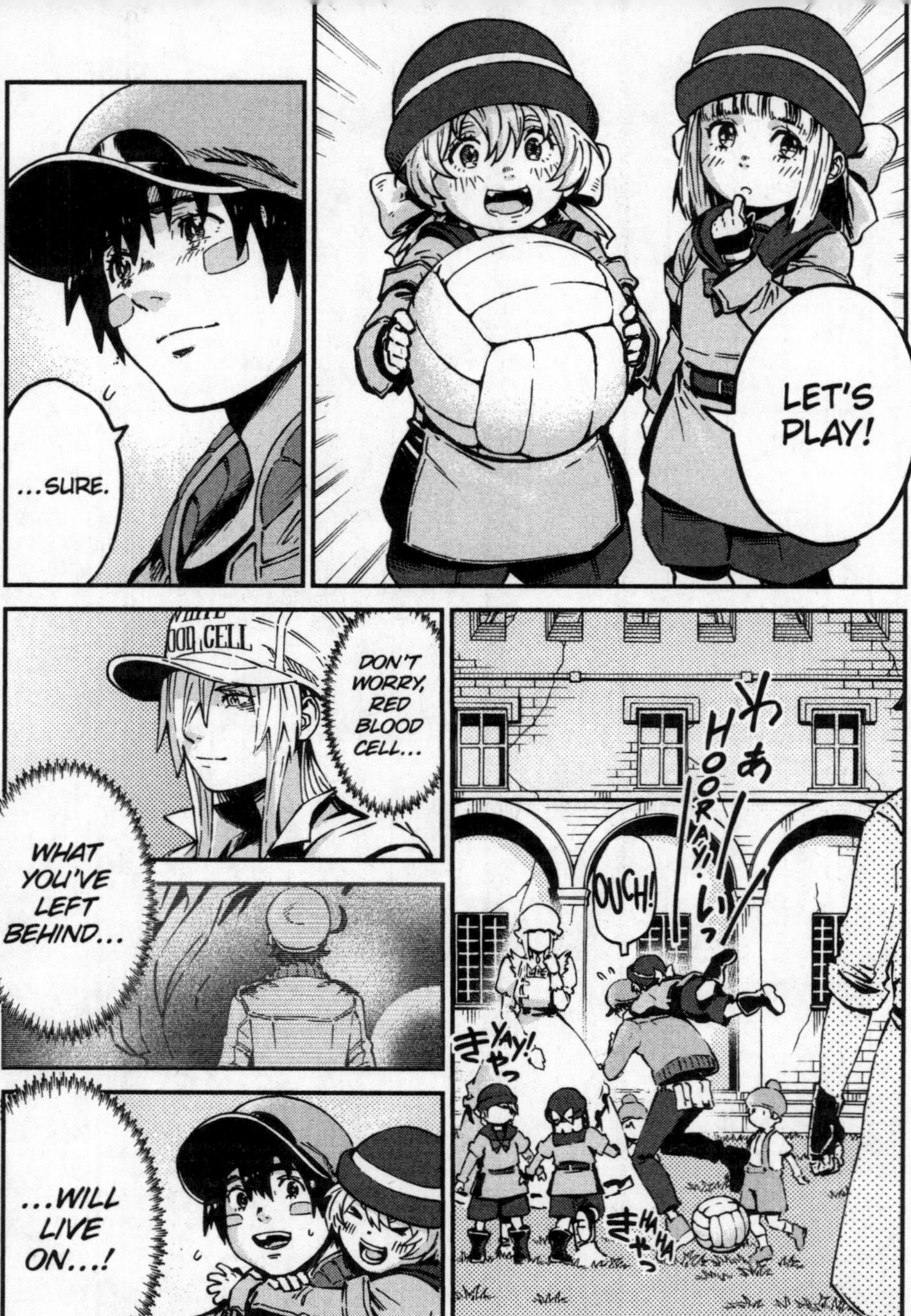
LET'S PLAY!
...SURE.
わぁ HOORAY!
OUCH!
いっ
きゃっ YAY!
きゃっ HAHA
DON'T WORRY, RED BLOOD CELL...
WHAT YOU'VE LEFT BEHIND...
...WILL LIVE ON...!

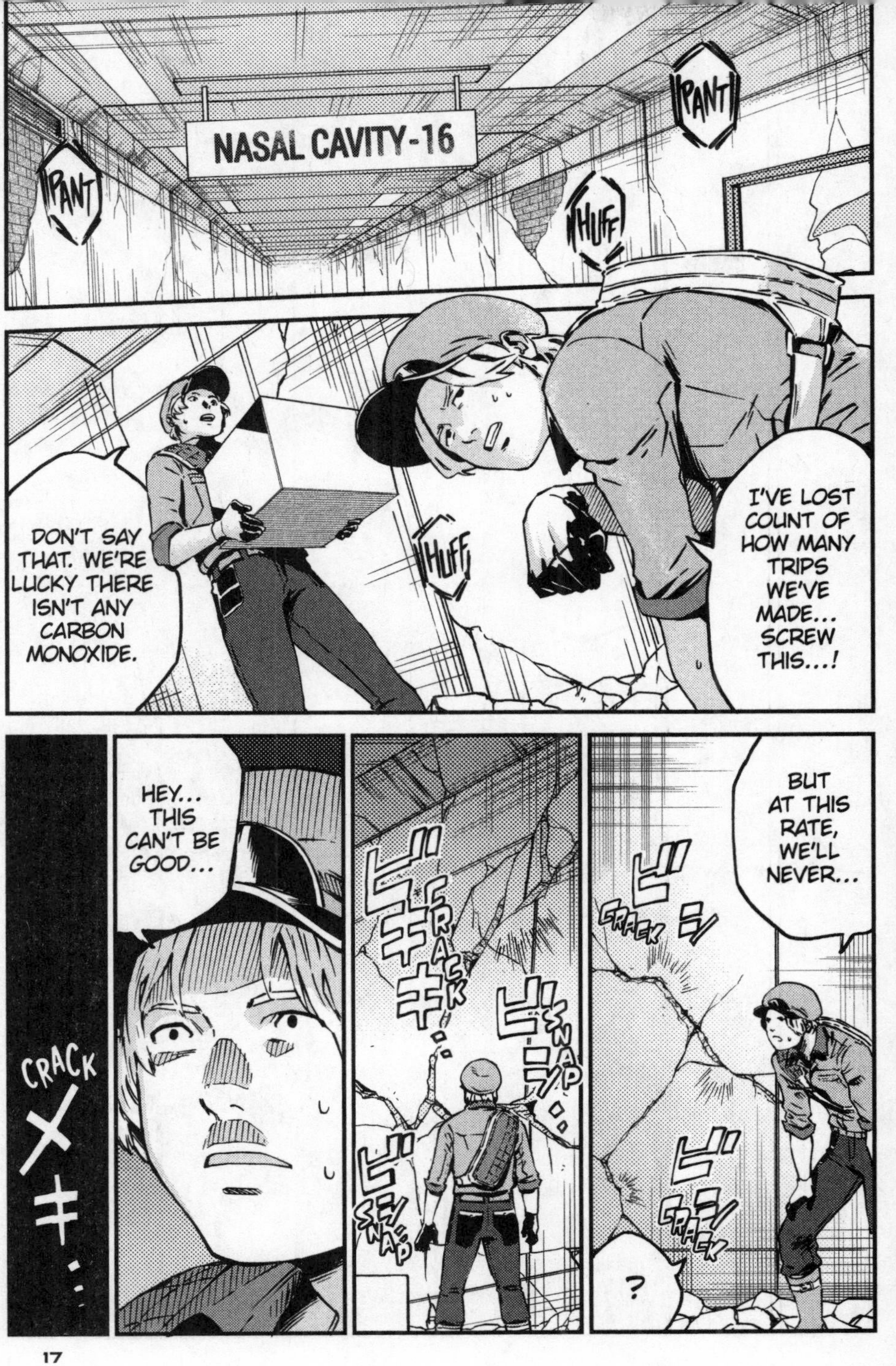
PANT
NASAL CAVITY-16
HUFF
PANT
I'VE LOST COUNT OF HOW MANY TRIPS WE'VE MADE... SCREW THIS...!
HUFF
DON'T SAY THAT. WE'RE LUCKY THERE ISN'T ANY CARBON MONOXIDE.
BUT AT THIS RATE, WE'LL NEVER...
CRACK
CRACK
?
CRACK
SNAP
SNAP
HEY... THIS CAN'T BE GOOD...
CRACK

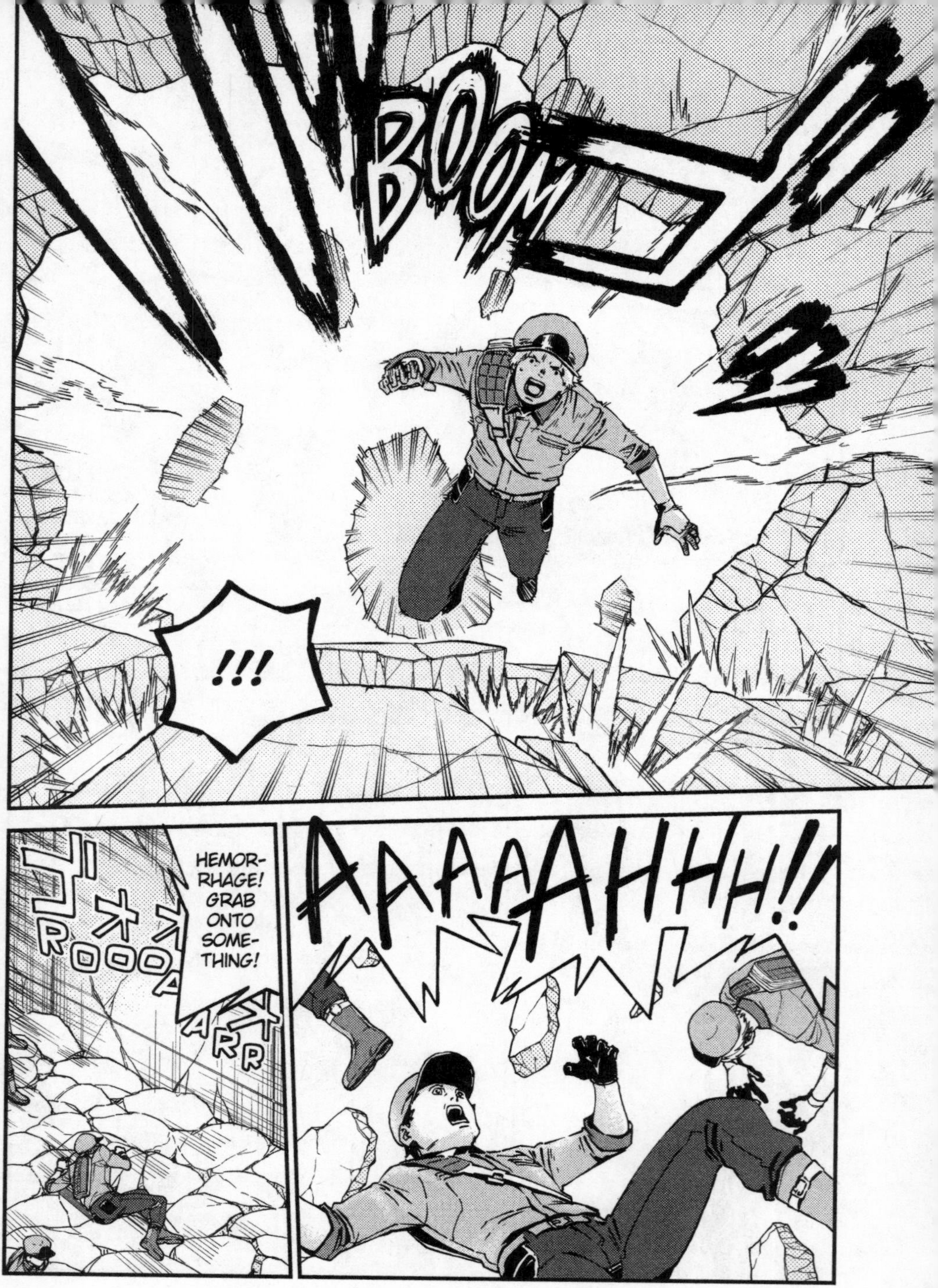
BOOM
!!!
AAAAHHH!!
HEMORRHAGE! GRAB ONTO SOMETHING!
ROOOAARRR

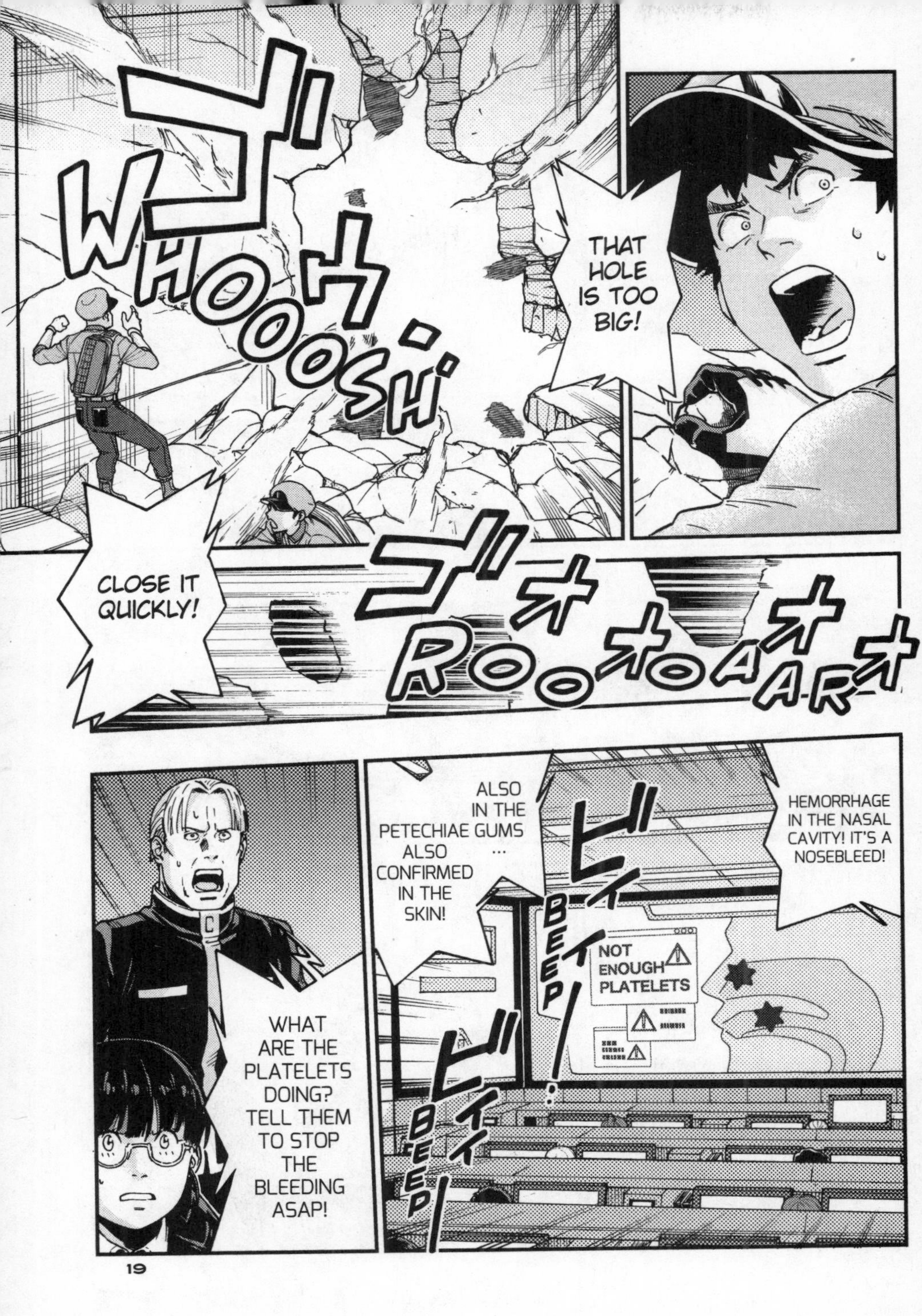
THAT HOLE IS TOO BIG!
ゴ
WHOOOSH
CLOSE IT QUICKLY!
ゴオオオオオ
ROOOOAAAR
HEMORRHAGE IN THE NASAL CAVITY! IT'S A NOSEBLEED!
ALSO IN THE GUMS...
PETECHIAE ALSO CONFIRMED IN THE SKIN!
ビイイ
BEEP
NOT ENOUGH PLATELETS
ビイイ
BEEP
WHAT ARE THE PLATELETS DOING? TELL THEM TO STOP THE BLEEDING ASAP!

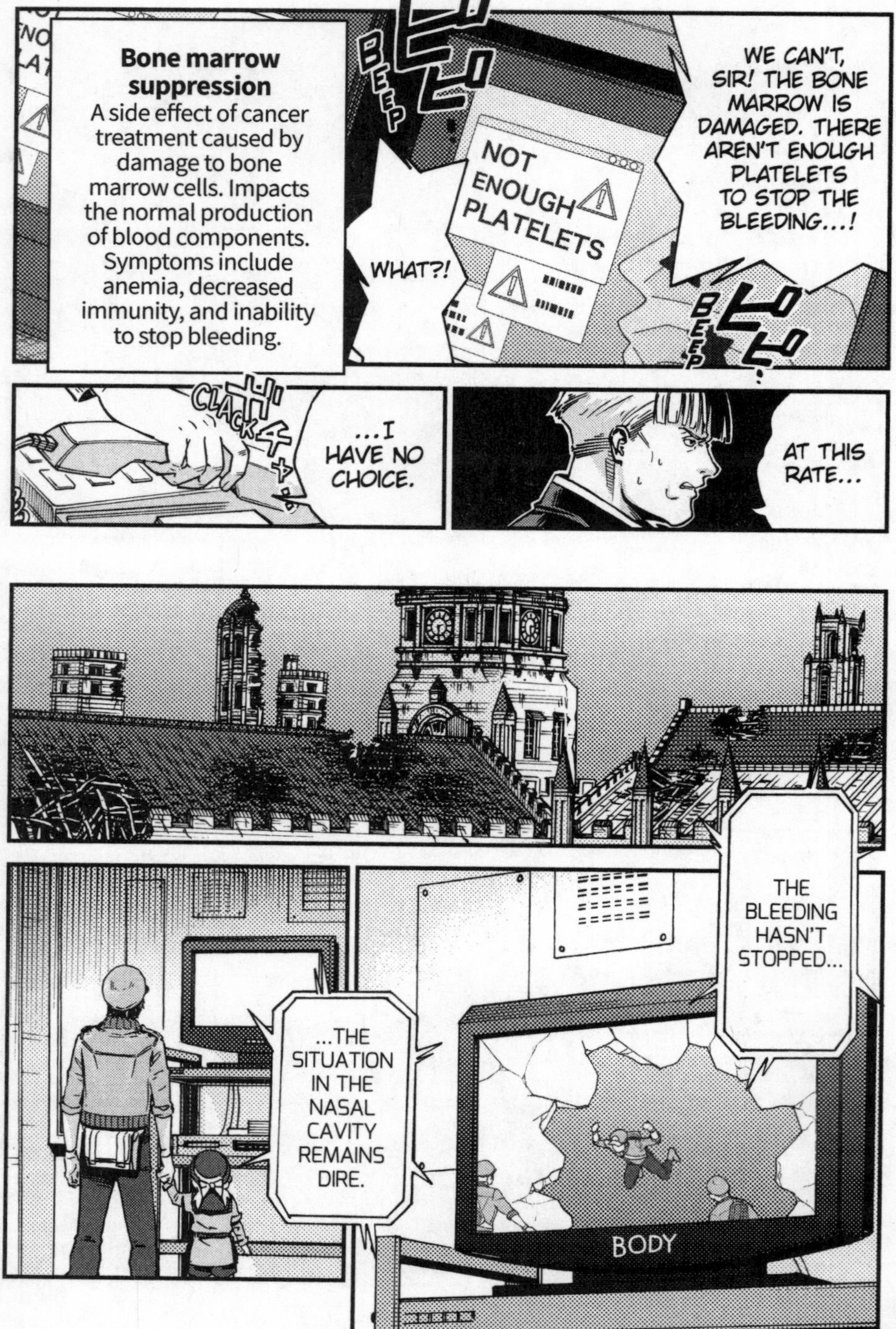
BEEP
WE CAN'T, SIR! THE BONE MARROW IS DAMAGED. THERE AREN'T ENOUGH PLATELETS TO STOP THE BLEEDING...!
BEEP
NOT ENOUGH PLATELETS
WHAT?!
Bone marrow suppression
A side effect of cancer treatment caused by damage to bone marrow cells. Impacts the normal production of blood components. Symptoms include anemia, decreased immunity, and inability to stop bleeding.
AT THIS RATE...
...I HAVE NO CHOICE.
CLACK
THE BLEEDING HASN'T STOPPED...
...THE SITUATION IN THE NASAL CAVITY REMAINS DIRE.
BODY

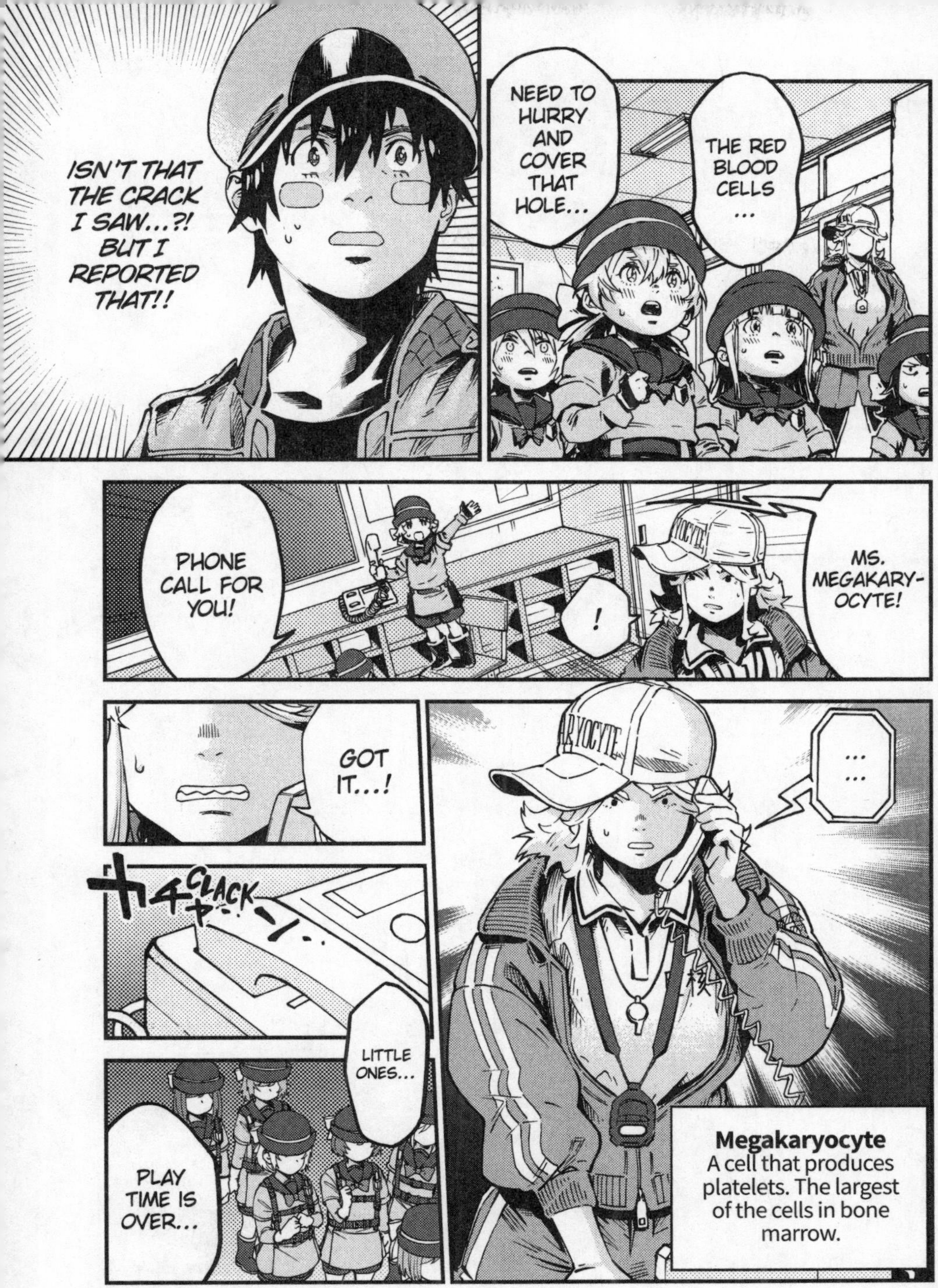
THE RED BLOOD CELLS ...
NEED TO HURRY AND COVER THAT HOLE...
ISN'T THAT THE CRACK I SAW...?! BUT I REPORTED THAT!!
MS. MEGAKARYOCYTE!
!
PHONE CALL FOR YOU!
... ...
Megakaryocyte
A cell that produces platelets. The largest of the cells in bone marrow.
GOT IT...!
CLACK
LITTLE ONES...
PLAY TIME IS OVER...

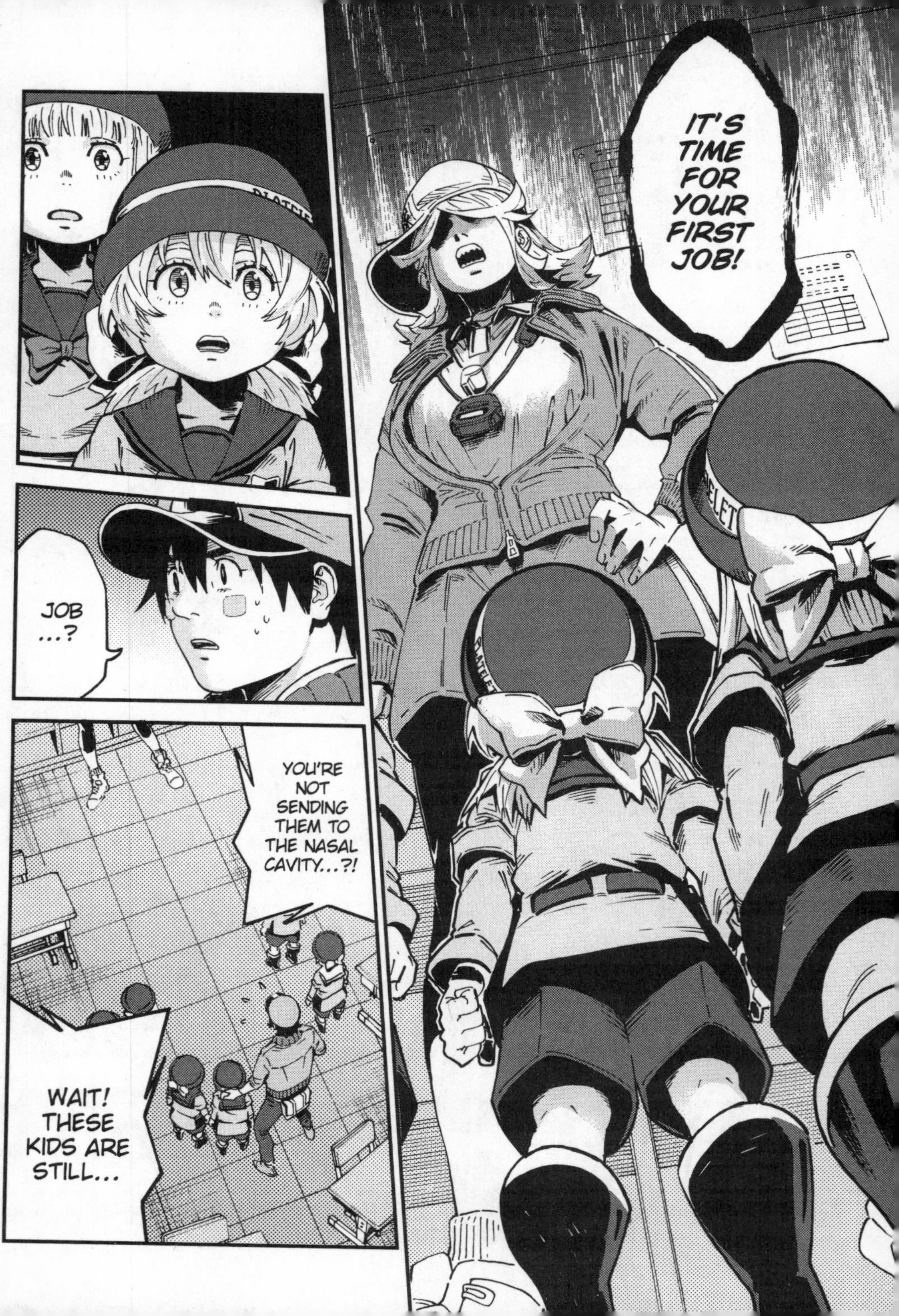
IT'S TIME FOR YOUR FIRST JOB!
JOB ...?
YOU'RE NOT SENDING THEM TO THE NASAL CAVITY...?!
WAIT! THESE KIDS ARE STILL...

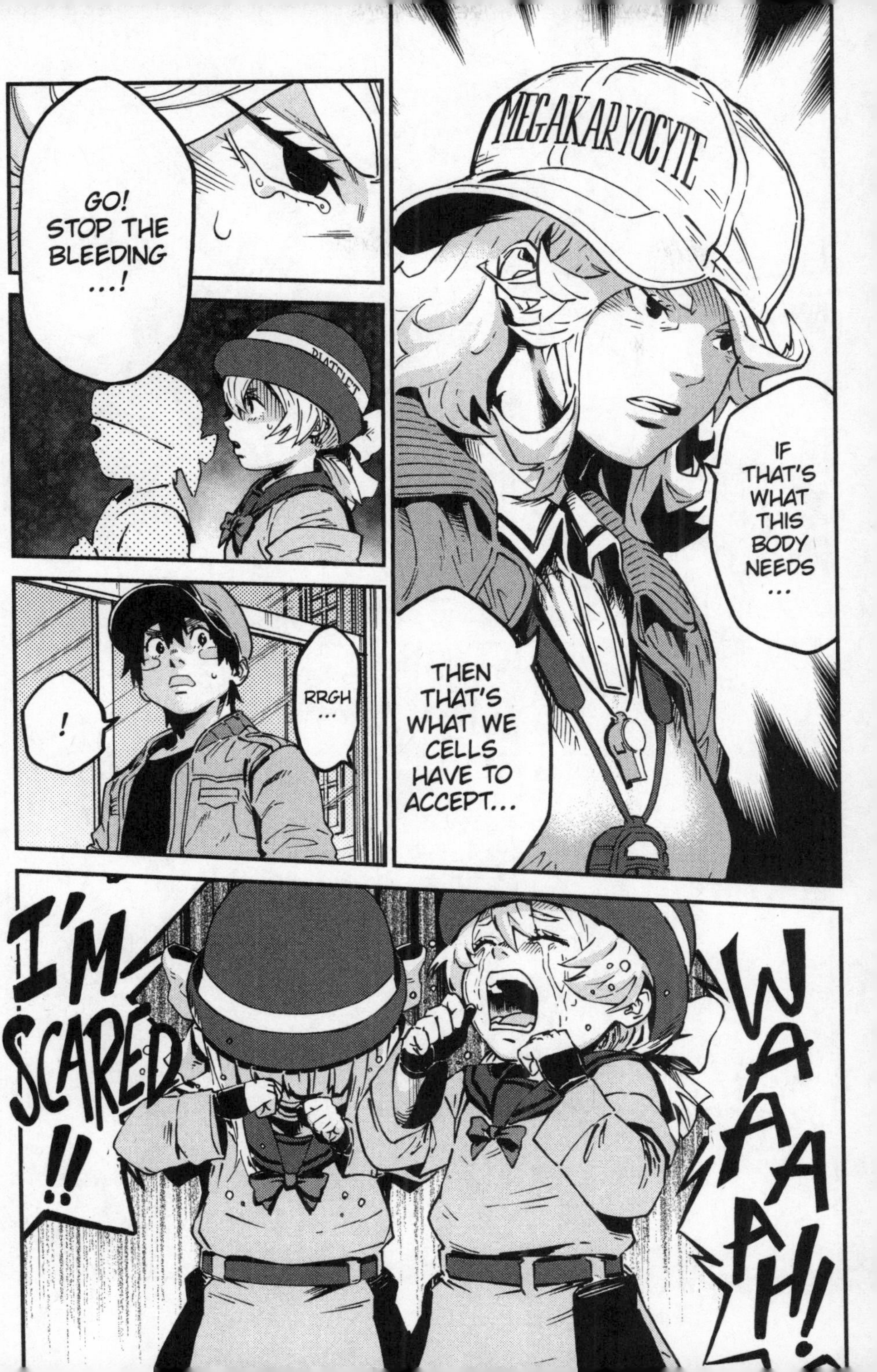
MEGAKARYOCYTE
IF THAT'S WHAT THIS BODY NEEDS...
THEN THAT'S WHAT WE CELLS HAVE TO ACCEPT...
GO! STOP THE BLEEDING...!
RRGH...
!
WAAAAH!
I'M SCARED!!

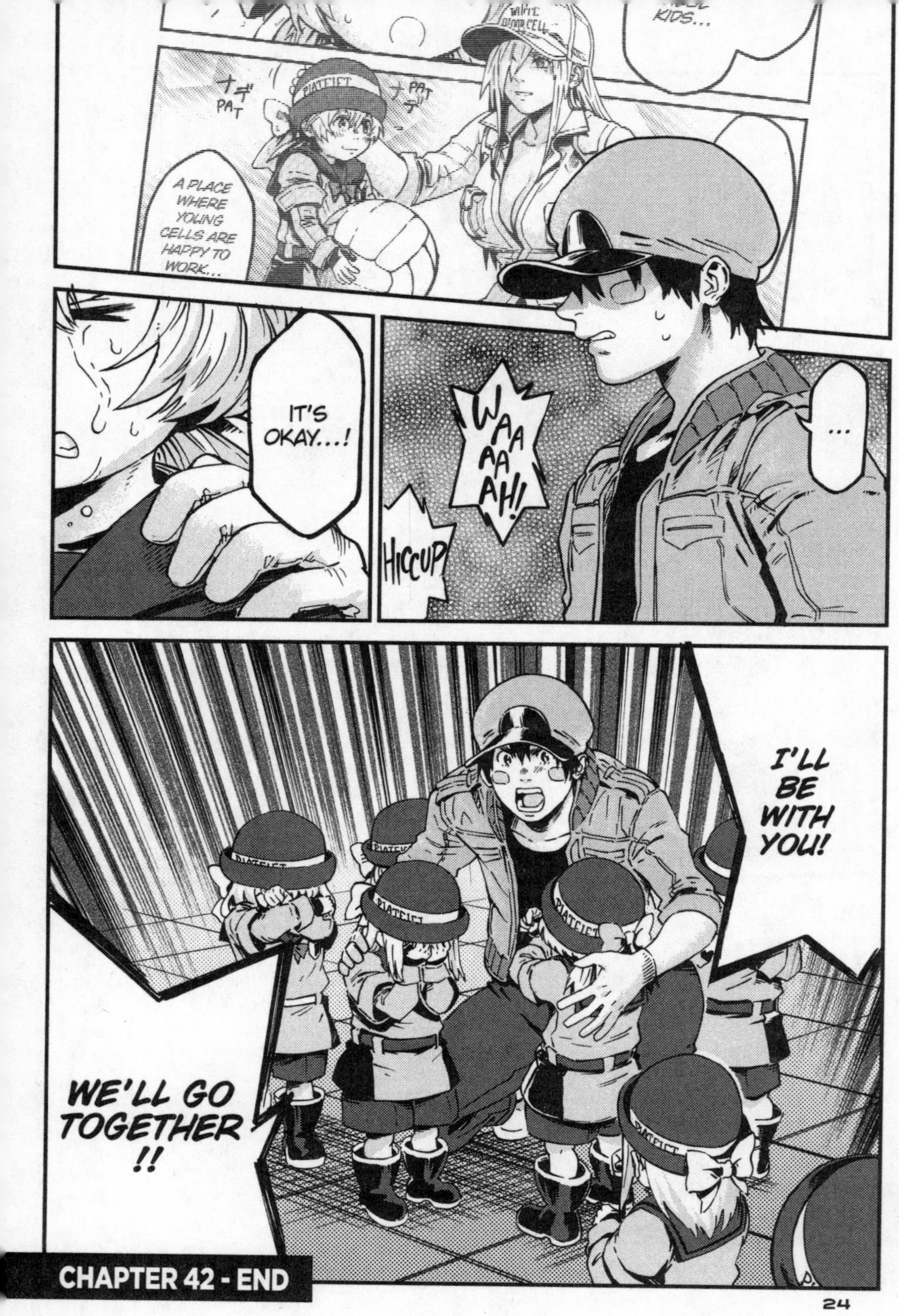
KIDS...
PAT PAT
A PLACE WHERE YOUNG CELLS ARE HAPPY TO WORK...
...
WAAAAAH!!
HICCUP
IT'S OKAY...!
I'LL BE WITH YOU!
WE'LL GO TOGETHER!!
CHAPTER 42 - END

# 43. HEMOSTASIS, TRUST, SEMPAI

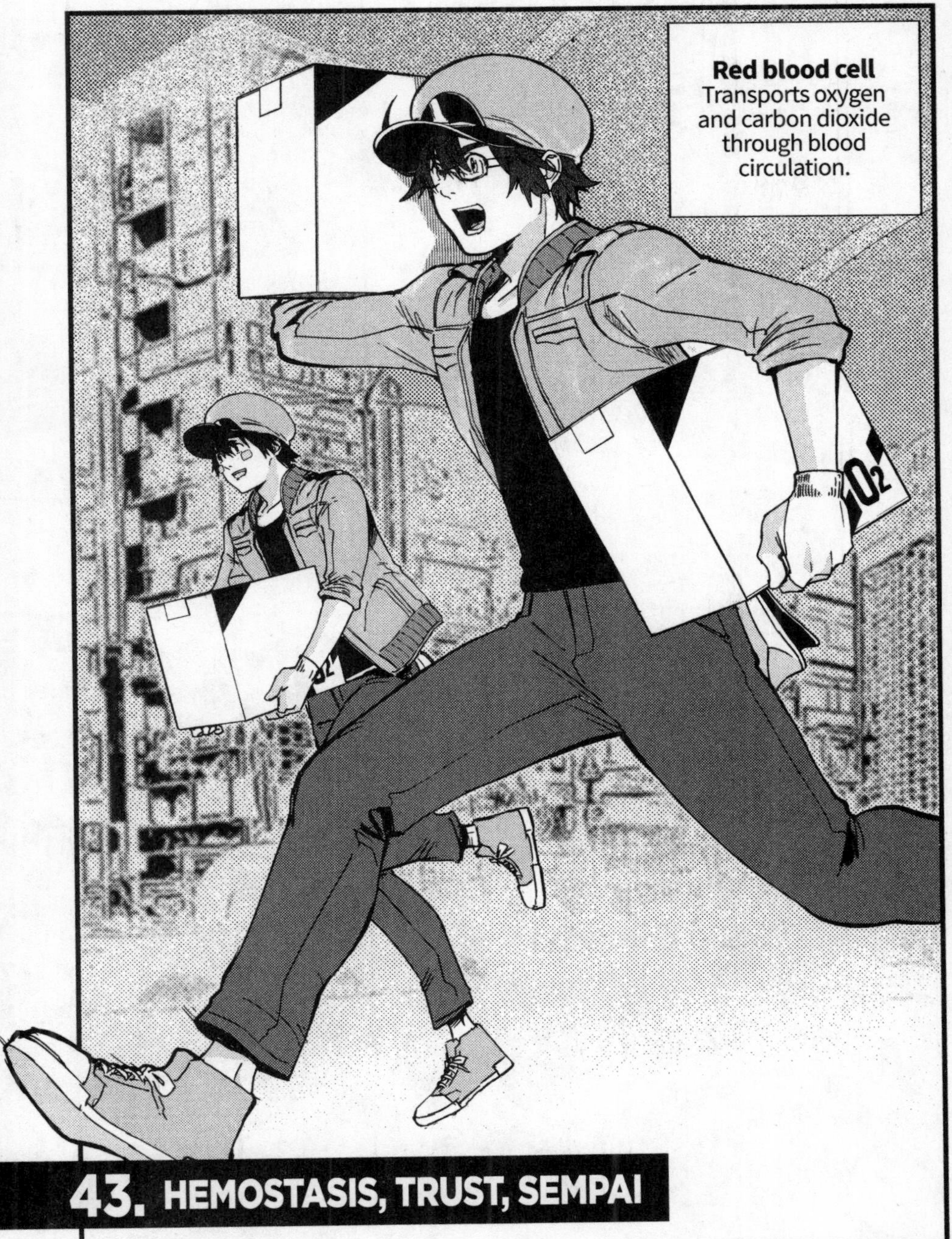
Red blood cell
Transports oxygen and carbon dioxide through blood circulation.
$O_2$

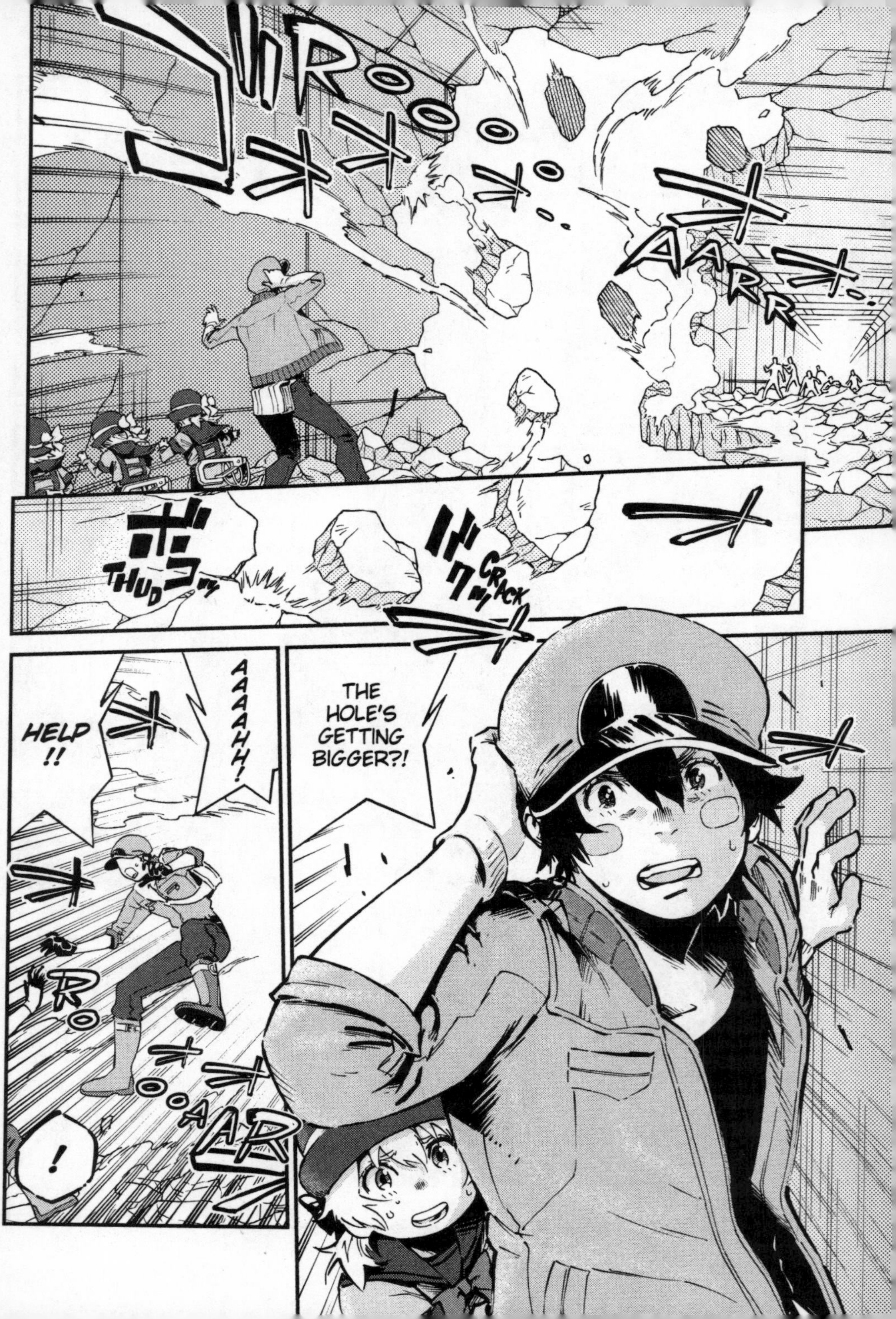

AARR
VROOOOO
THUD
CRACK
THE HOLE'S GETTING BIGGER?!
AAAAAHH!
HELP !!
ROOOAAR
!

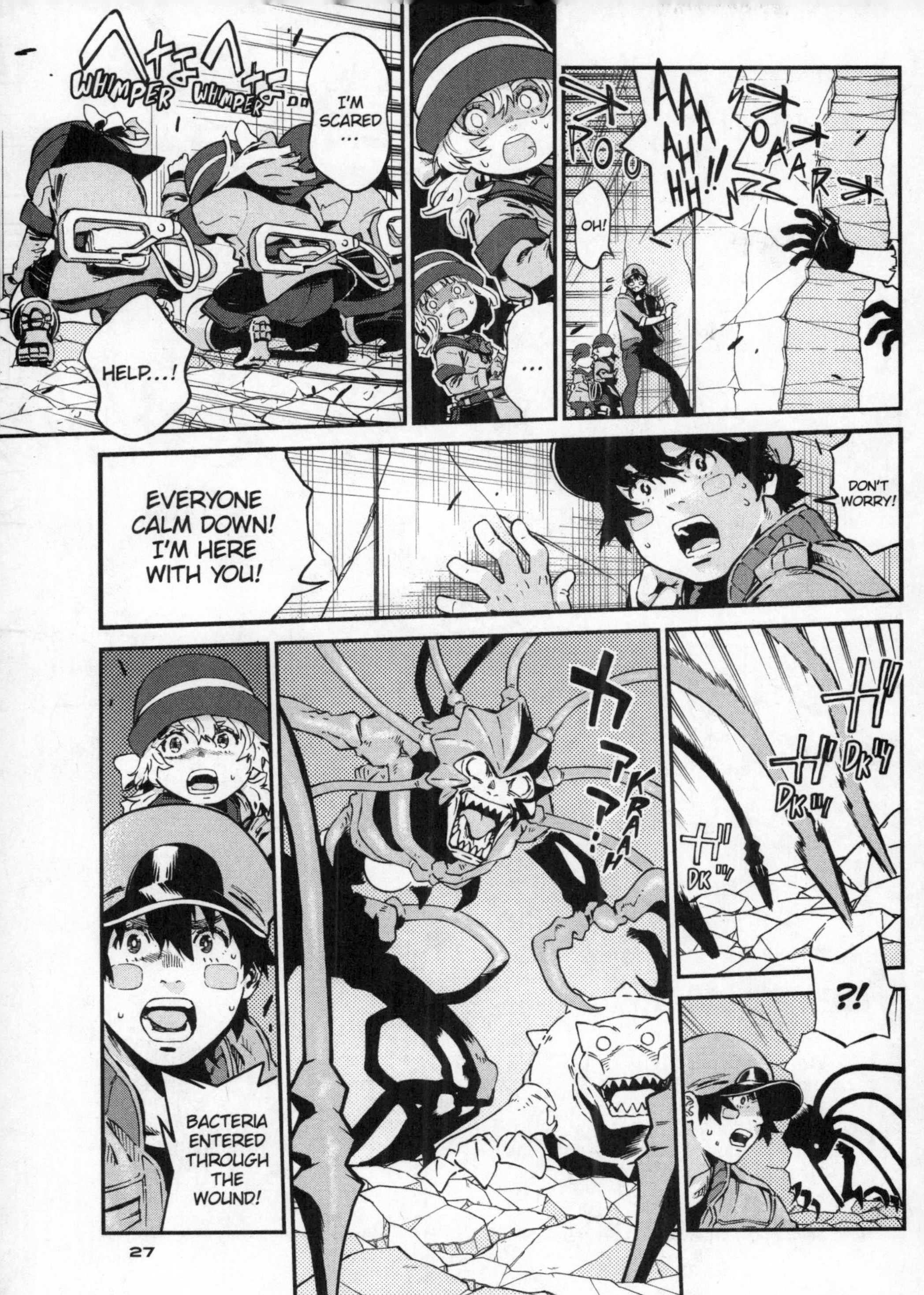
AAAAHHHH!!
ROOOAAR
OH!
...
I'M SCARED ...
WHIMPER WHIMPER...
HELP...!
DON'T WORRY!
EVERYONE CALM DOWN! I'M HERE WITH YOU!
DK DK
DK
?!
KRAAH!!
BACTERIA ENTERED THROUGH THE WOUND!

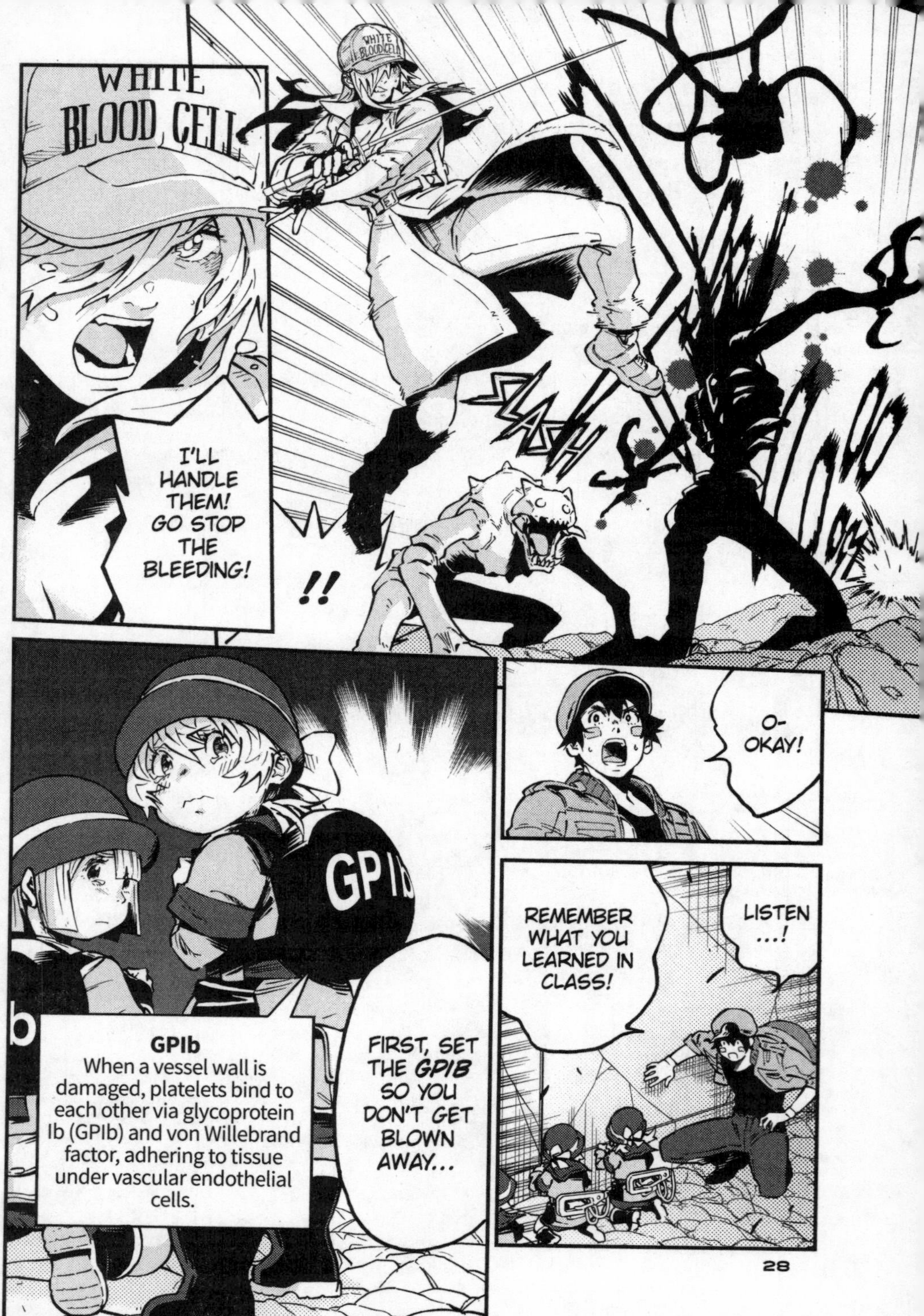

SLASH
!!
I'LL HANDLE THEM! GO STOP THE BLEEDING!
O-OKAY!
LISTEN...!
REMEMBER WHAT YOU LEARNED IN CLASS!
FIRST, SET THE *GPIB* SO YOU DON'T GET BLOWN AWAY...
GPIb
**GPIb**
When a vessel wall is damaged, platelets bind to each other via glycoprotein Ib (GPIb) and von Willebrand factor, adhering to tissue under vascular endothelial cells.

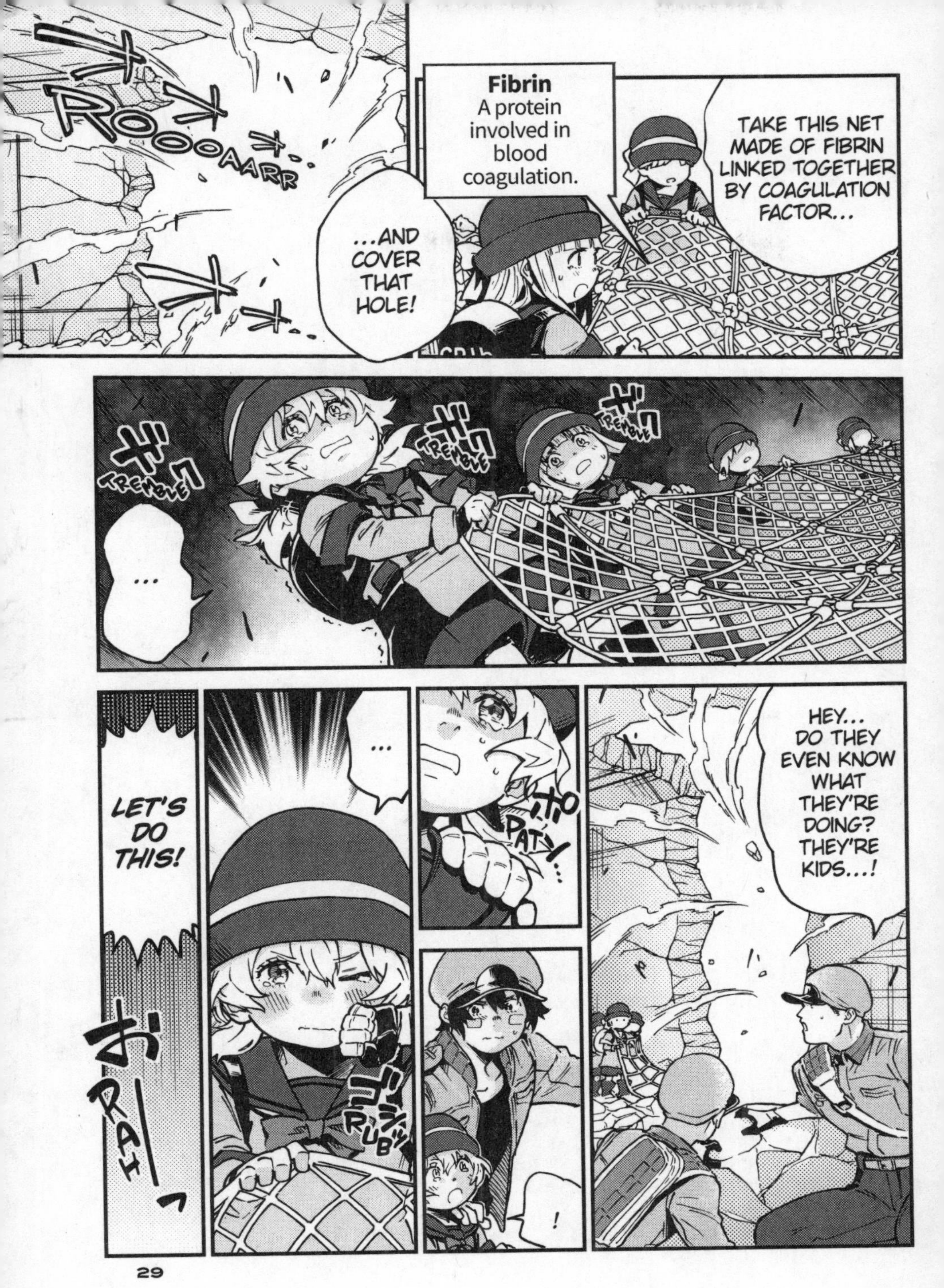
TAKE THIS NET MADE OF FIBRIN LINKED TOGETHER BY COAGULATION FACTOR...
**Fibrin** A protein involved in blood coagulation.
...AND COVER THAT HOLE!
ROOOOAARR
TREMBLE
TREMBLE
TREMBLE
...
HEY... DO THEY EVEN KNOW WHAT THEY'RE DOING? THEY'RE KIDS...!
PAT
!
...
LET'S DO THIS!
RUB
RAH

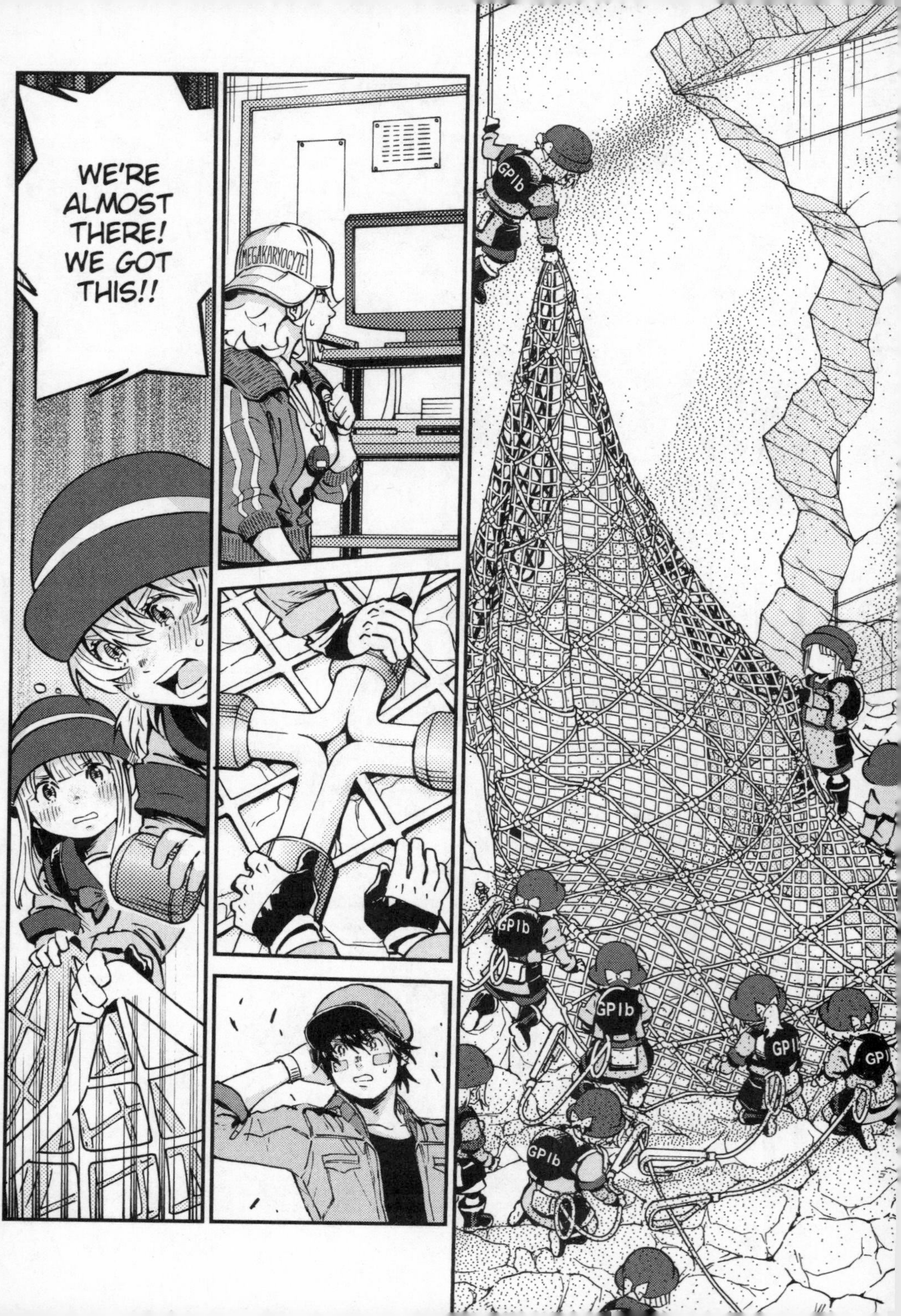
GPIb
MEGAKARYOCYTE
WE'RE ALMOST THERE! WE GOT THIS!!
GPIb
GPIb
GPI
GPI
GPIb

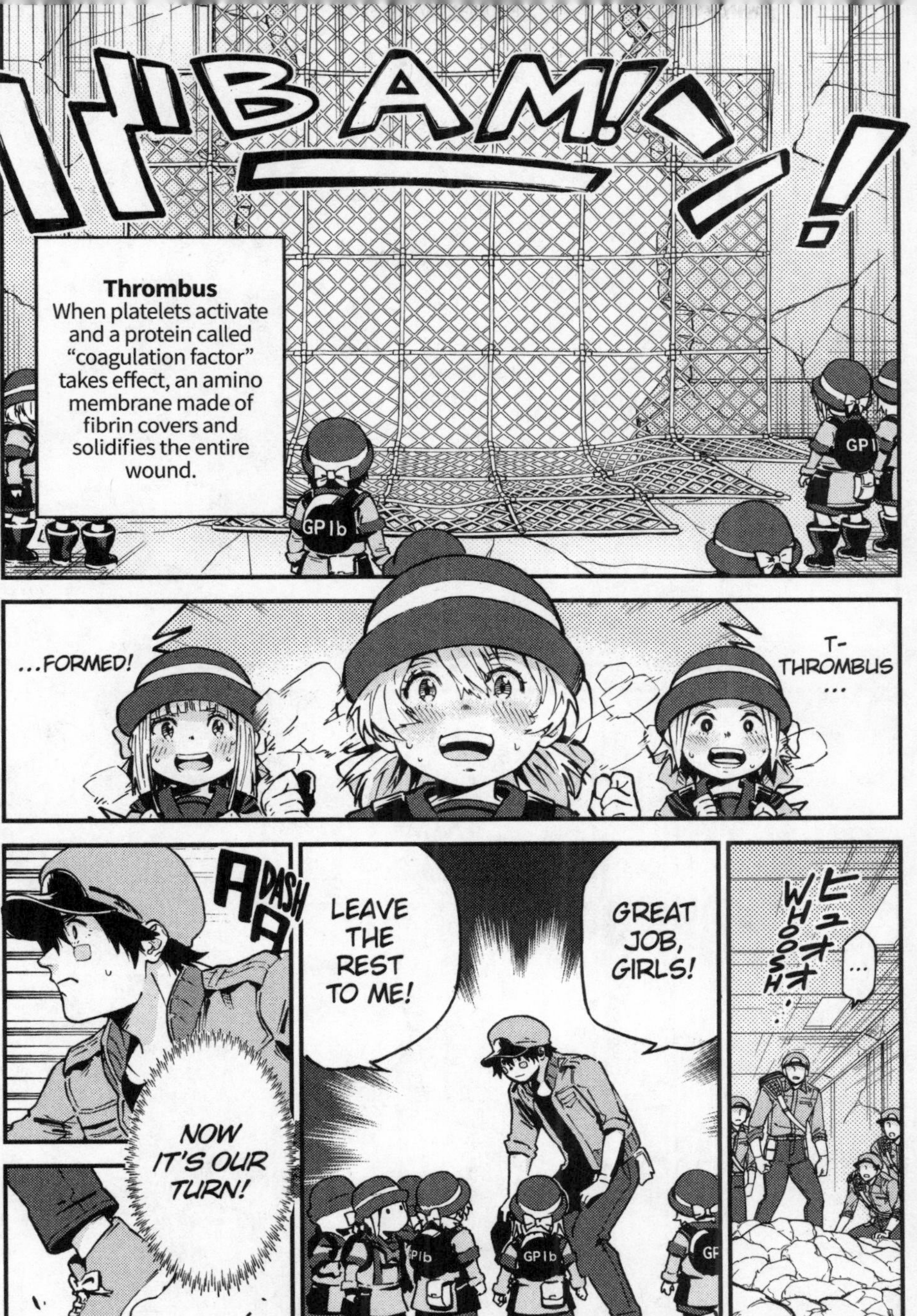
BAM!
Thrombus
When platelets activate and a protein called "coagulation factor" takes effect, an amino membrane made of fibrin covers and solidifies the entire wound.
GP Ib
GP I
T-THROMBUS...
...FORMED!
WHOOSH
...
GREAT JOB, GIRLS!
LEAVE THE REST TO ME!
DASH
NOW IT'S OUR TURN!

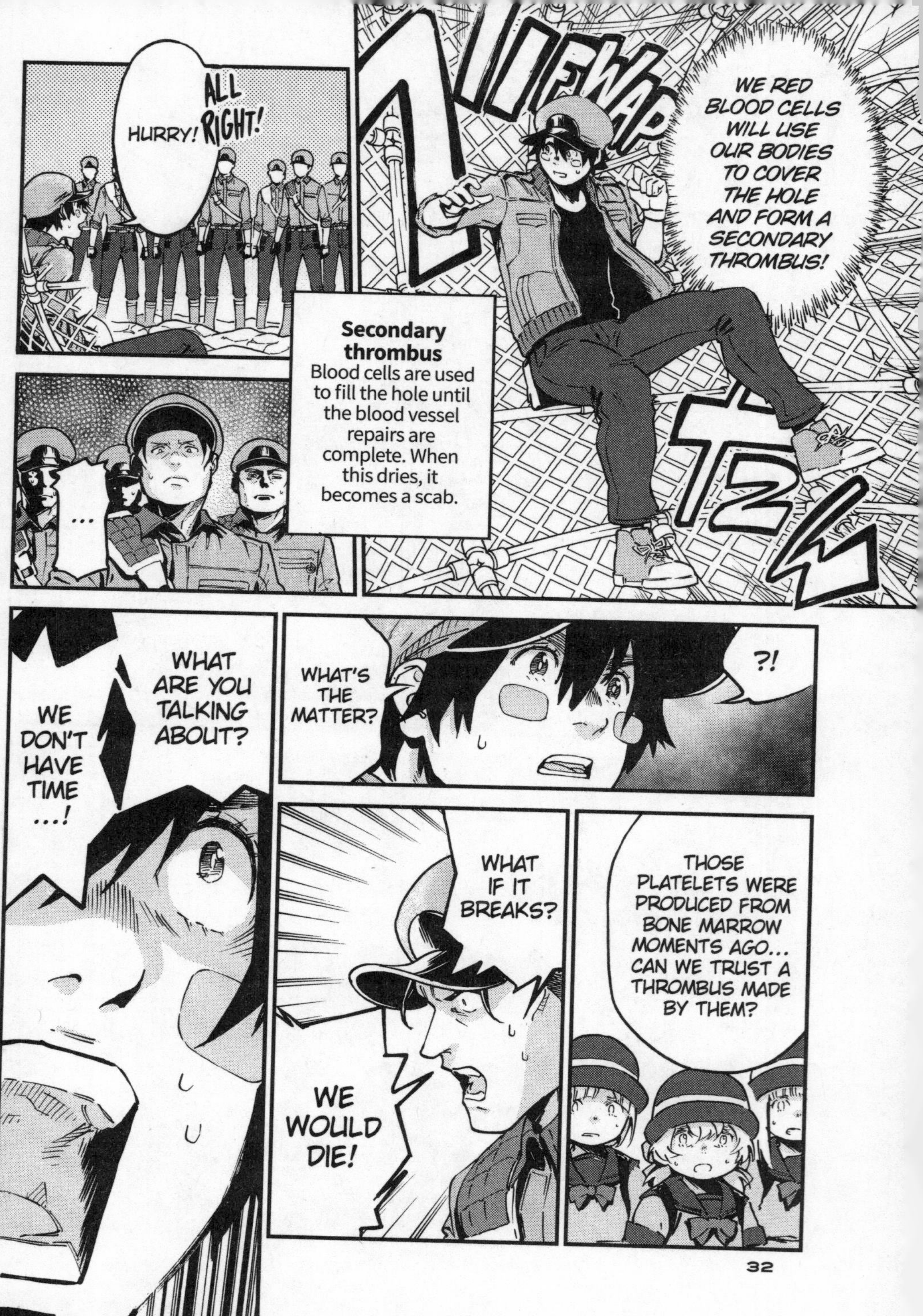
ZWAP
WE RED BLOOD CELLS WILL USE OUR BODIES TO COVER THE HOLE AND FORM A SECONDARY THROMBUS!
TZL
HURRY!
ALL RIGHT!
**Secondary thrombus**
Blood cells are used to fill the hole until the blood vessel repairs are complete. When this dries, it becomes a scab.
...
?!
WHAT'S THE MATTER?
THOSE PLATELETS WERE PRODUCED FROM BONE MARROW MOMENTS AGO... CAN WE TRUST A THROMBUS MADE BY THEM?
WHAT IF IT BREAKS?
WE WOULD DIE!
WHAT ARE YOU TALKING ABOUT?
WE DON'T HAVE TIME ...!

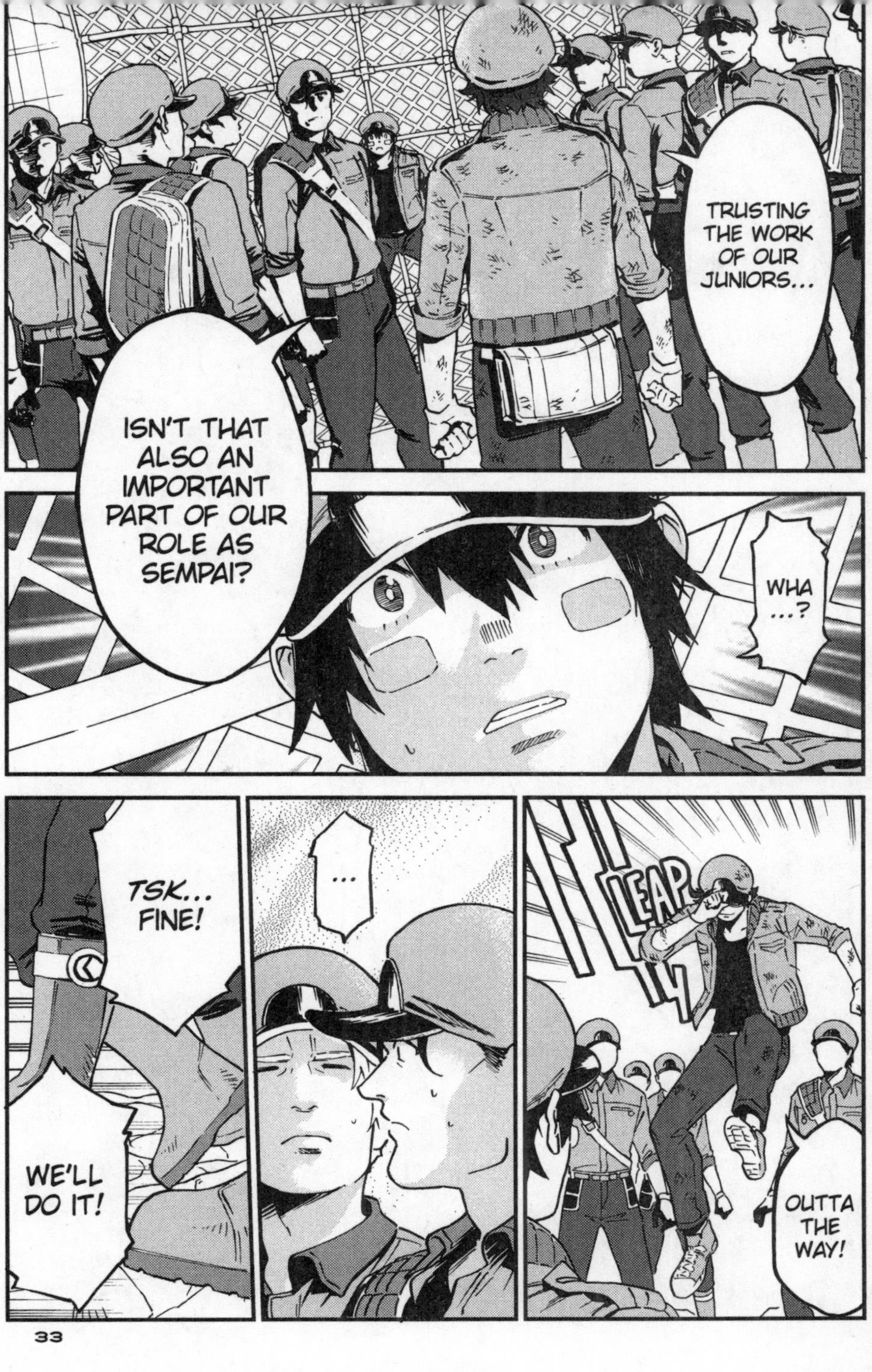
TRUSTING THE WORK OF OUR JUNIORS...
ISN'T THAT ALSO AN IMPORTANT PART OF OUR ROLE AS SEMPAI?
WHA ...?
LEAP
OUTTA THE WAY!
...
TSK... FINE!
WE'LL DO IT!

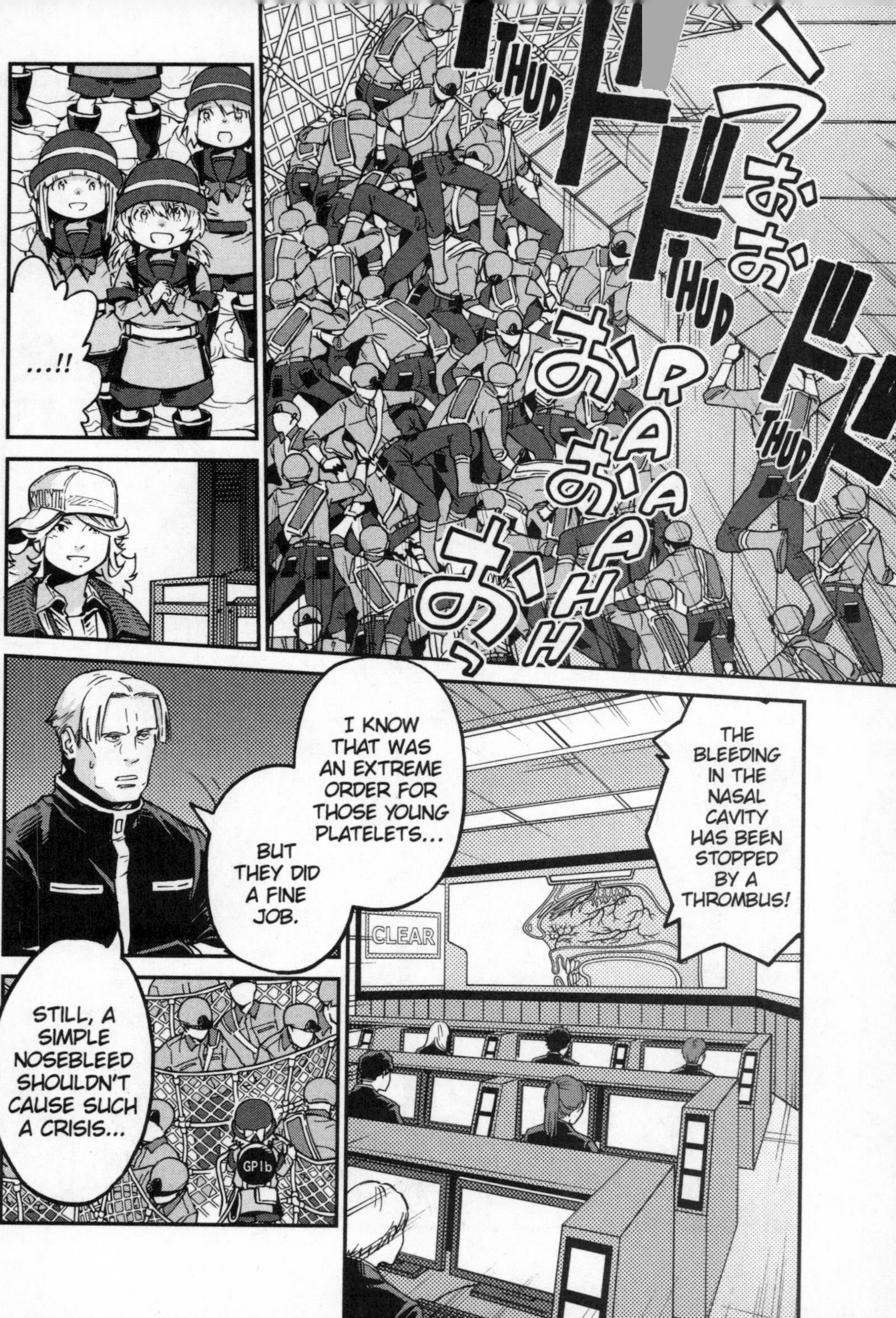
ドドド
THUD
THUD
ドドド
THUD
THUD
うおおおおお
RAAAHH
...!!
RYOCYTE
CLEAR
THE BLEEDING IN THE NASAL CAVITY HAS BEEN STOPPED BY A THROMBUS!
I KNOW THAT WAS AN EXTREME ORDER FOR THOSE YOUNG PLATELETS...
BUT THEY DID A FINE JOB.
STILL, A SIMPLE NOSEBLEED SHOULDN'T CAUSE SUCH A CRISIS...
GPIb

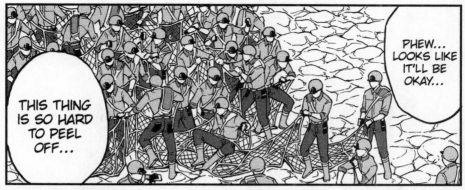

PHEW... LOOKS LIKE IT'LL BE OKAY...

THIS THING IS SO HARD TO PEEL OFF...

THAT VOICE ...!!

EXCUSE ME! I NEED TO GET THROUGH!

HEY ...!

!

I'M SURE THAT WAS ...!!

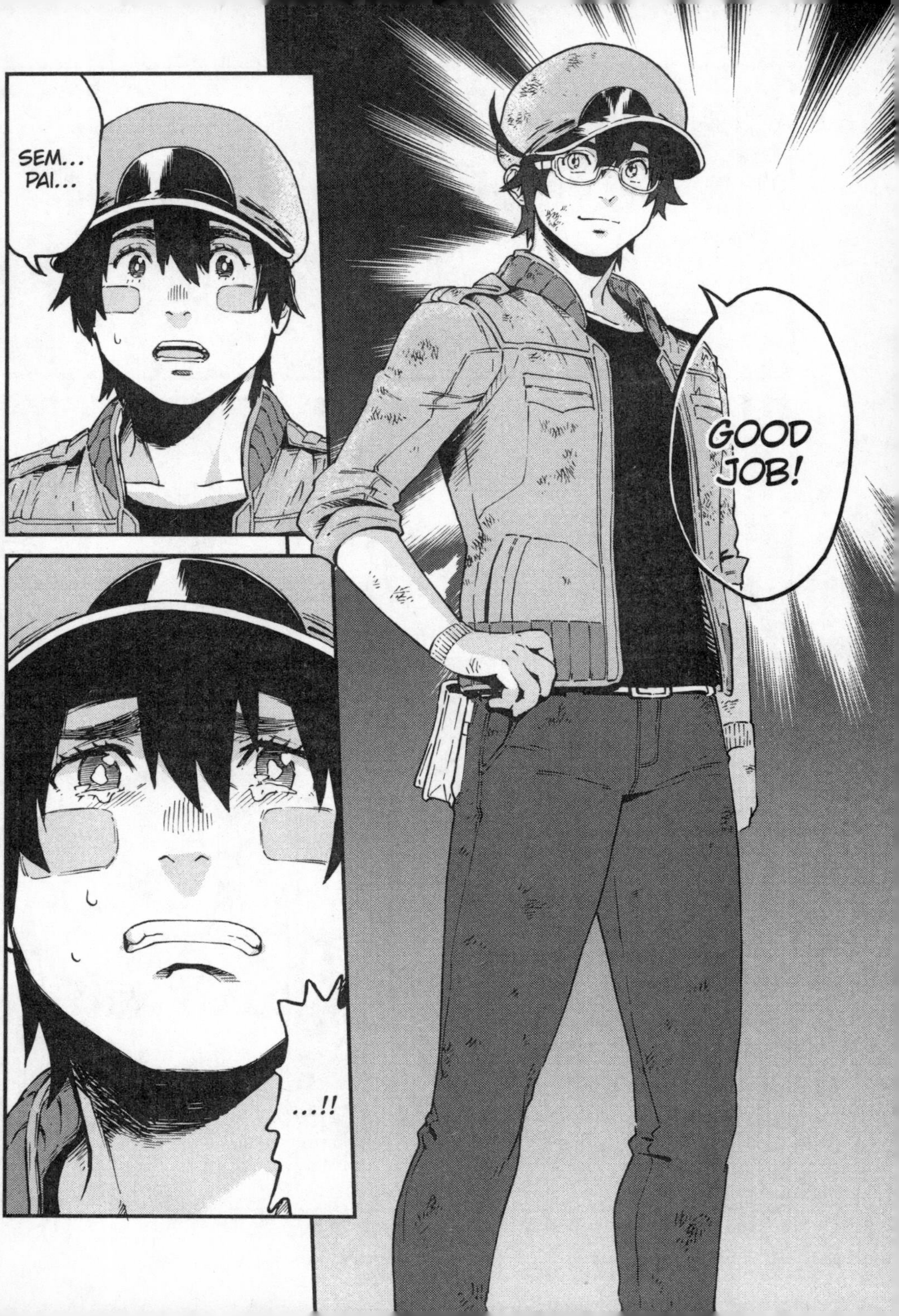
GOOD JOB!
SEM... PAI...
...!!

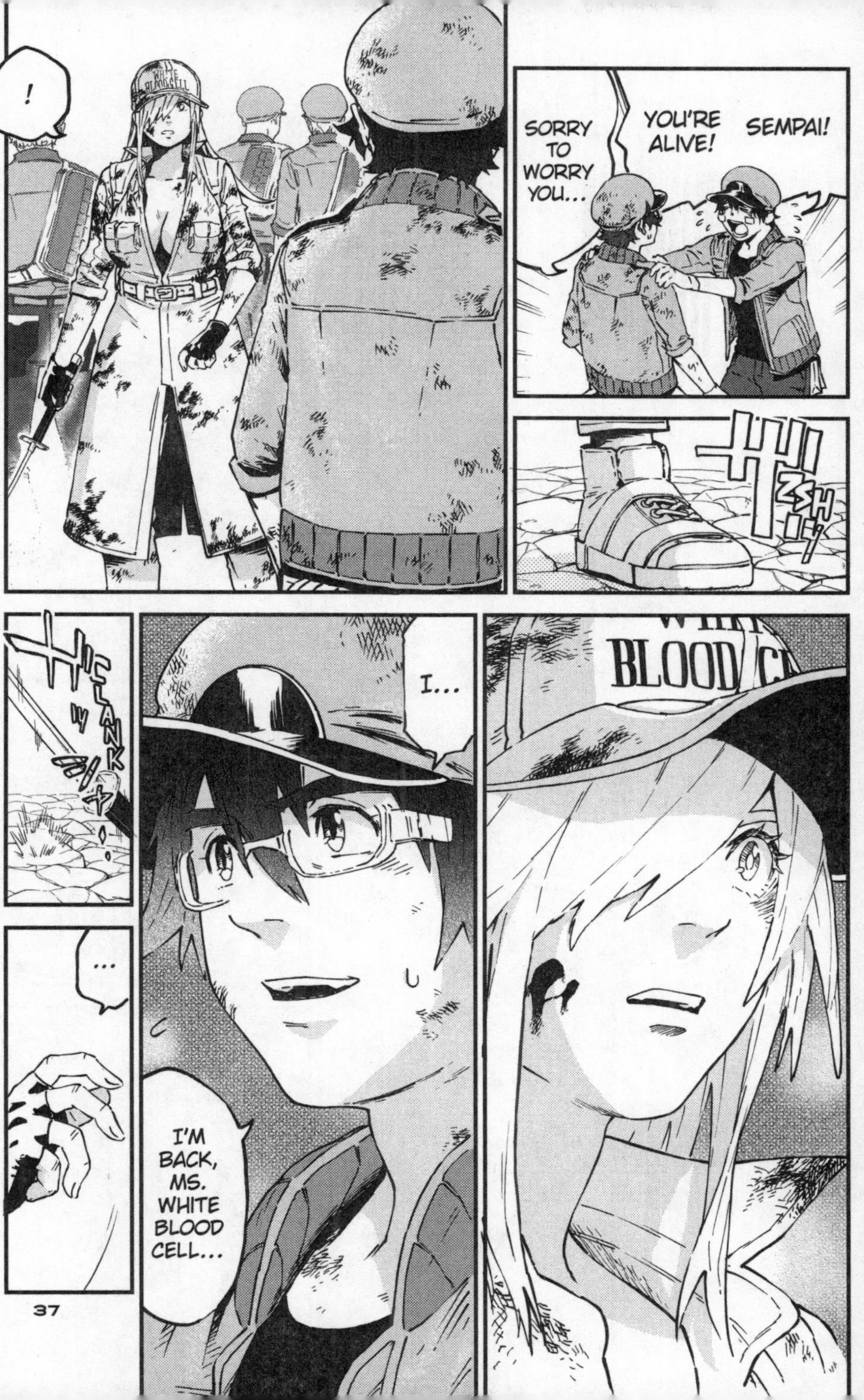
SEMPAI!
YOU'RE ALIVE!
SORRY TO WORRY YOU...
ZSH
!
BLOOD
I...
I'M BACK, MS. WHITE BLOOD CELL...
CLANK
...

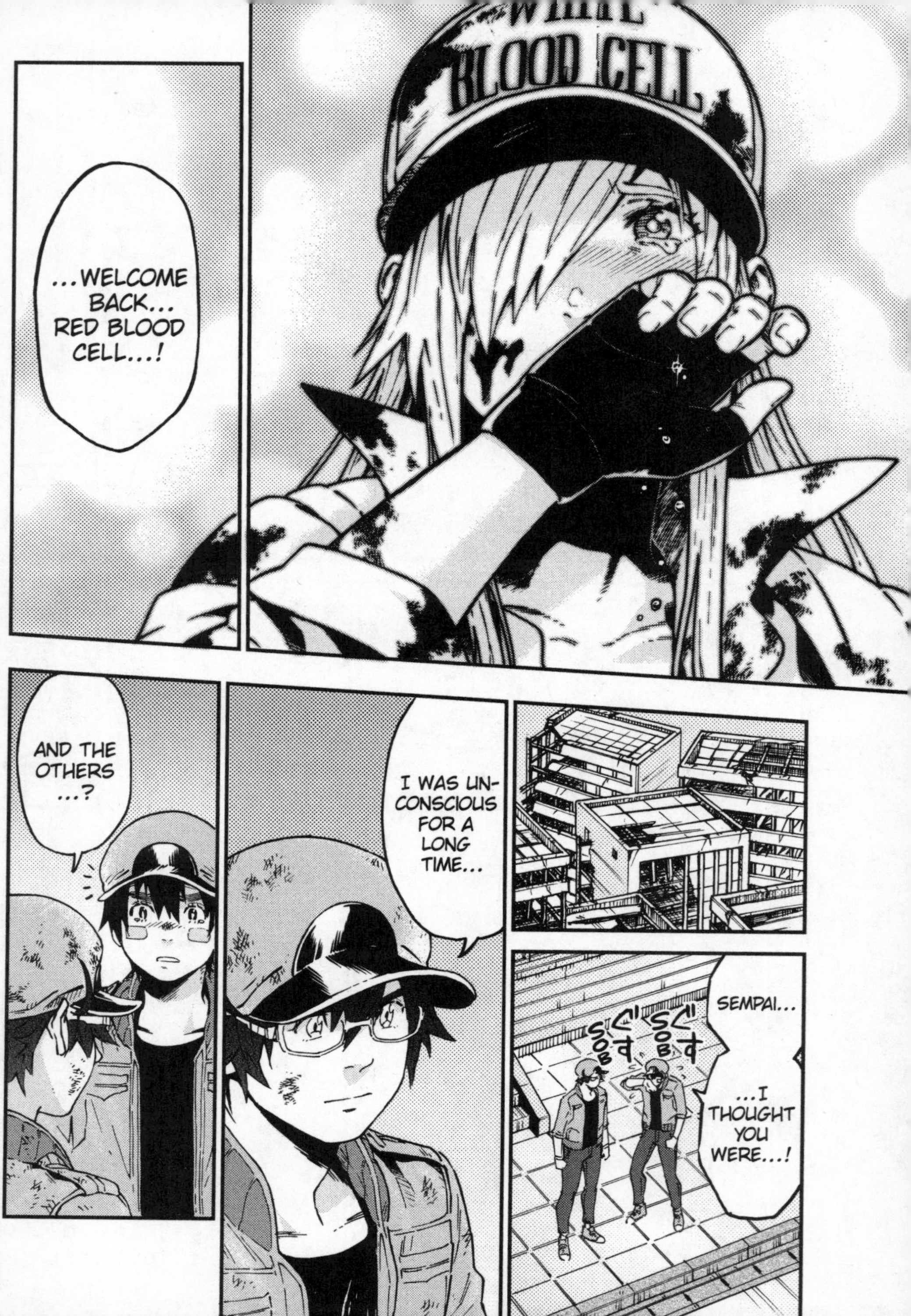
BLOOD CELL
...WELCOME BACK... RED BLOOD CELL...!
SEMPAI...
ぐす SOB
ぐす SOB
...I THOUGHT YOU WERE...!
I WAS UN-CONSCIOUS FOR A LONG TIME...
AND THE OTHERS ...?

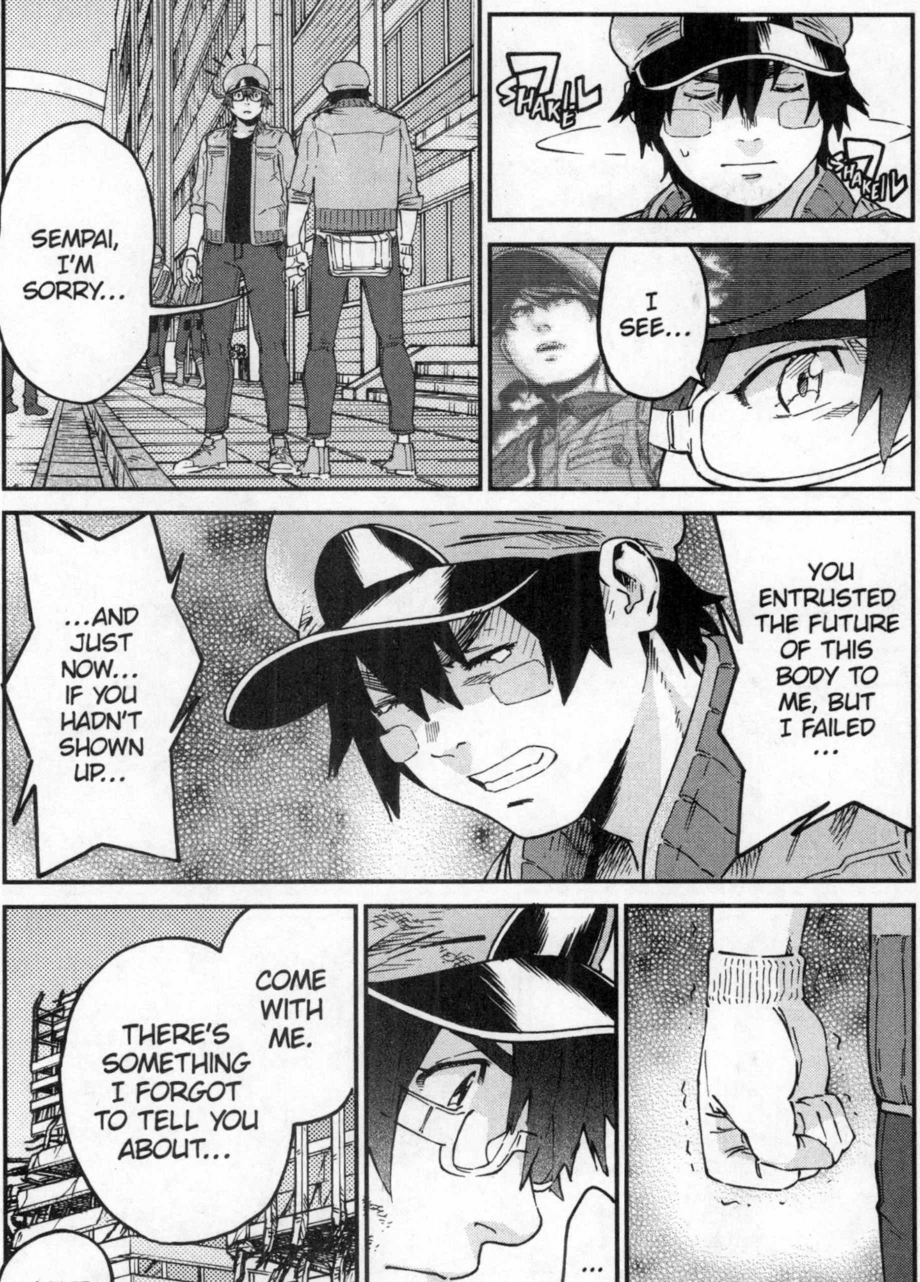
SHAKE
SHAKE
I SEE…
SEMPAI, I'M SORRY…
YOU ENTRUSTED THE FUTURE OF THIS BODY TO ME, BUT I FAILED …
…AND JUST NOW… IF YOU HADN'T SHOWN UP…
…
COME WITH ME.
THERE'S SOMETHING I FORGOT TO TELL YOU ABOUT…
WHAT?

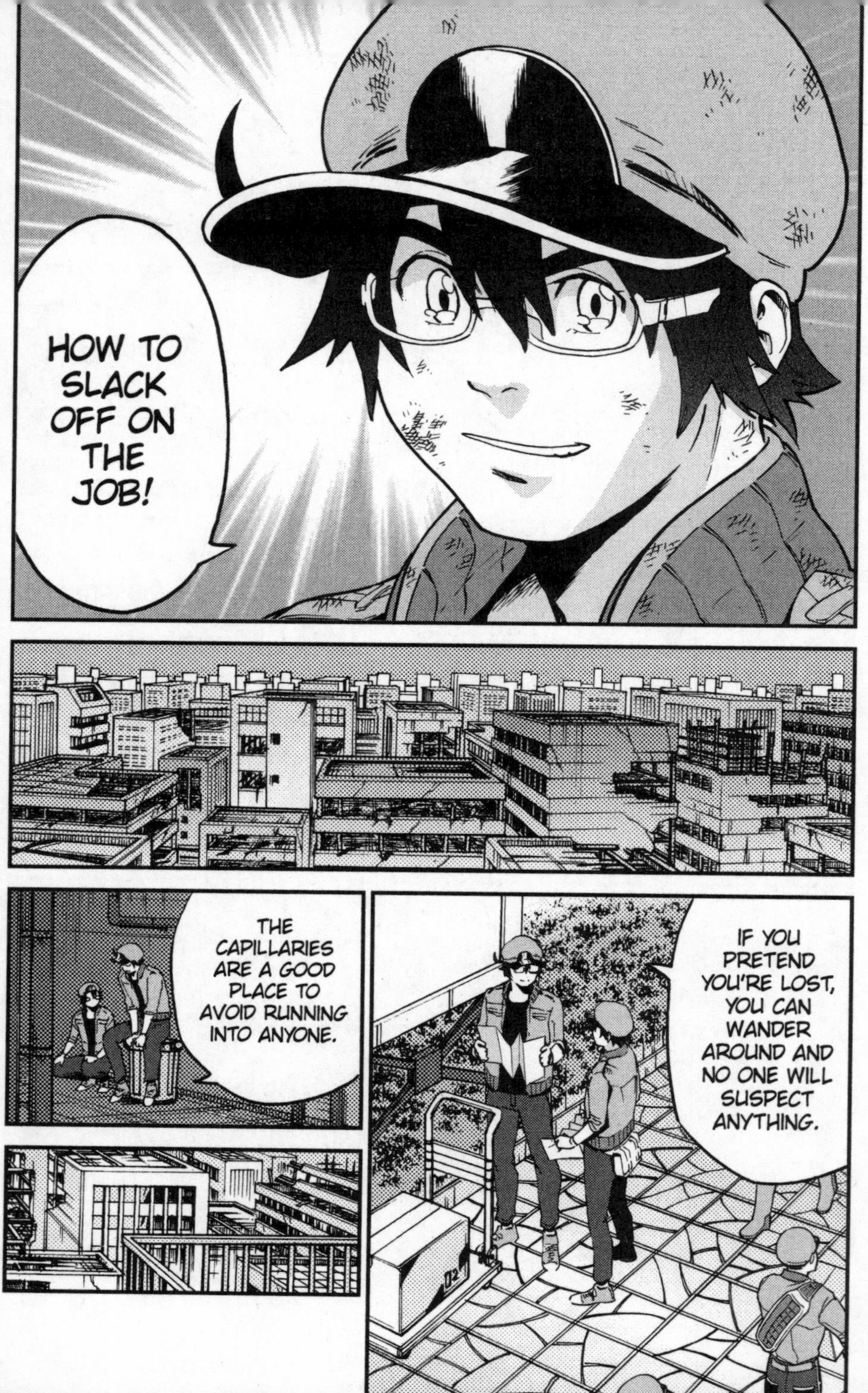
HOW TO SLACK OFF ON THE JOB!
IF YOU PRETEND YOU'RE LOST, YOU CAN WANDER AROUND AND NO ONE WILL SUSPECT ANYTHING.
THE CAPILLARIES ARE A GOOD PLACE TO AVOID RUNNING INTO ANYONE.

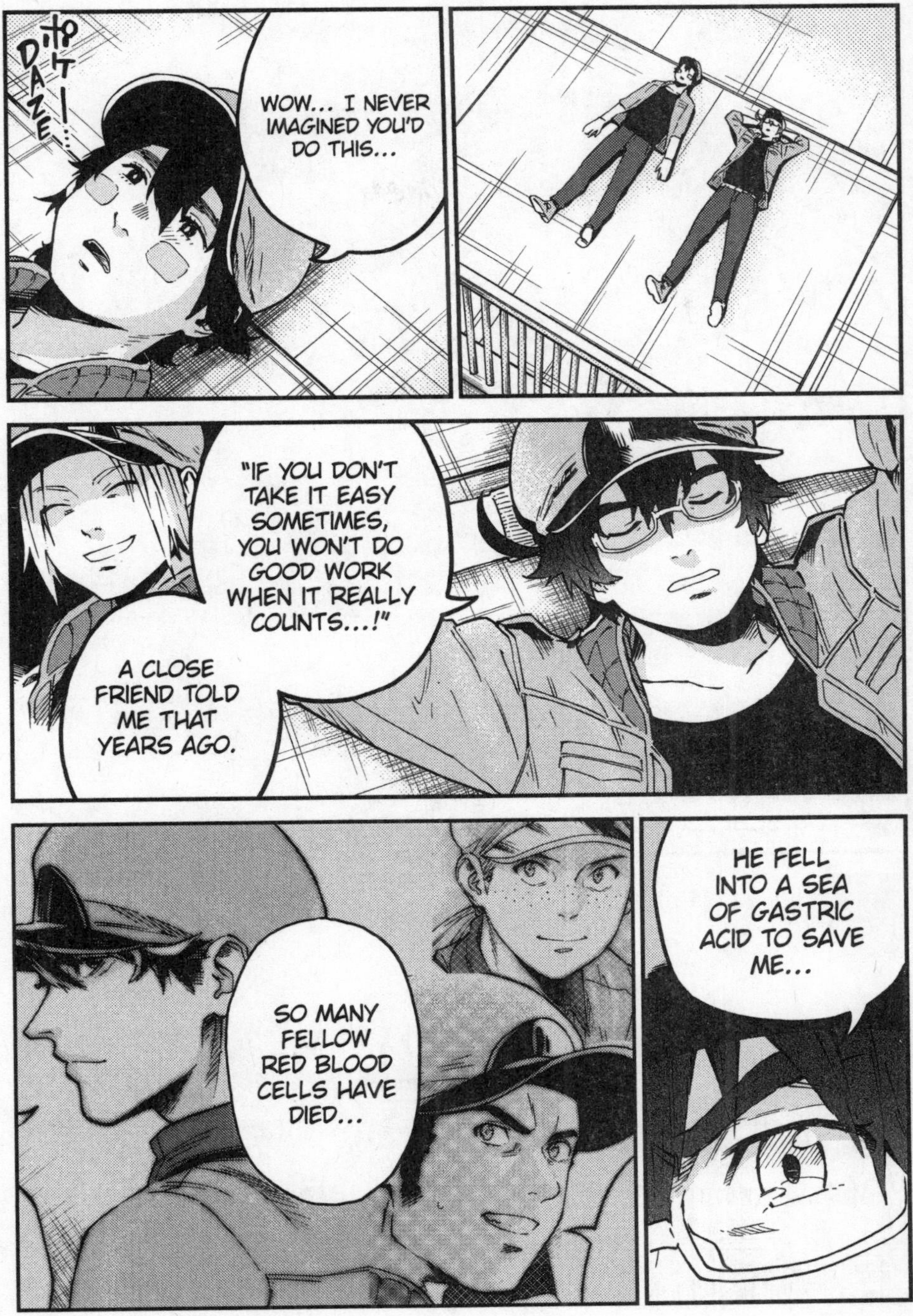
DAZE
WOW... I NEVER IMAGINED YOU'D DO THIS...
"IF YOU DON'T TAKE IT EASY SOMETIMES, YOU WON'T DO GOOD WORK WHEN IT REALLY COUNTS...!"
A CLOSE FRIEND TOLD ME THAT YEARS AGO.
HE FELL INTO A SEA OF GASTRIC ACID TO SAVE ME...
SO MANY FELLOW RED BLOOD CELLS HAVE DIED...

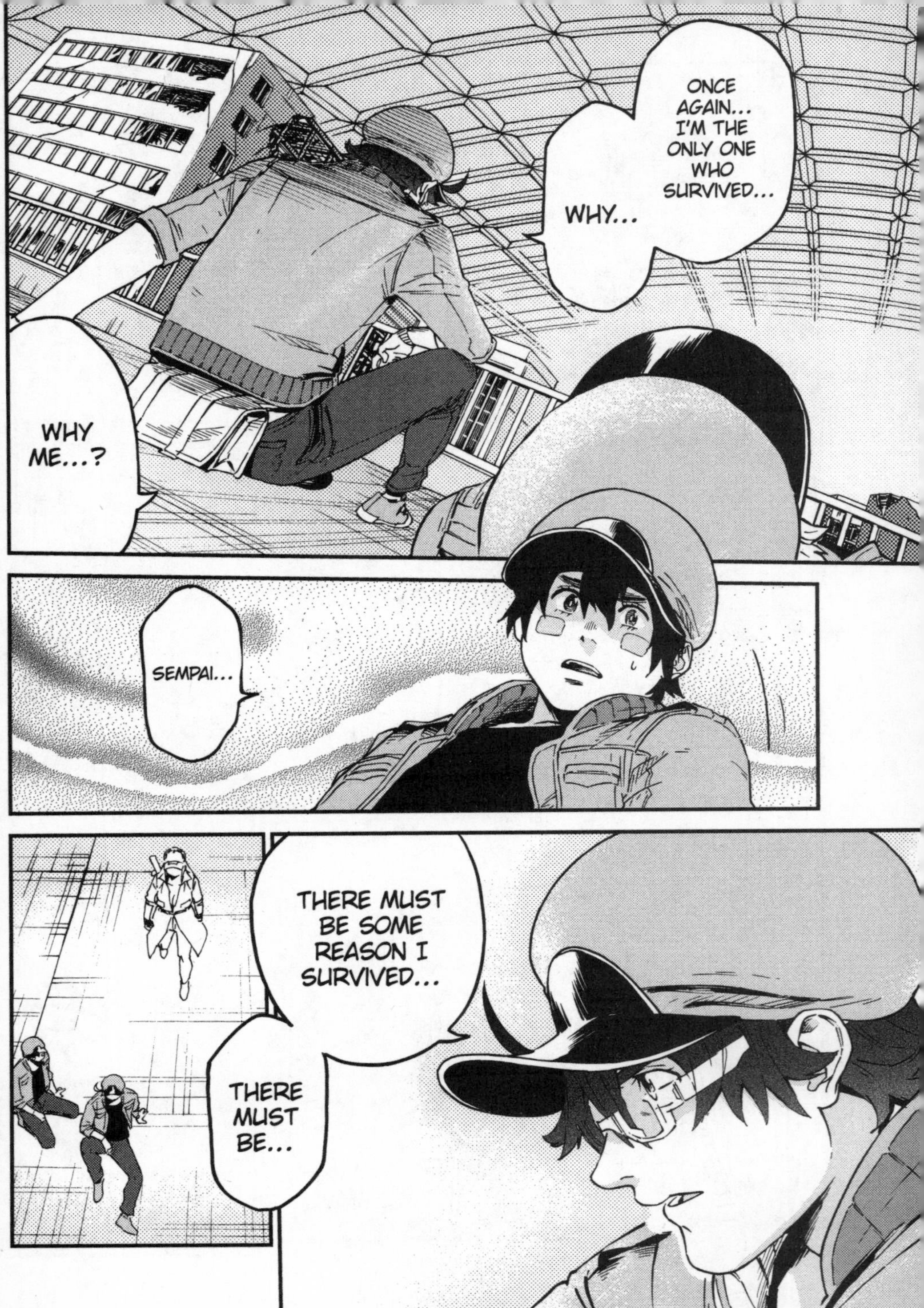
ONCE AGAIN... I'M THE ONLY ONE WHO SURVIVED...
WHY...
WHY ME...?
SEMPAI...
THERE MUST BE SOME REASON I SURVIVED...
THERE MUST BE...

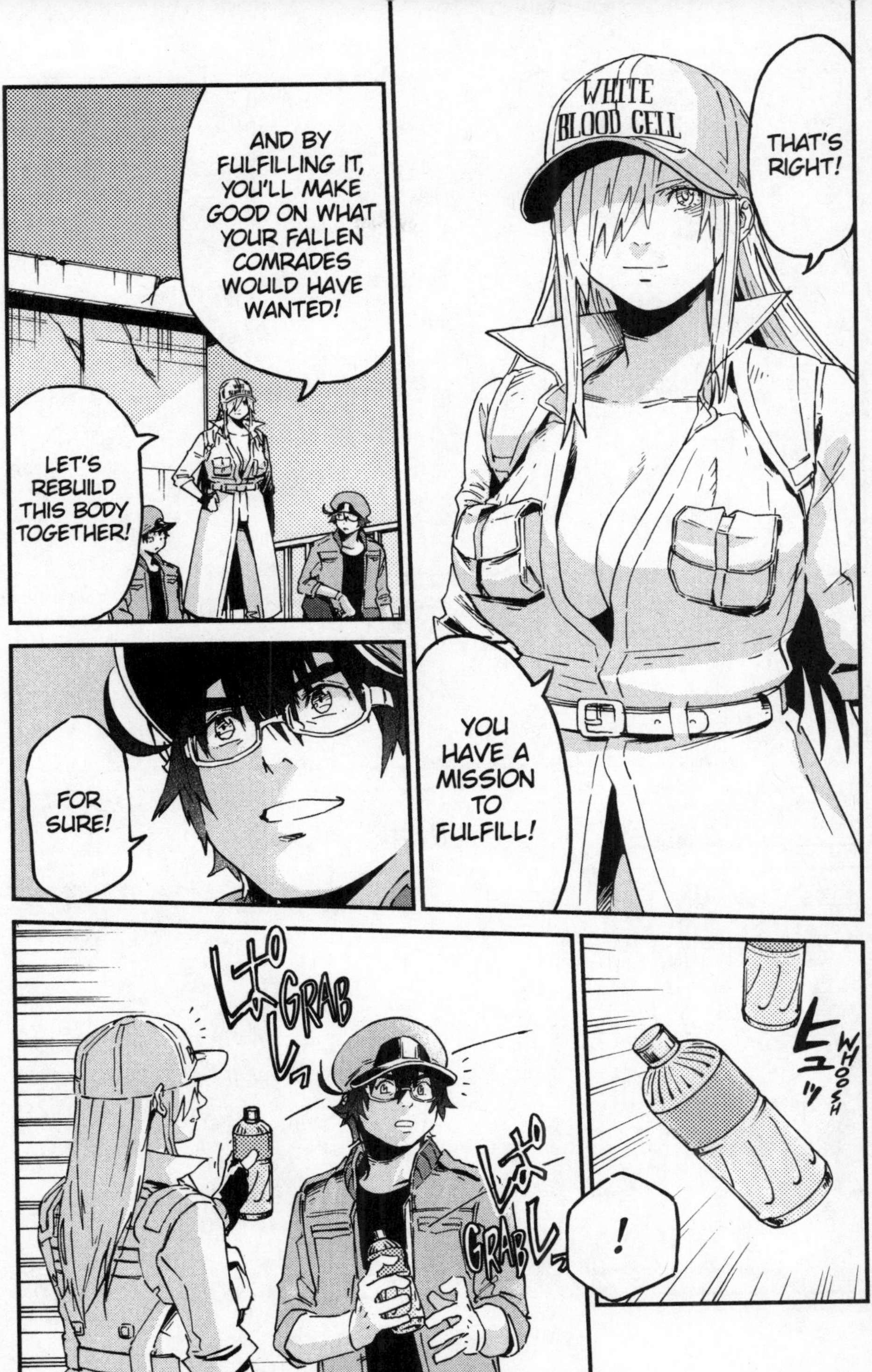
WHITE BLOOD CELL
THAT'S RIGHT!
YOU HAVE A MISSION TO FULFILL!
AND BY FULFILLING IT, YOU'LL MAKE GOOD ON WHAT YOUR FALLEN COMRADES WOULD HAVE WANTED!
LET'S REBUILD THIS BODY TOGETHER!
FOR SURE!
ヒュッ WHOOSH
ぱしっ GRAB
!
ぱしっ GRAB

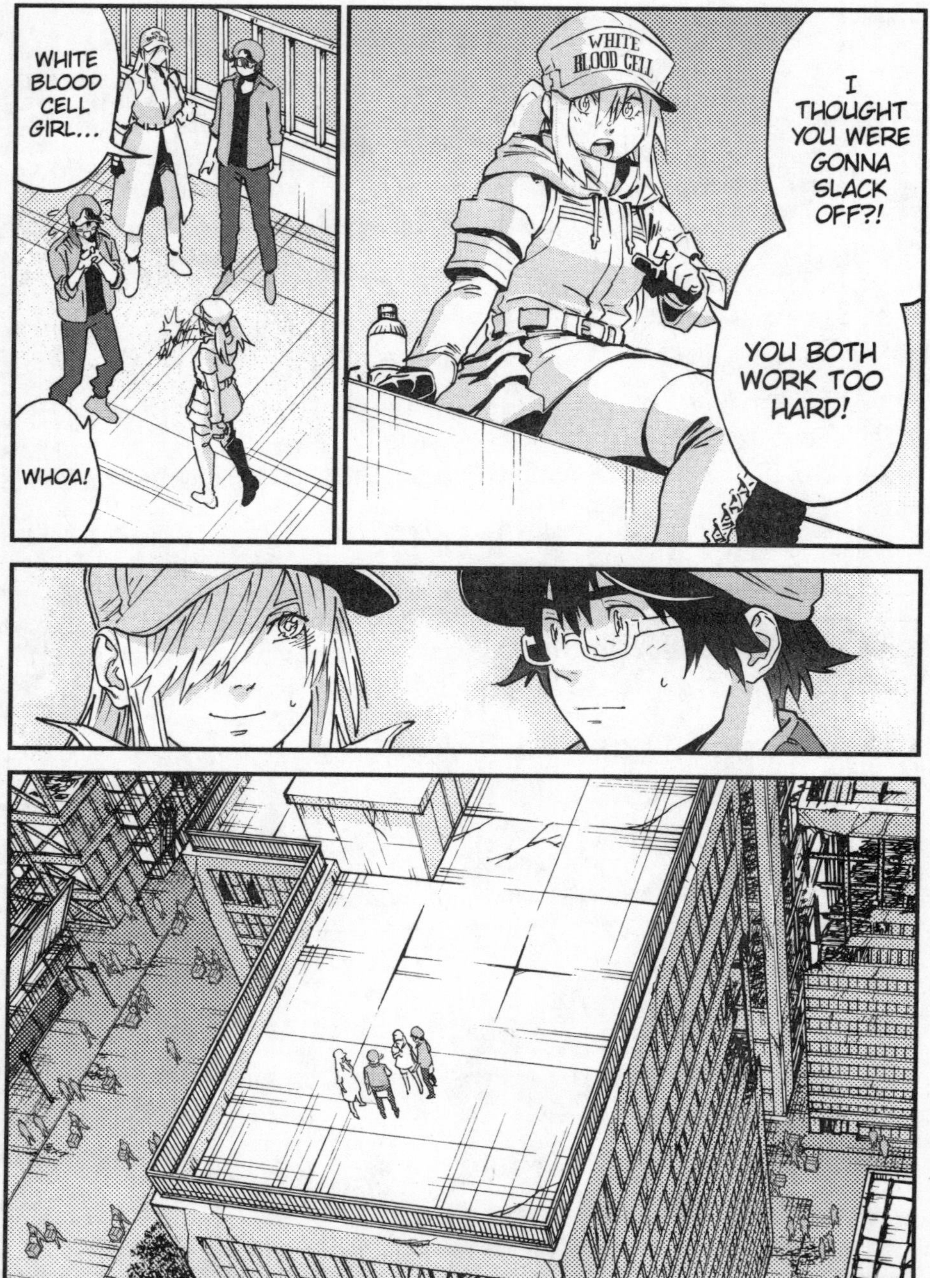
WHITE BLOOD CELL
I THOUGHT YOU WERE GONNA SLACK OFF?!
YOU BOTH WORK TOO HARD!
WHITE BLOOD CELL GIRL...
WHOA!

CHAPTER 43 - END

# 44. HERO, EDUCATION, STRIKE

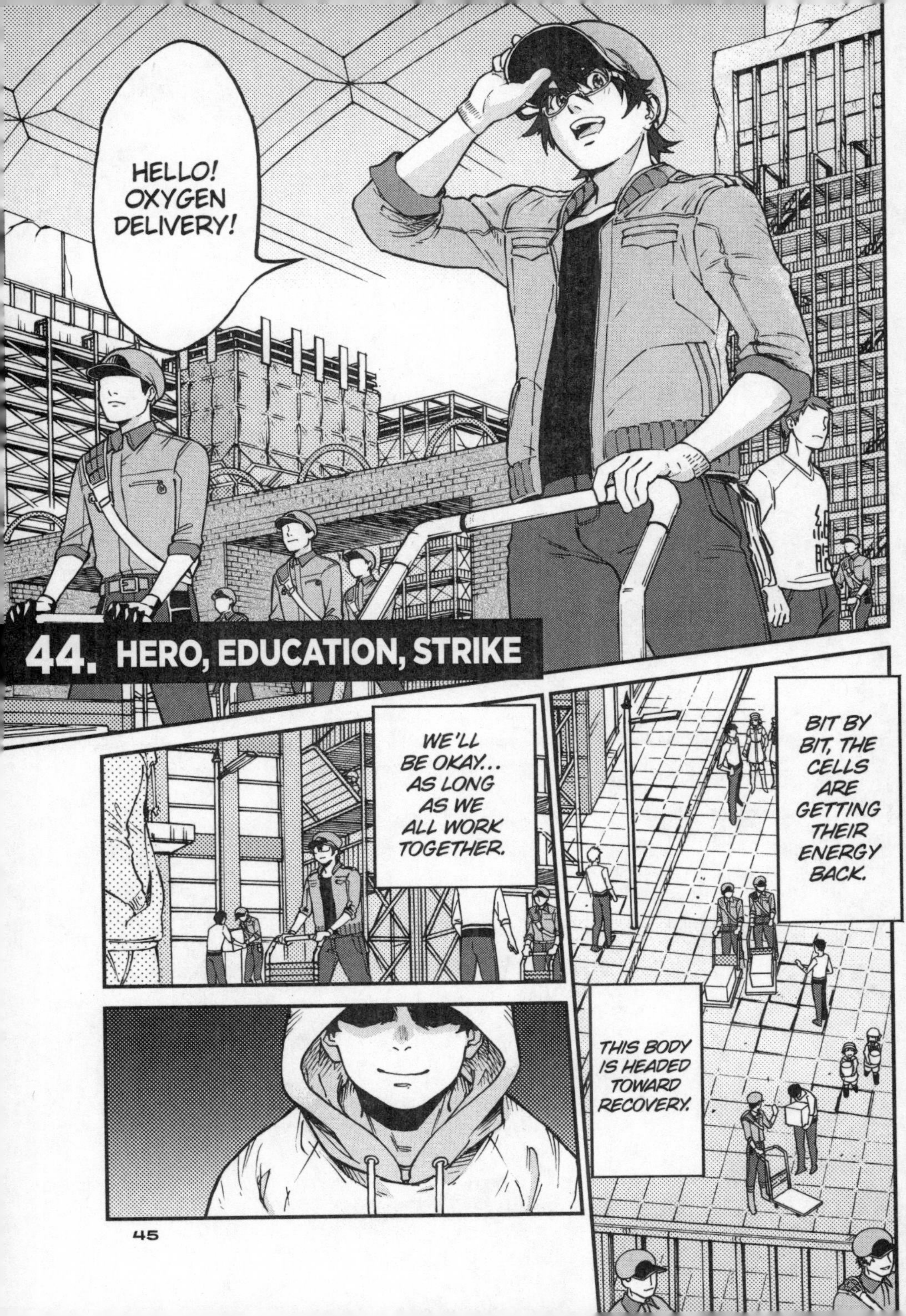
HELLO! OXYGEN DELIVERY!
BIT BY BIT, THE CELLS ARE GETTING THEIR ENERGY BACK.
THIS BODY IS HEADED TOWARD RECOVERY.
WE'LL BE OKAY... AS LONG AS WE ALL WORK TOGETHER.

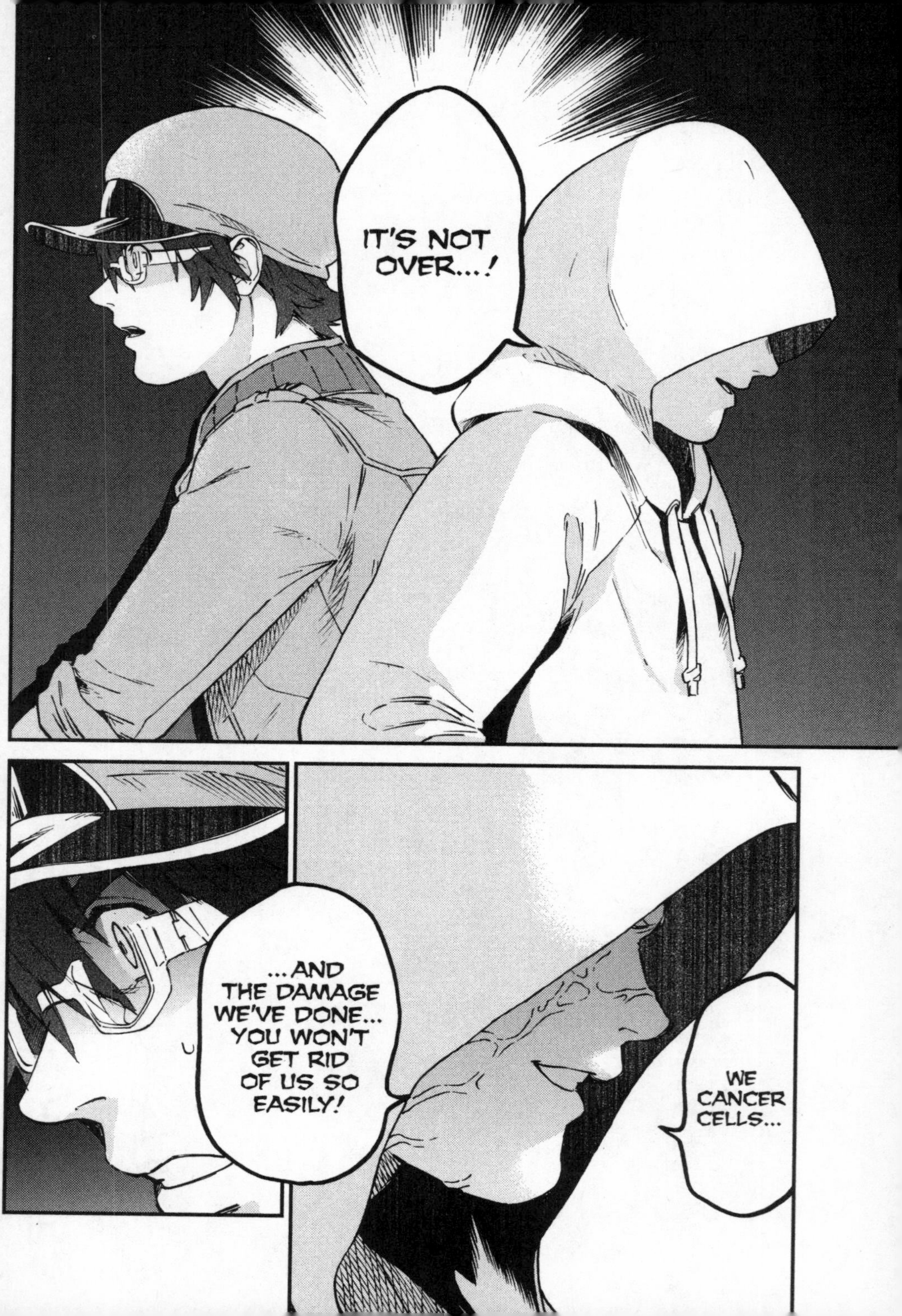
IT'S NOT OVER...!
WE CANCER CELLS...
...AND THE DAMAGE WE'VE DONE... YOU WON'T GET RID OF US SO EASILY!

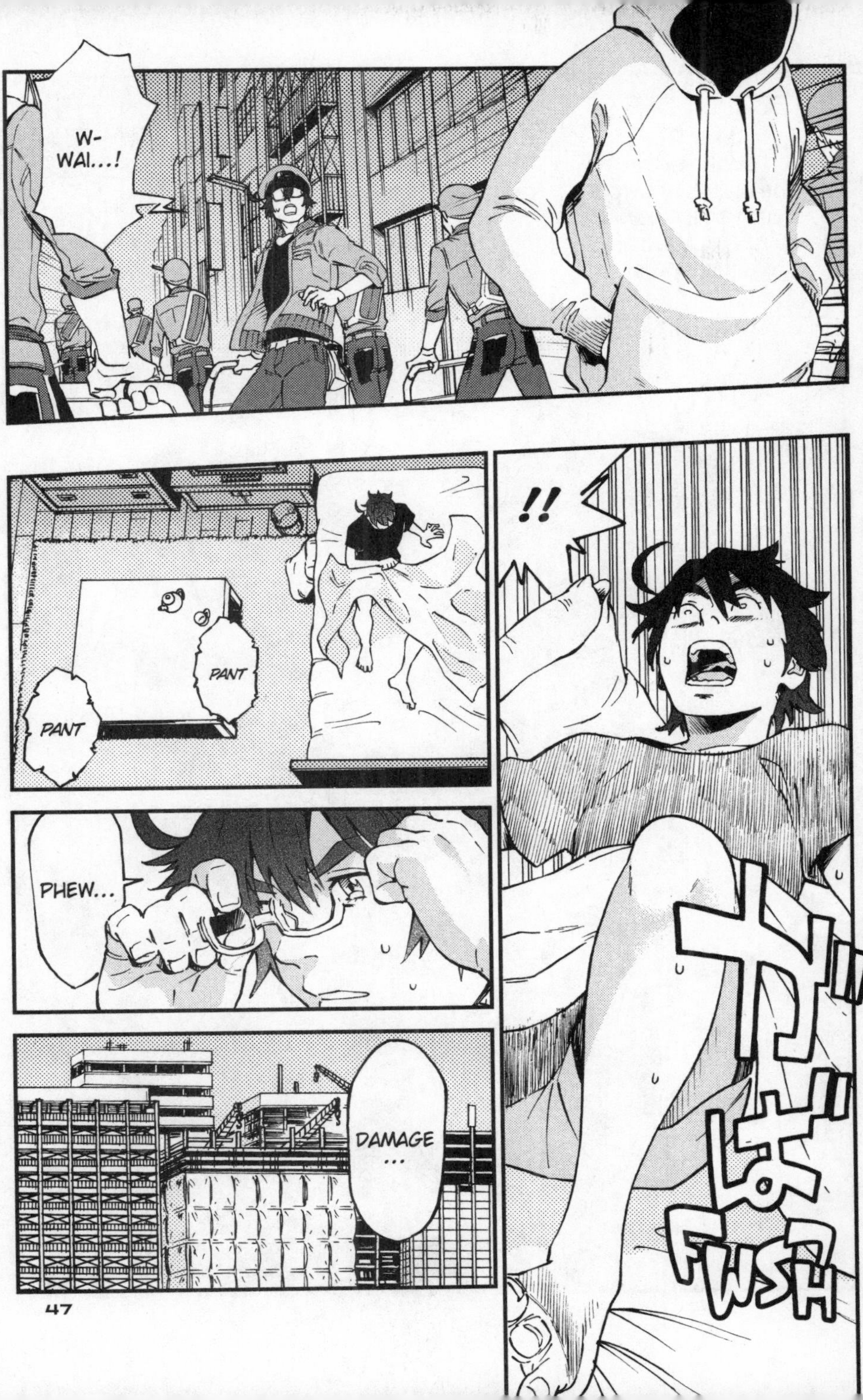
W-
WAI...!
!!
FWSH
PANT
PANT
PHEW...
DAMAGE
...

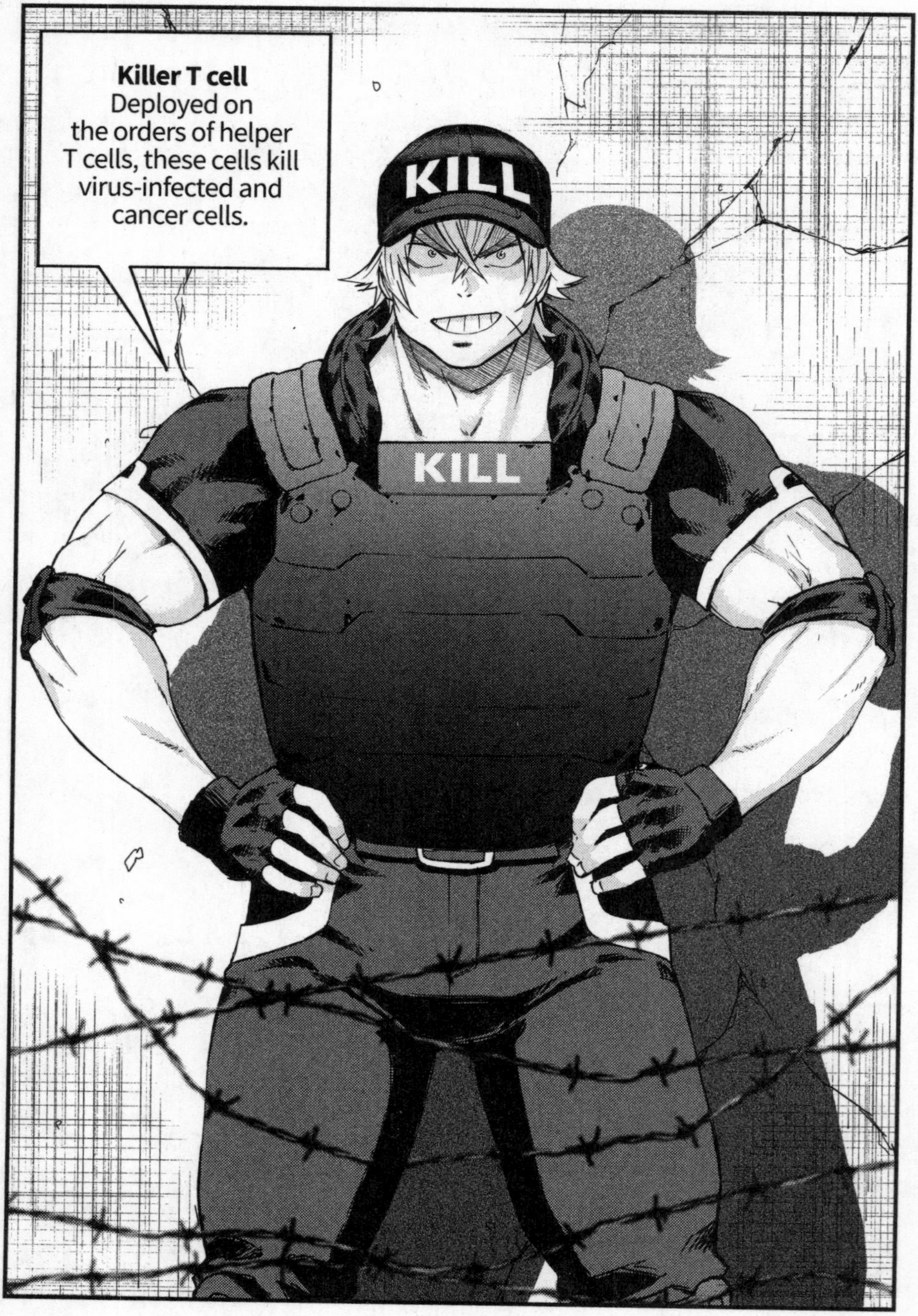
**Killer T cell**
Deployed on the orders of helper T cells, these cells kill virus-infected and cancer cells.
KILL
KILL

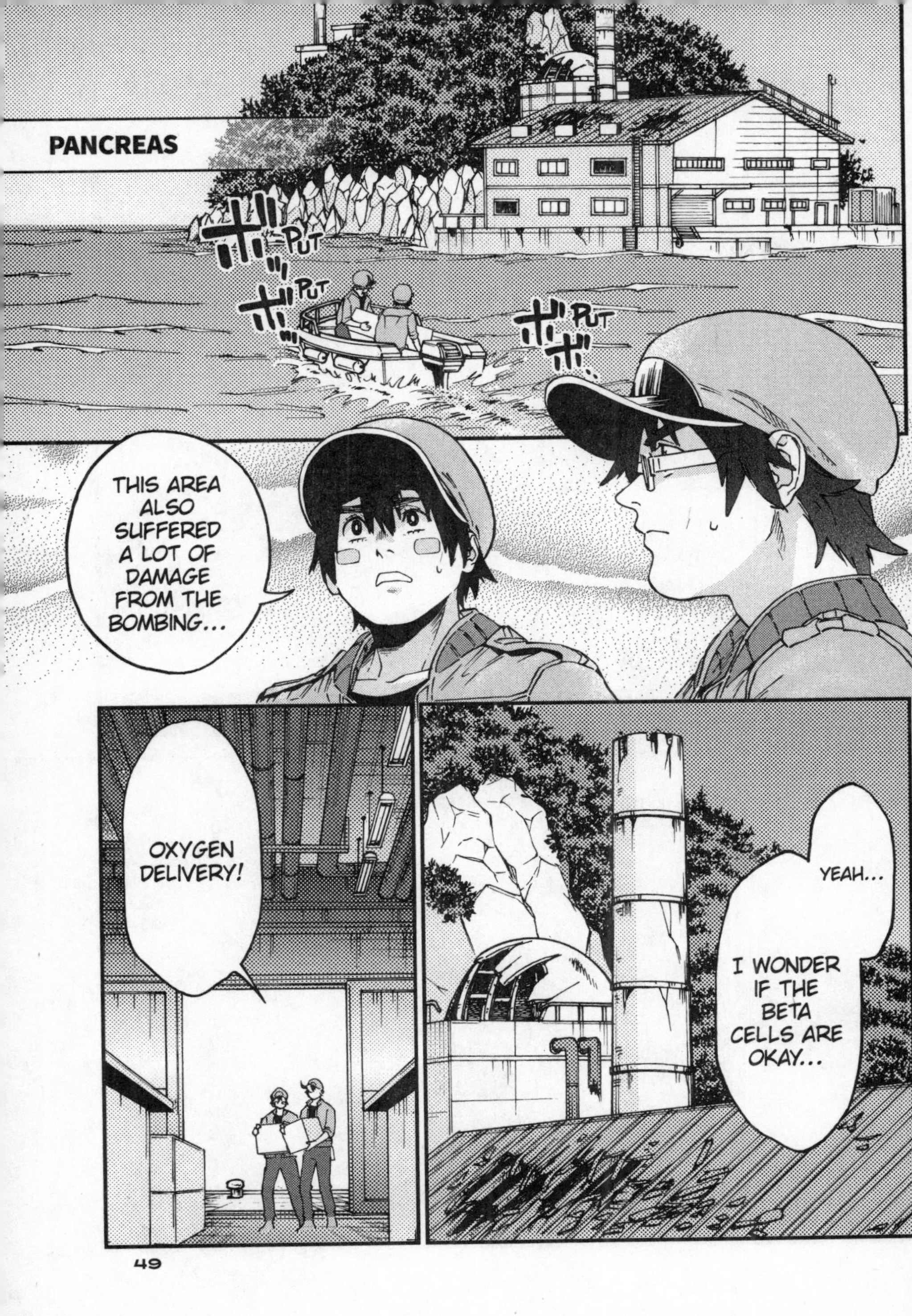
PANCREAS
PUT
PUT
PUT
THIS AREA ALSO SUFFERED A LOT OF DAMAGE FROM THE BOMBING...
YEAH...
I WONDER IF THE BETA CELLS ARE OKAY...
OXYGEN DELIVERY!

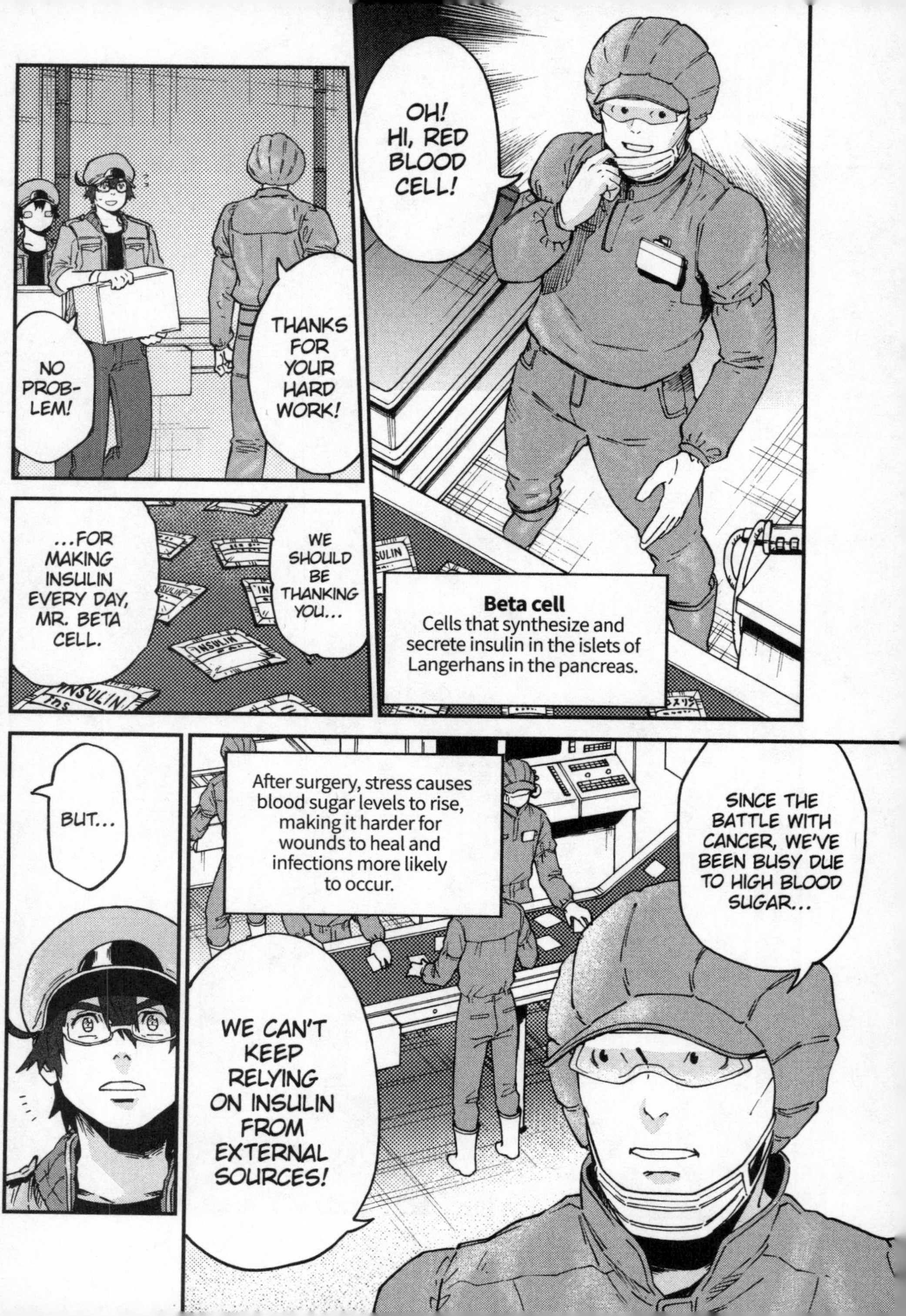

OH! HI, RED BLOOD CELL!
Beta cell
Cells that synthesize and secrete insulin in the islets of Langerhans in the pancreas.
THANKS FOR YOUR HARD WORK!
NO PROBLEM!
WE SHOULD BE THANKING YOU...
...FOR MAKING INSULIN EVERY DAY, MR. BETA CELL.
SINCE THE BATTLE WITH CANCER, WE'VE BEEN BUSY DUE TO HIGH BLOOD SUGAR...
After surgery, stress causes blood sugar levels to rise, making it harder for wounds to heal and infections more likely to occur.
WE CAN'T KEEP RELYING ON INSULIN FROM EXTERNAL SOURCES!
BUT...

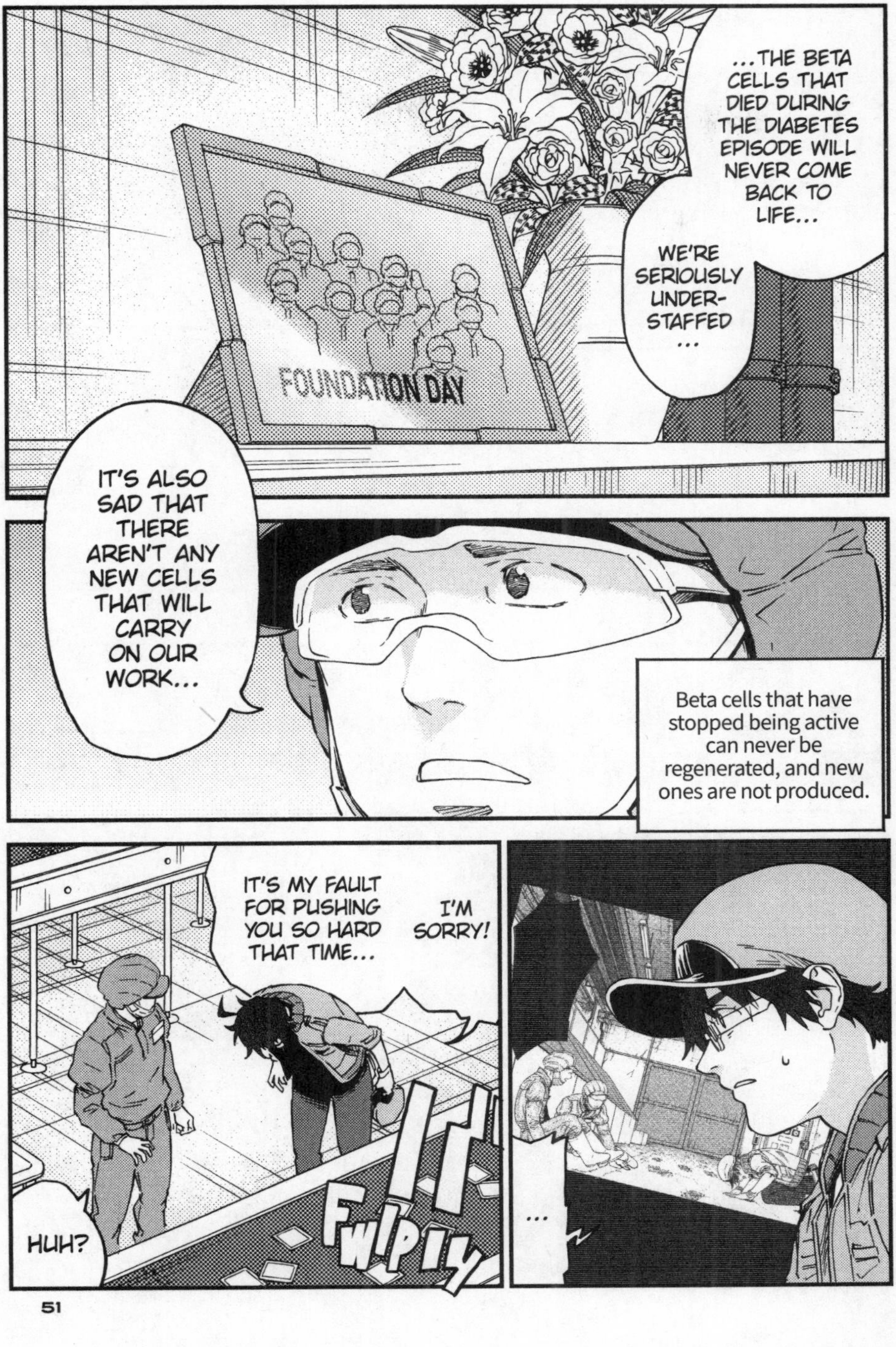
...THE BETA CELLS THAT DIED DURING THE DIABETES EPISODE WILL NEVER COME BACK TO LIFE...
WE'RE SERIOUSLY UNDER-STAFFED ...
FOUNDATION DAY
IT'S ALSO SAD THAT THERE AREN'T ANY NEW CELLS THAT WILL CARRY ON OUR WORK...
Beta cells that have stopped being active can never be regenerated, and new ones are not produced.
...
I'M SORRY!
IT'S MY FAULT FOR PUSHING YOU SO HARD THAT TIME...
HUH?

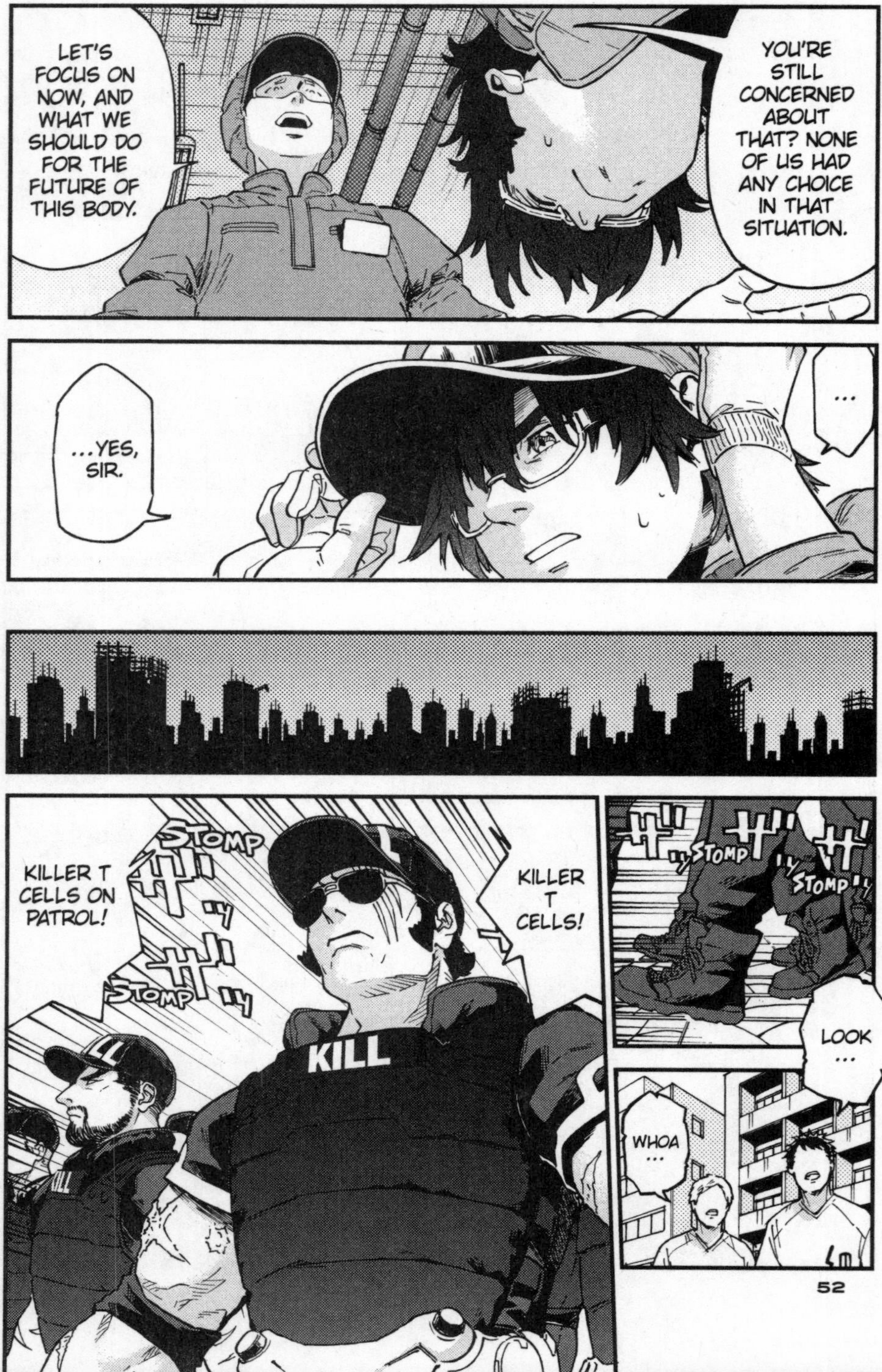
YOU'RE STILL CONCERNED ABOUT THAT? NONE OF US HAD ANY CHOICE IN THAT SITUATION.
LET'S FOCUS ON NOW, AND WHAT WE SHOULD DO FOR THE FUTURE OF THIS BODY.
...
...YES, SIR.
STOMP
STOMP
LOOK ...
WHOA ...
KILLER T CELLS!
KILLER T CELLS ON PATROL!
STOMP
STOMP
KILL

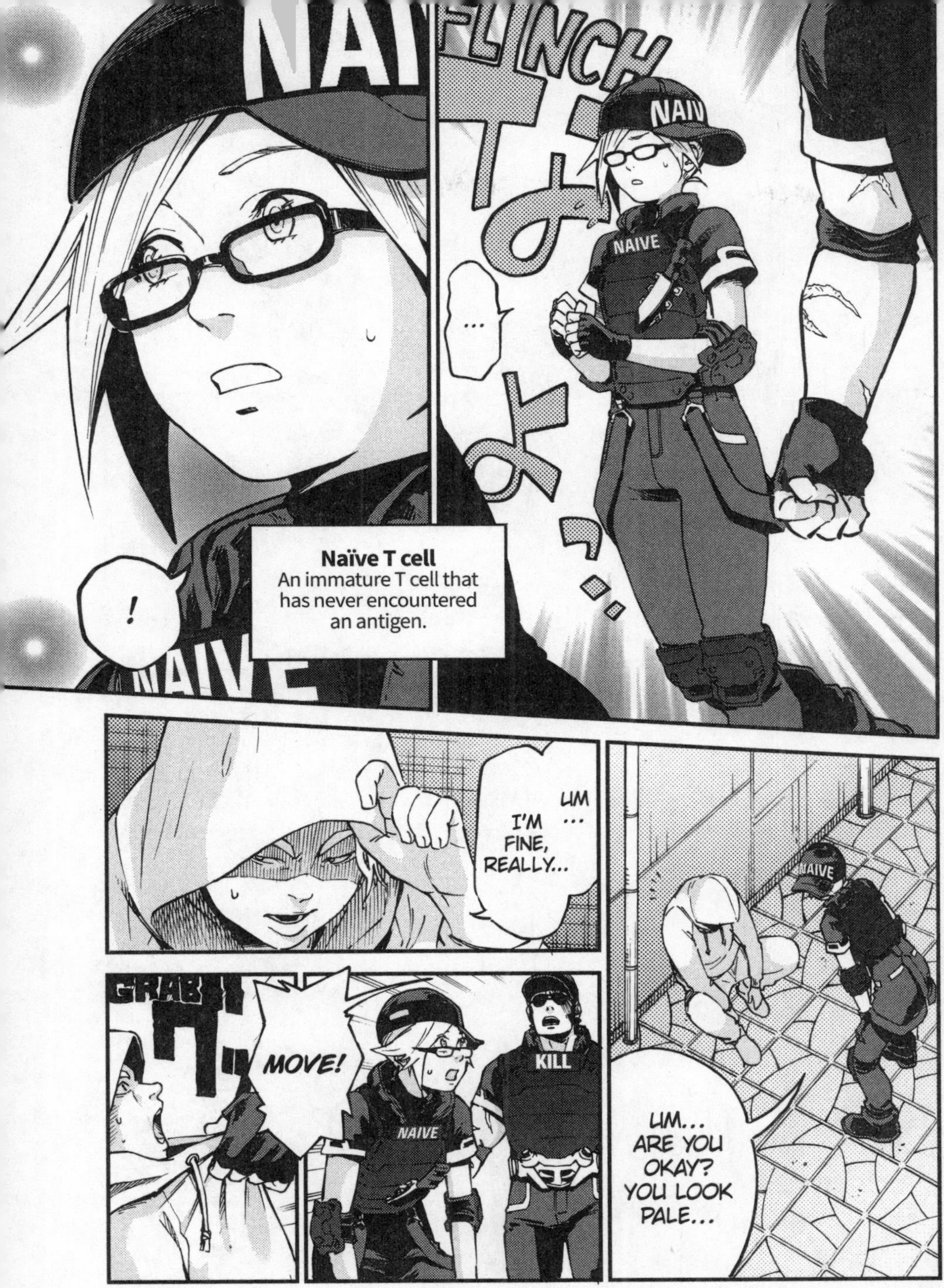
FLINCH
...
Naïve T cell
An immature T cell that has never encountered an antigen.
!
UM... ARE YOU OKAY? YOU LOOK PALE...
UM... I'M FINE, REALLY...
GRAB!!
MOVE!

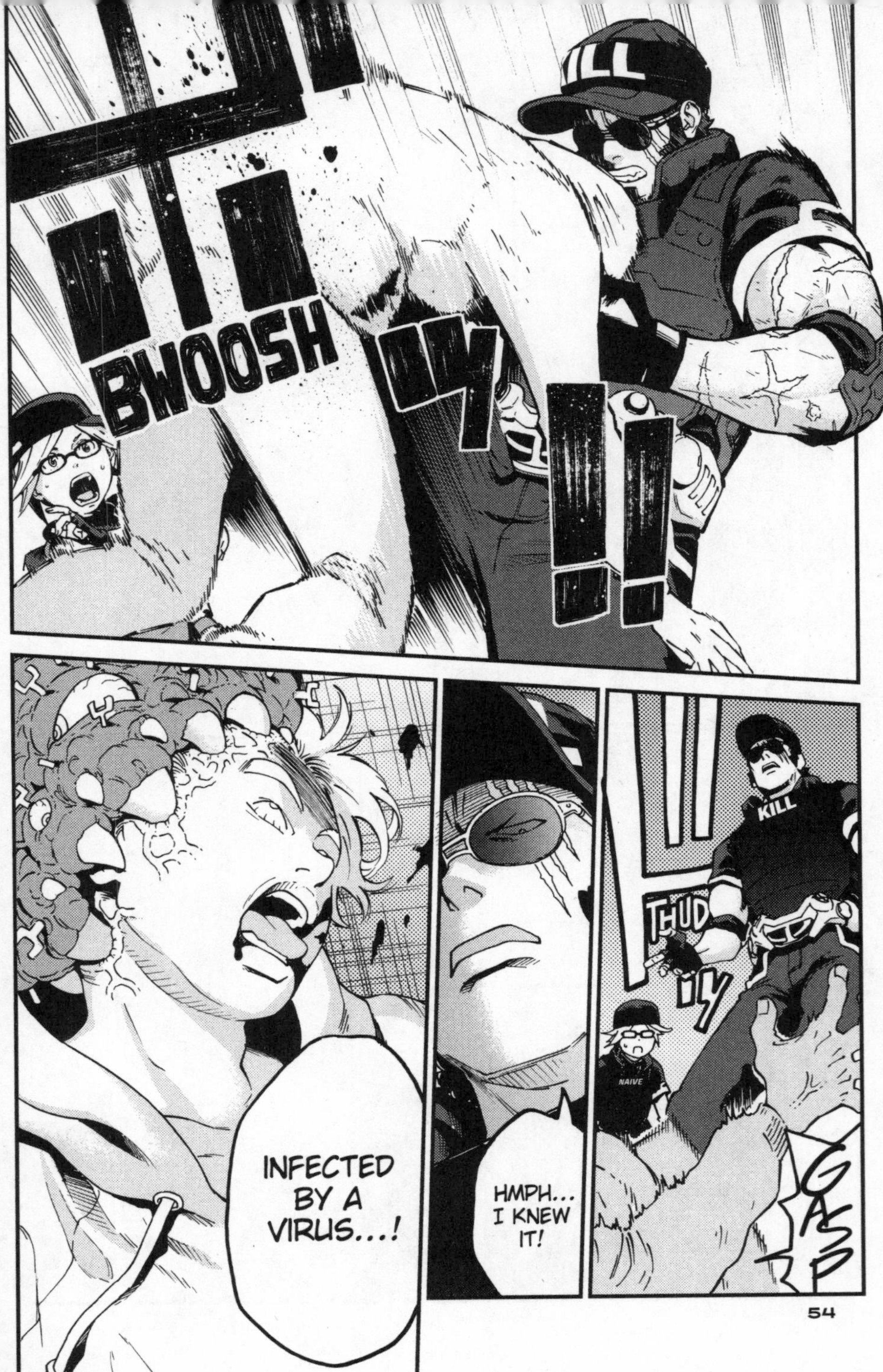
BWOOSH
KILL
THUD
NAIVE
GASP
HMPH... I KNEW IT!
INFECTED BY A VIRUS...!

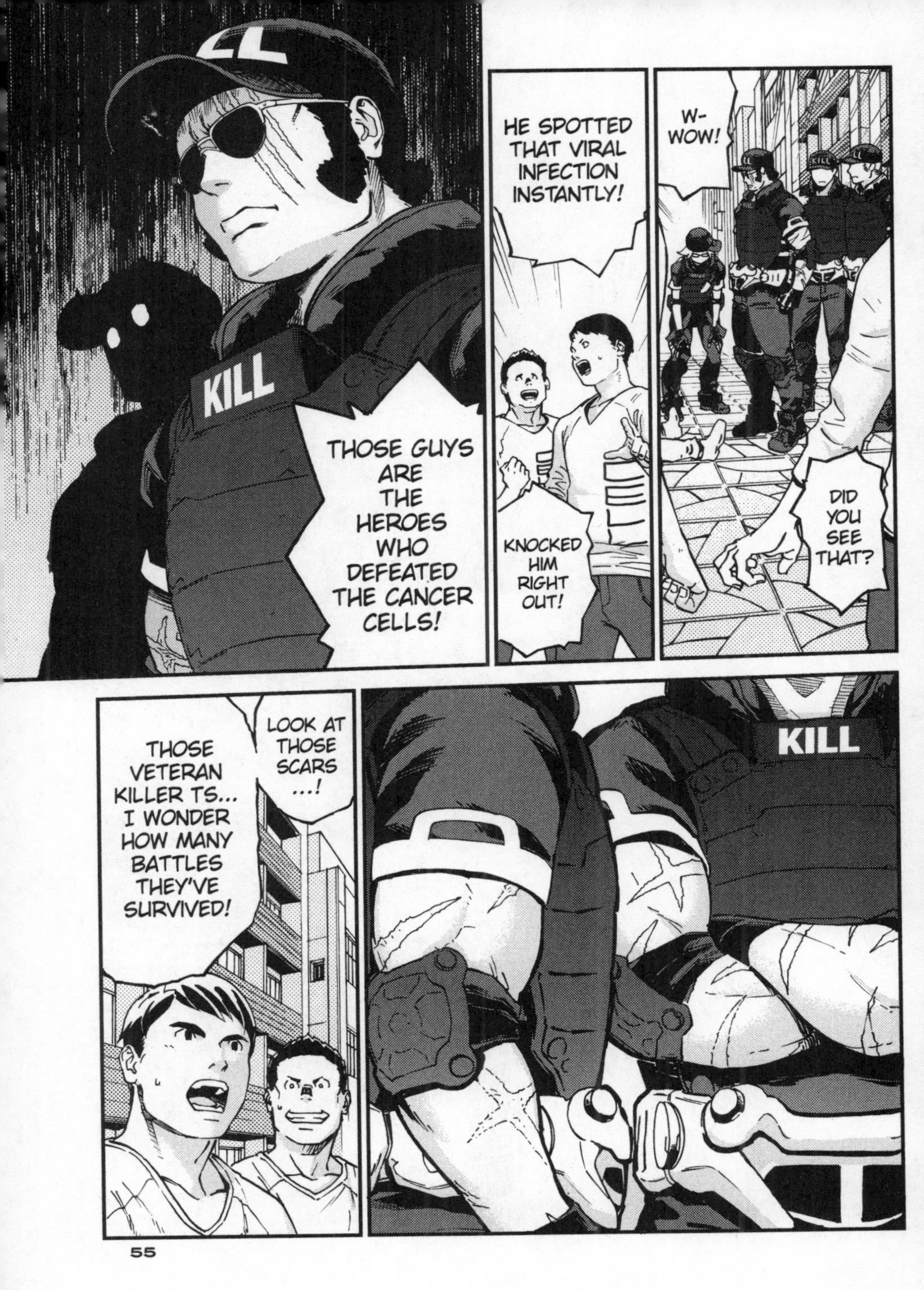
W-WOW!
DID YOU SEE THAT?
HE SPOTTED THAT VIRAL INFECTION INSTANTLY!
KNOCKED HIM RIGHT OUT!
KILL
THOSE GUYS ARE THE HEROES WHO DEFEATED THE CANCER CELLS!
KILL
LOOK AT THOSE SCARS ...!
THOSE VETERAN KILLER TS... I WONDER HOW MANY BATTLES THEY'VE SURVIVED!

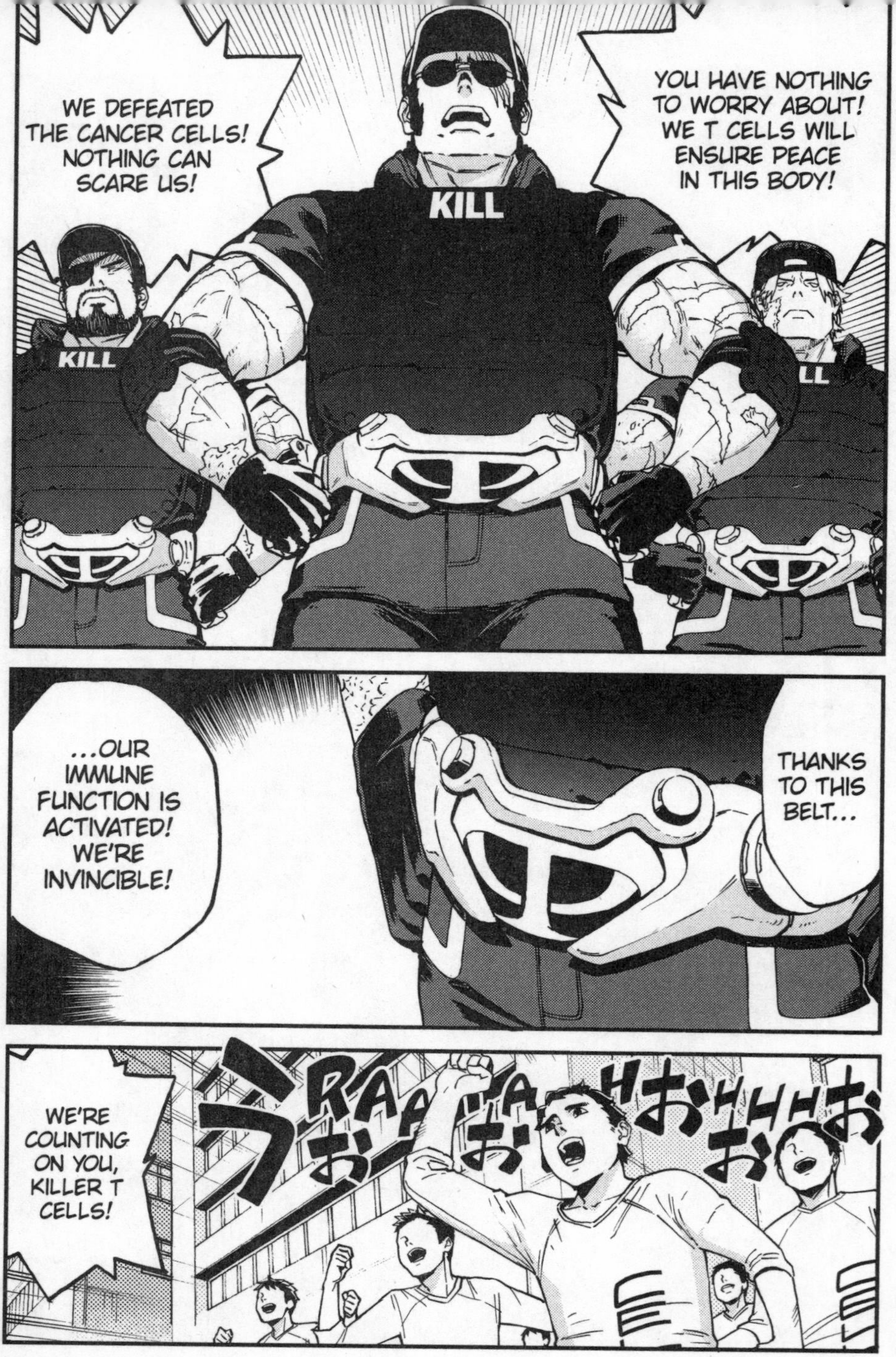
YOU HAVE NOTHING TO WORRY ABOUT! WE T CELLS WILL ENSURE PEACE IN THIS BODY!
WE DEFEATED THE CANCER CELLS! NOTHING CAN SCARE US!
KILL
KILL
THANKS TO THIS BELT...
...OUR IMMUNE FUNCTION IS ACTIVATED! WE'RE INVINCIBLE!
RAAAHHHH
WE'RE COUNTING ON YOU, KILLER T CELLS!

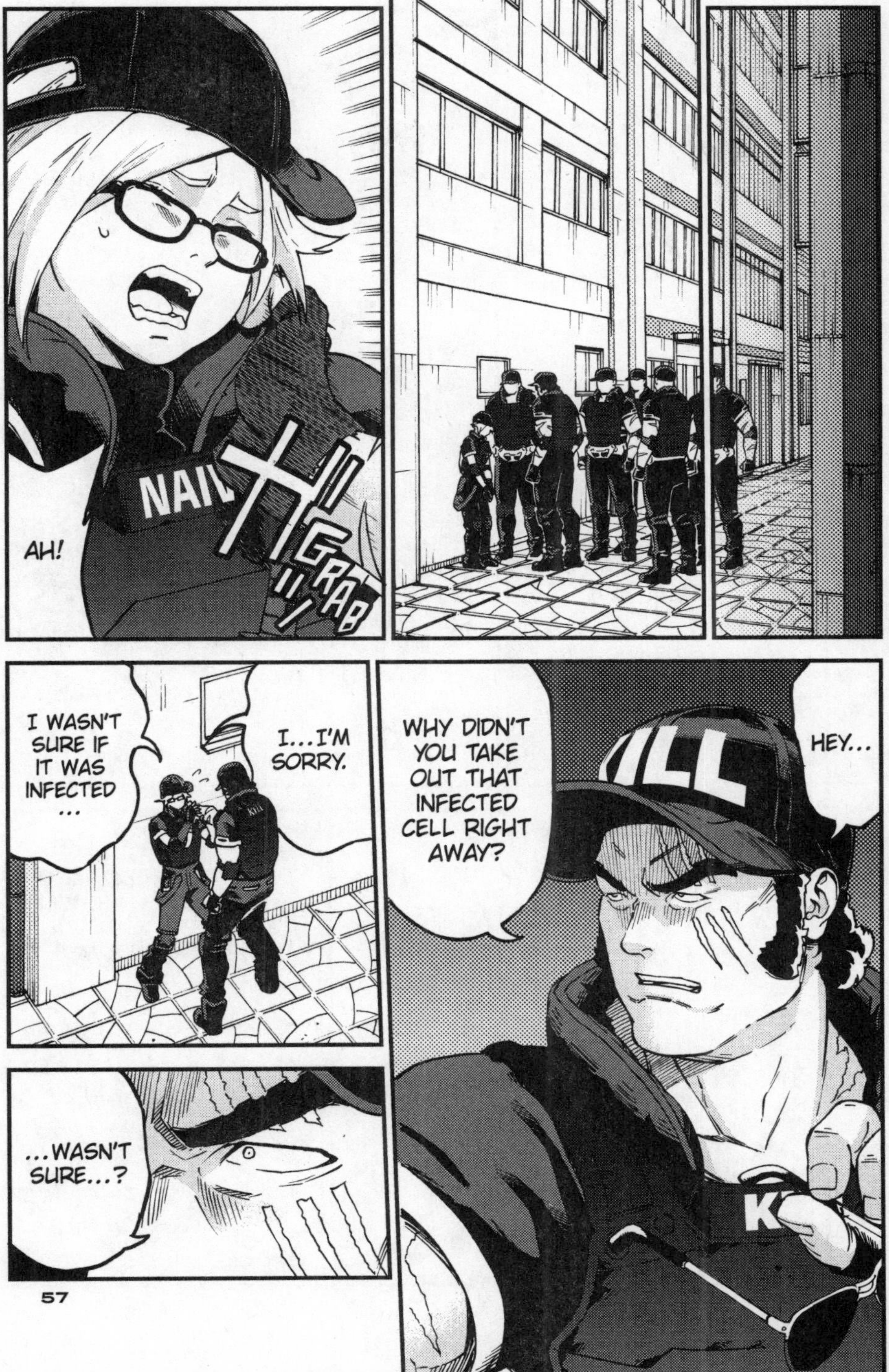
GRAB
AH!
HEY...
WHY DIDN'T YOU TAKE OUT THAT INFECTED CELL RIGHT AWAY?
I...I'M SORRY.
I WASN'T SURE IF IT WAS INFECTED ...
...WASN'T SURE...?

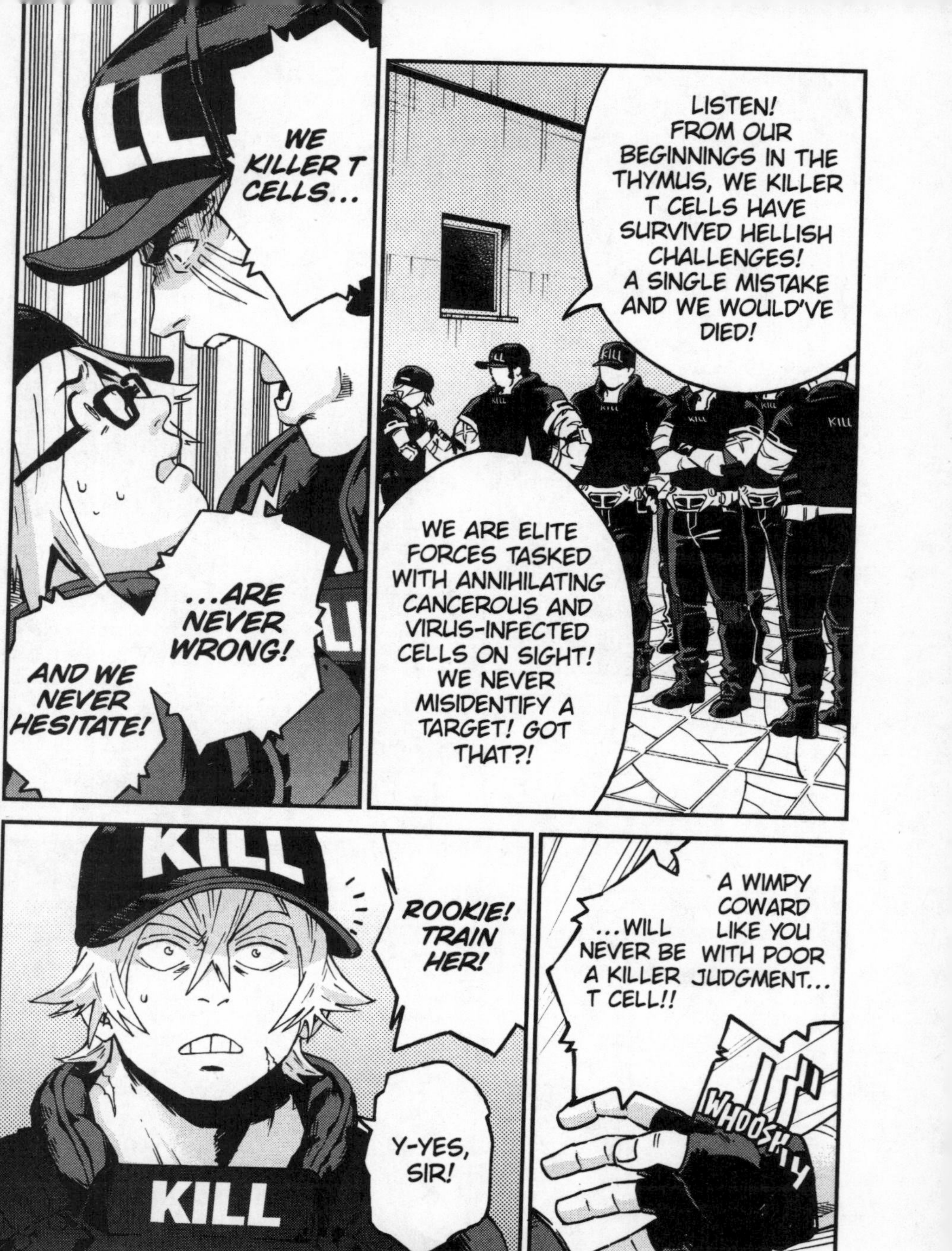
LISTEN! FROM OUR BEGINNINGS IN THE THYMUS, WE KILLER T CELLS HAVE SURVIVED HELLISH CHALLENGES! A SINGLE MISTAKE AND WE WOULD'VE DIED!
WE ARE ELITE FORCES TASKED WITH ANNIHILATING CANCEROUS AND VIRUS-INFECTED CELLS ON SIGHT! WE NEVER MISIDENTIFY A TARGET! GOT THAT?!
KILL
WE KILLER T CELLS...
...ARE NEVER WRONG!
AND WE NEVER HESITATE!
A WIMPY COWARD LIKE YOU WITH POOR JUDGMENT...
...WILL NEVER BE A KILLER T CELL!!
WHOOSH
KILL
ROOKIE! TRAIN HER!
Y-YES, SIR!
KILL

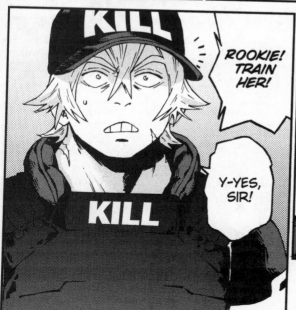

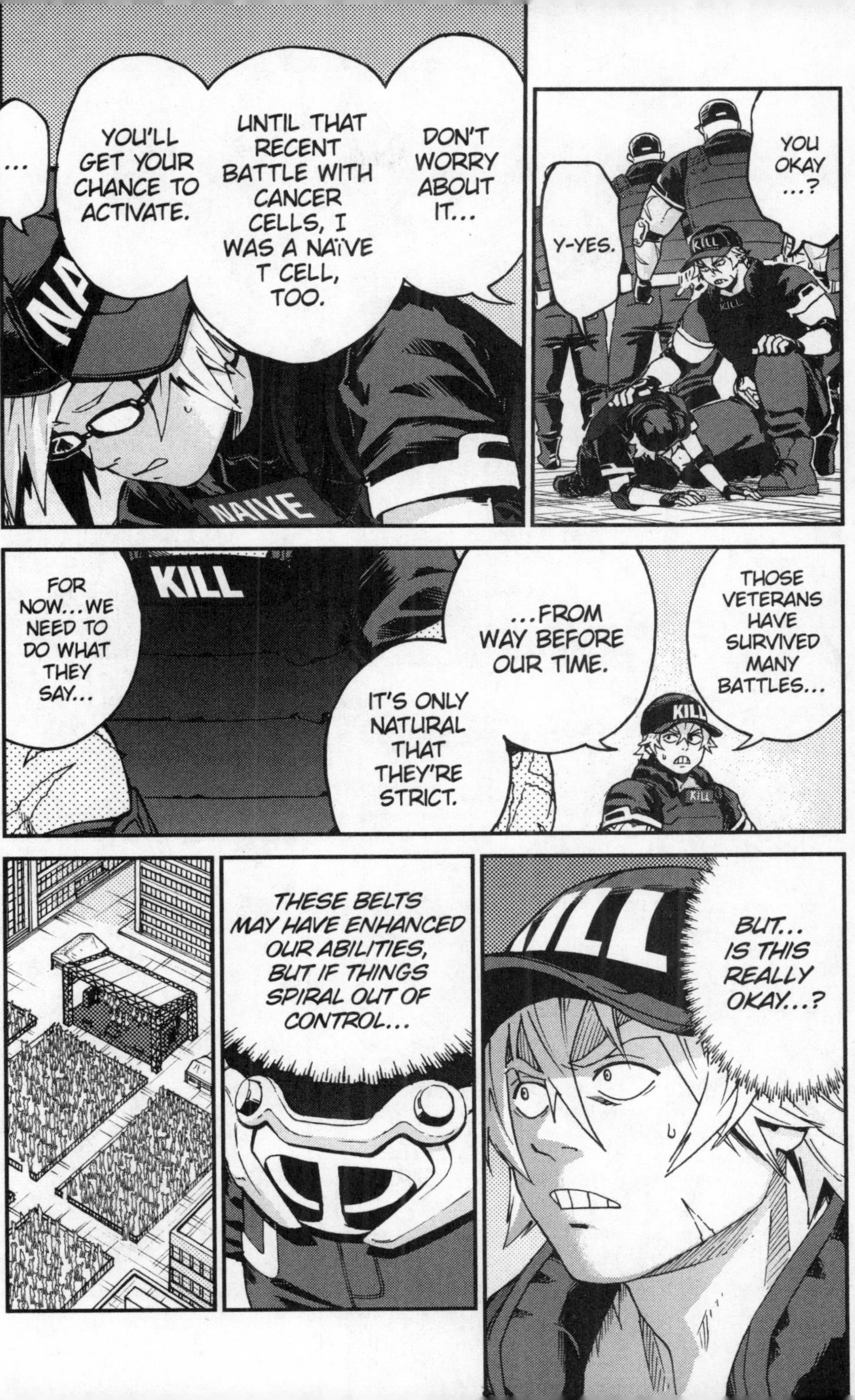
YOU OKAY ...?
Y-YES.
DON'T WORRY ABOUT IT...
UNTIL THAT RECENT BATTLE WITH CANCER CELLS, I WAS A NAÏVE T CELL, TOO.
YOU'LL GET YOUR CHANCE TO ACTIVATE.
...
THOSE VETERANS HAVE SURVIVED MANY BATTLES...
...FROM WAY BEFORE OUR TIME.
IT'S ONLY NATURAL THAT THEY'RE STRICT.
FOR NOW...WE NEED TO DO WHAT THEY SAY...
BUT... IS THIS REALLY OKAY...?
THESE BELTS MAY HAVE ENHANCED OUR ABILITIES, BUT IF THINGS SPIRAL OUT OF CONTROL...

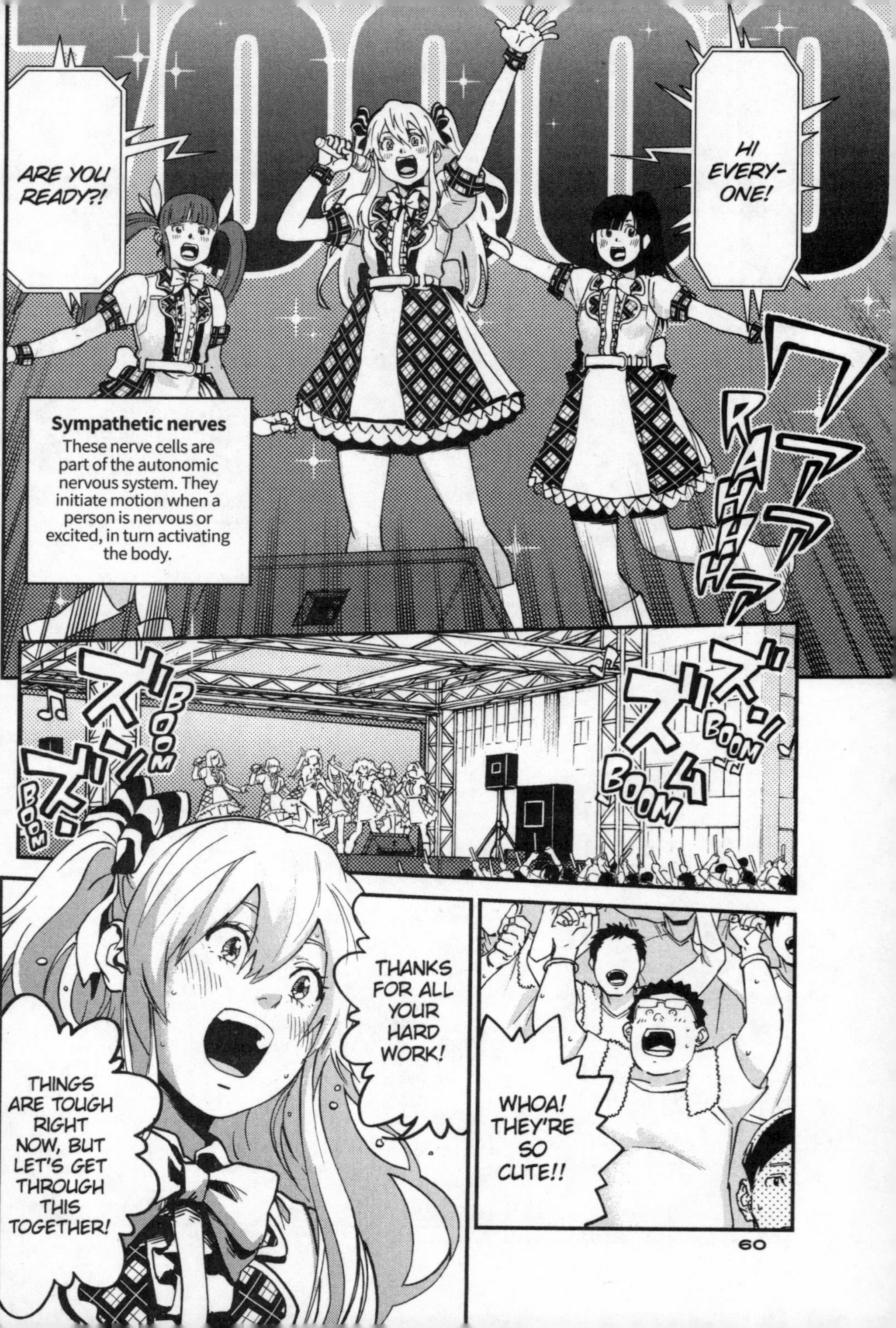
HI EVERY-ONE!
ARE YOU READY?!
RAHHHH
Sympathetic nerves
These nerve cells are part of the autonomic nervous system. They initiate motion when a person is nervous or excited, in turn activating the body.
BOOM
BOOM
BOOM
BOOM
BOOM
WHOA! THEY'RE SO CUTE!!
THANKS FOR ALL YOUR HARD WORK!
THINGS ARE TOUGH RIGHT NOW, BUT LET'S GET THROUGH THIS TOGETHER!

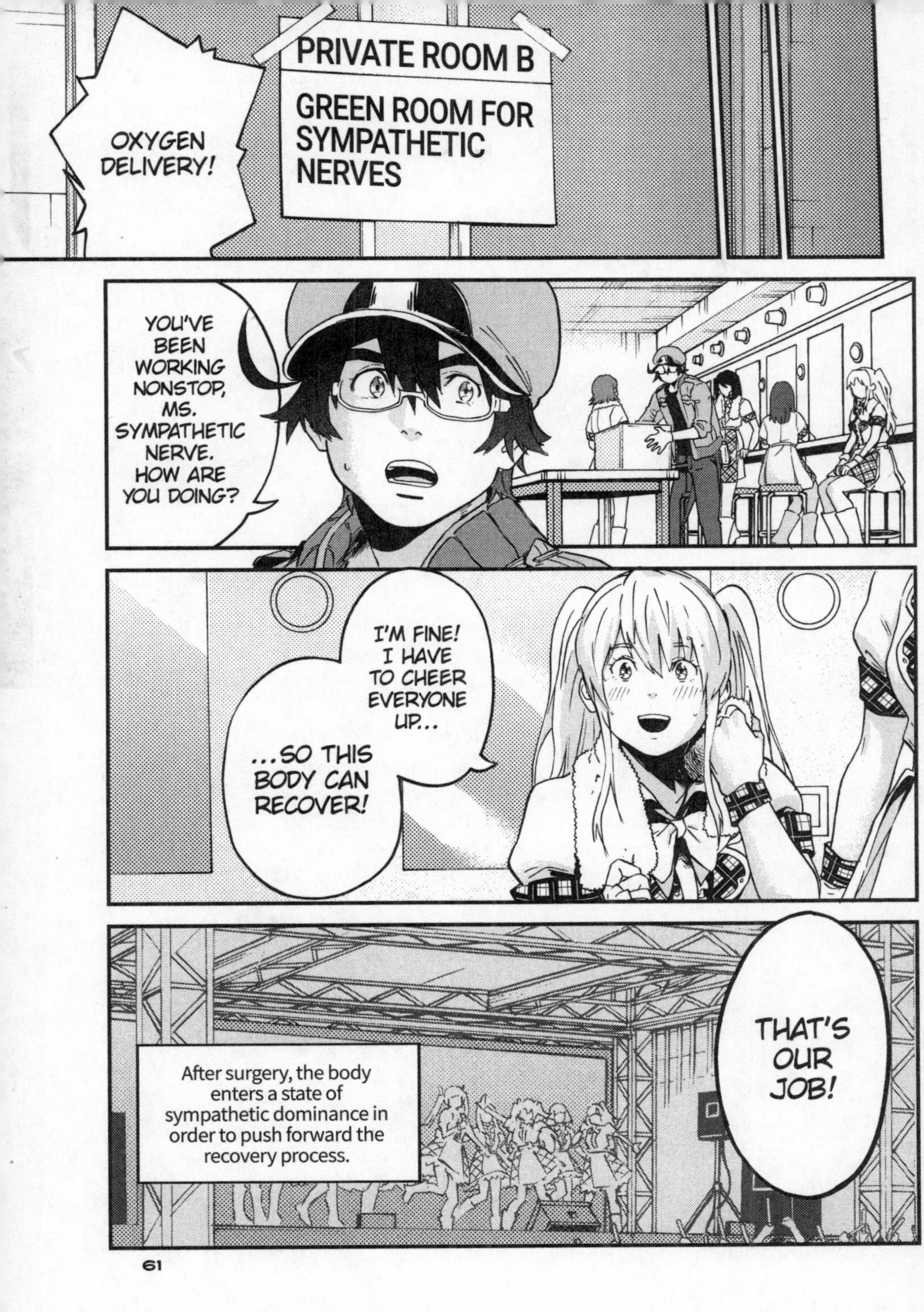
PRIVATE ROOM B
GREEN ROOM FOR SYMPATHETIC NERVES
OXYGEN DELIVERY!
YOU'VE BEEN WORKING NONSTOP, MS. SYMPATHETIC NERVE. HOW ARE YOU DOING?
I'M FINE! I HAVE TO CHEER EVERYONE UP...
...SO THIS BODY CAN RECOVER!
THAT'S OUR JOB!
After surgery, the body enters a state of sympathetic dominance in order to push forward the recovery process.

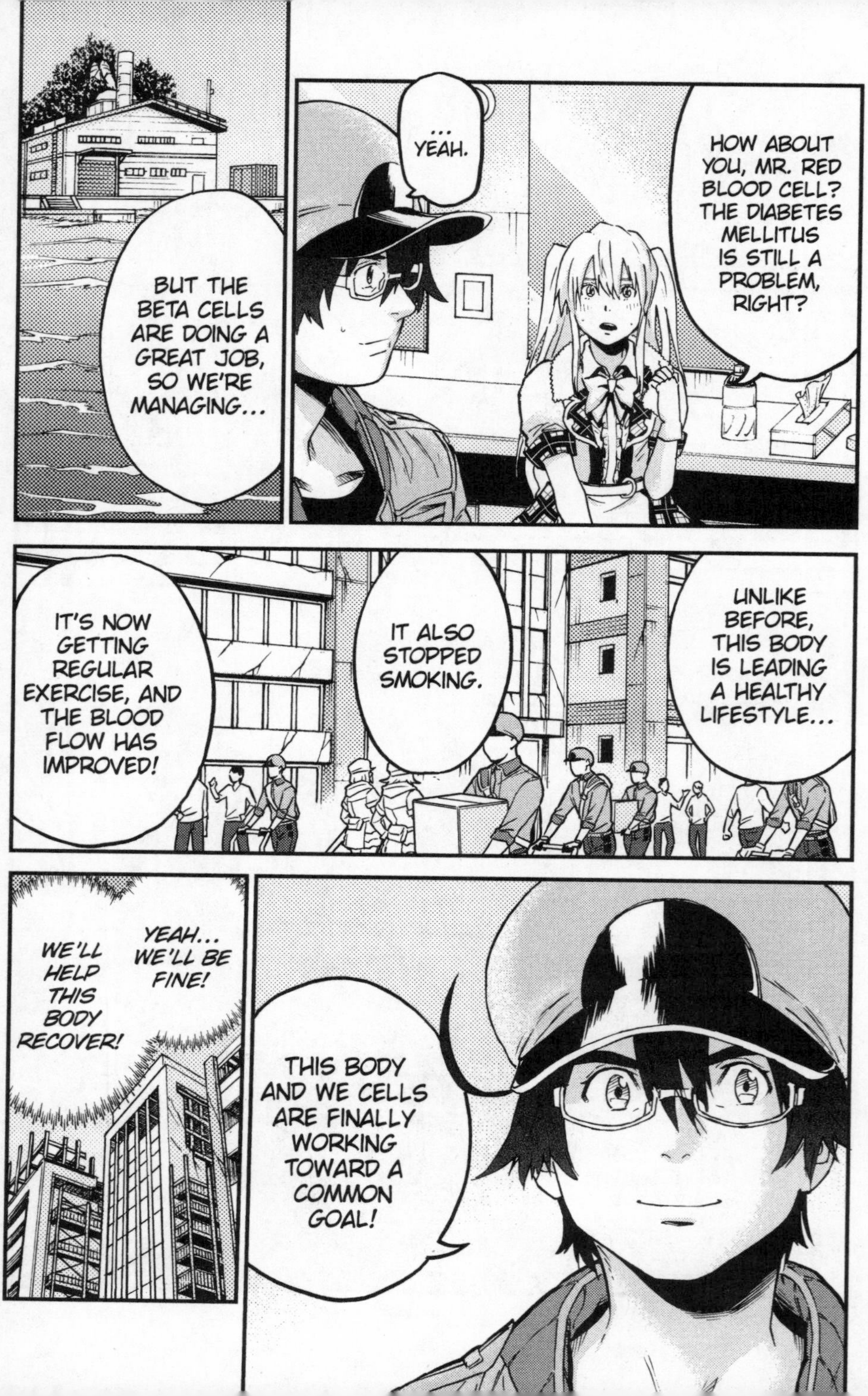
HOW ABOUT YOU, MR. RED BLOOD CELL? THE DIABETES MELLITUS IS STILL A PROBLEM, RIGHT?
... YEAH.
BUT THE BETA CELLS ARE DOING A GREAT JOB, SO WE'RE MANAGING...
UNLIKE BEFORE, THIS BODY IS LEADING A HEALTHY LIFESTYLE...
IT ALSO STOPPED SMOKING.
IT'S NOW GETTING REGULAR EXERCISE, AND THE BLOOD FLOW HAS IMPROVED!
THIS BODY AND WE CELLS ARE FINALLY WORKING TOWARD A COMMON GOAL!
YEAH... WE'LL BE FINE!
WE'LL HELP THIS BODY RECOVER!

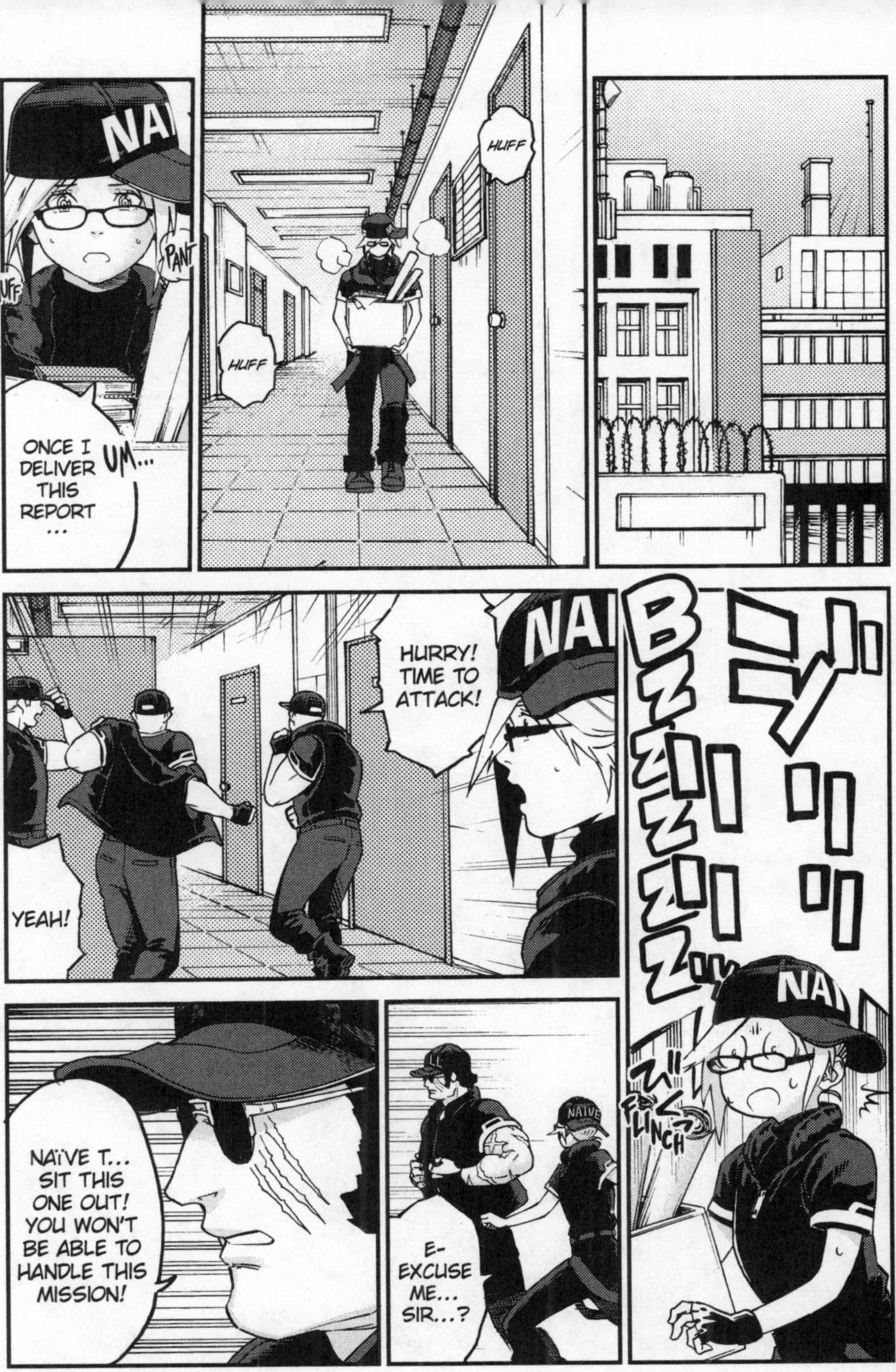
HUFF
HUFF
NAI
PANT
HUFF
UM...
ONCE I DELIVER THIS REPORT ...
BZZZZZZZZ
FLINCH
NAI
HURRY! TIME TO ATTACK!
YEAH!
E-EXCUSE ME... SIR...?
NAÏVE
NAÏVE T... SIT THIS ONE OUT! YOU WON'T BE ABLE TO HANDLE THIS MISSION!

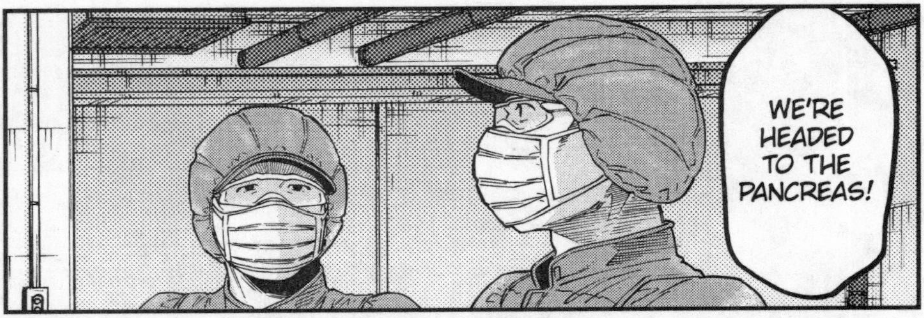
WE'RE HEADED TO THE PANCREAS!

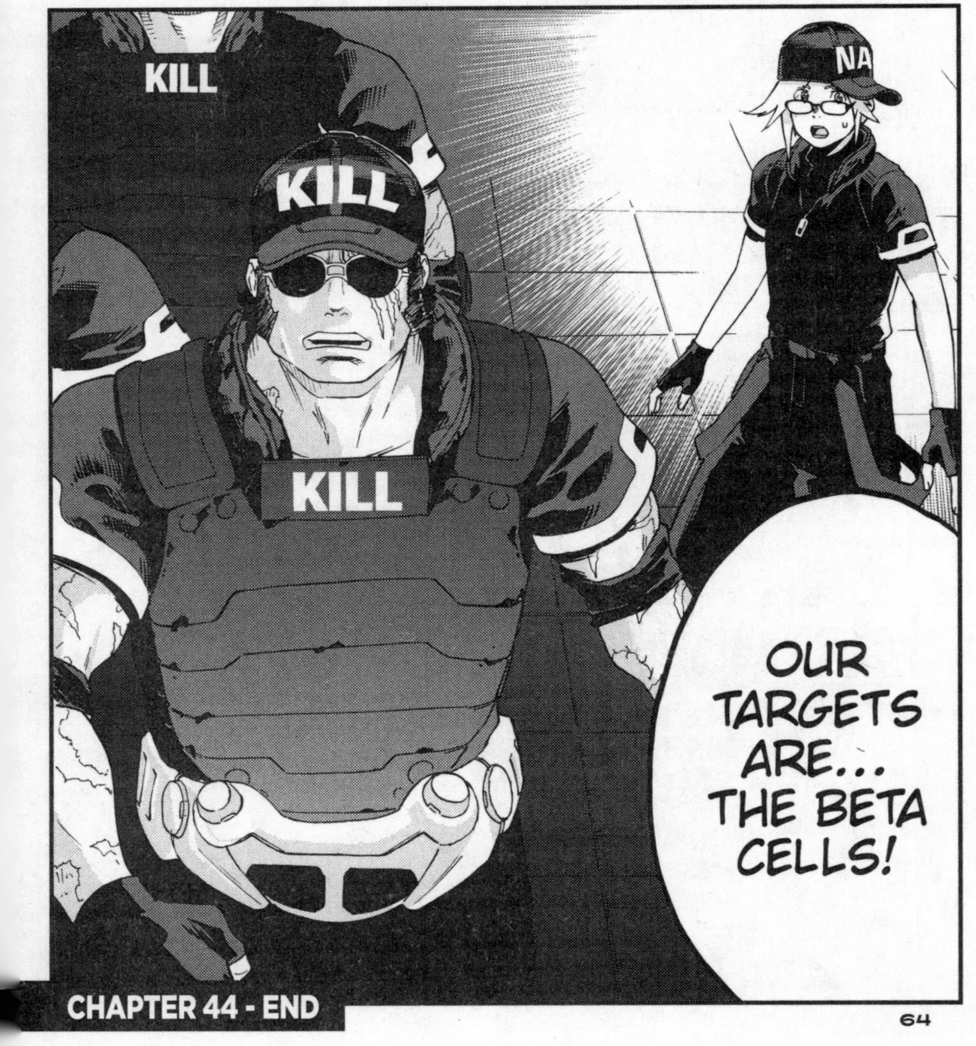
NA
KILL
KILL
KILL
OUR TARGETS ARE... THE BETA CELLS!

CHAPTER 44 - END

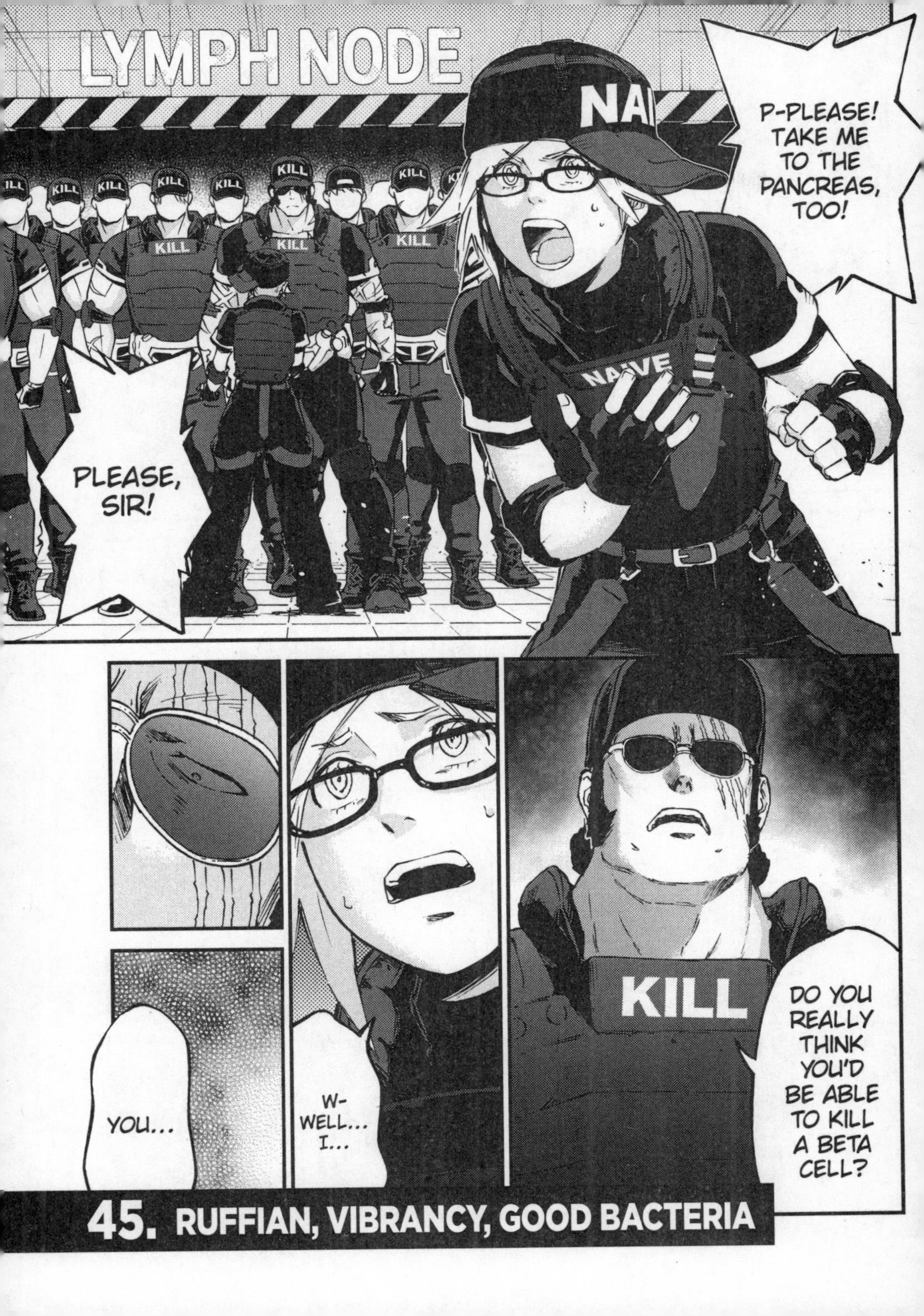
LYMPH NODE
P-PLEASE! TAKE ME TO THE PANCREAS, TOO!
PLEASE, SIR!
DO YOU REALLY THINK YOU'D BE ABLE TO KILL A BETA CELL?
KILL
W-WELL... I...
YOU...
45. RUFFIAN, VIBRANCY, GOOD BACTERIA

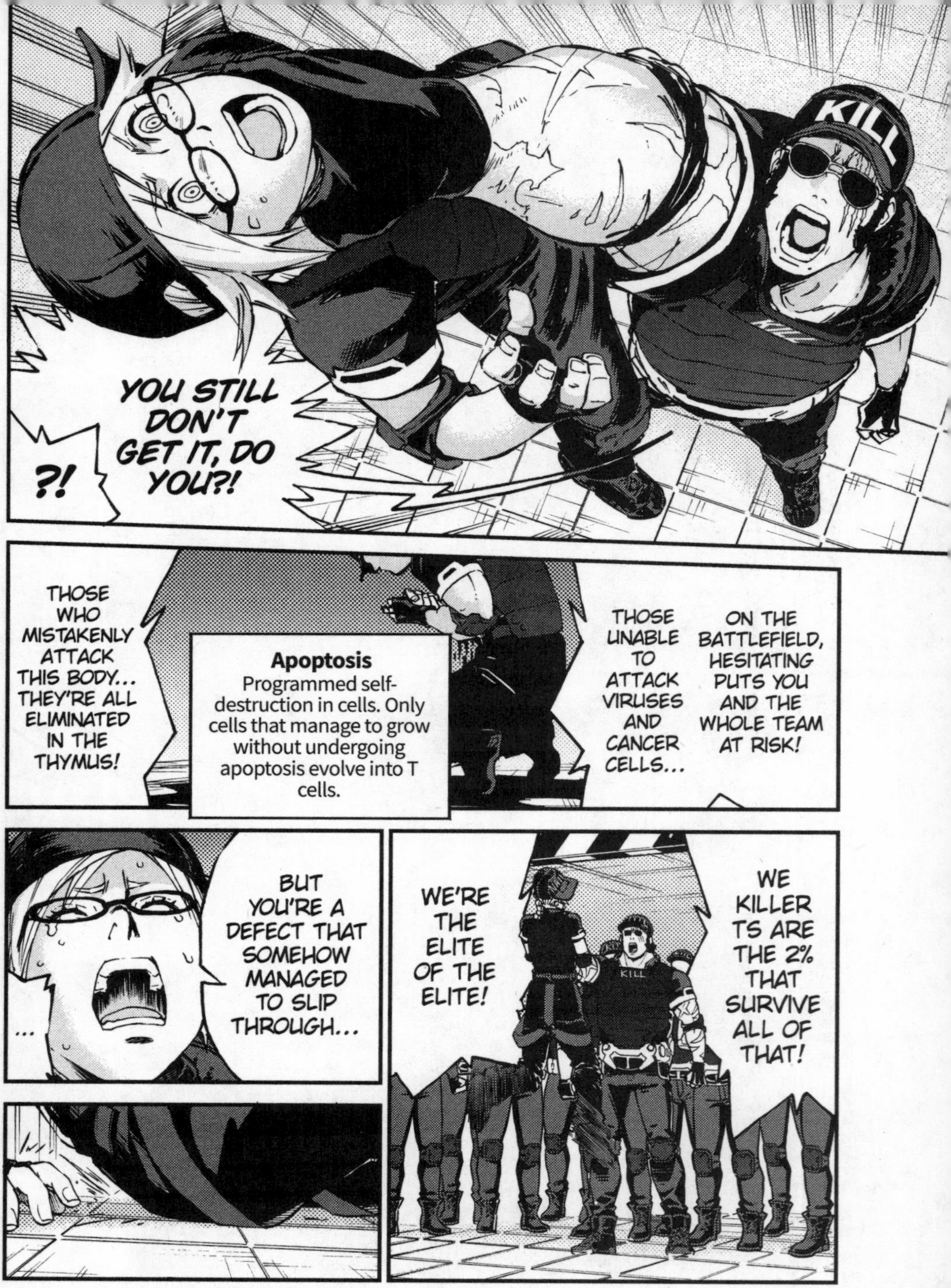
YOU STILL DON'T GET IT, DO YOU?!
?!
ON THE BATTLEFIELD, HESITATING PUTS YOU AND THE WHOLE TEAM AT RISK!
THOSE UNABLE TO ATTACK VIRUSES AND CANCER CELLS...
Apoptosis
Programmed self-destruction in cells. Only cells that manage to grow without undergoing apoptosis evolve into T cells.
THOSE WHO MISTAKENLY ATTACK THIS BODY... THEY'RE ALL ELIMINATED IN THE THYMUS!
WE KILLER TS ARE THE 2% THAT SURVIVE ALL OF THAT!
WE'RE THE ELITE OF THE ELITE!
BUT YOU'RE A DEFECT THAT SOMEHOW MANAGED TO SLIP THROUGH...
...

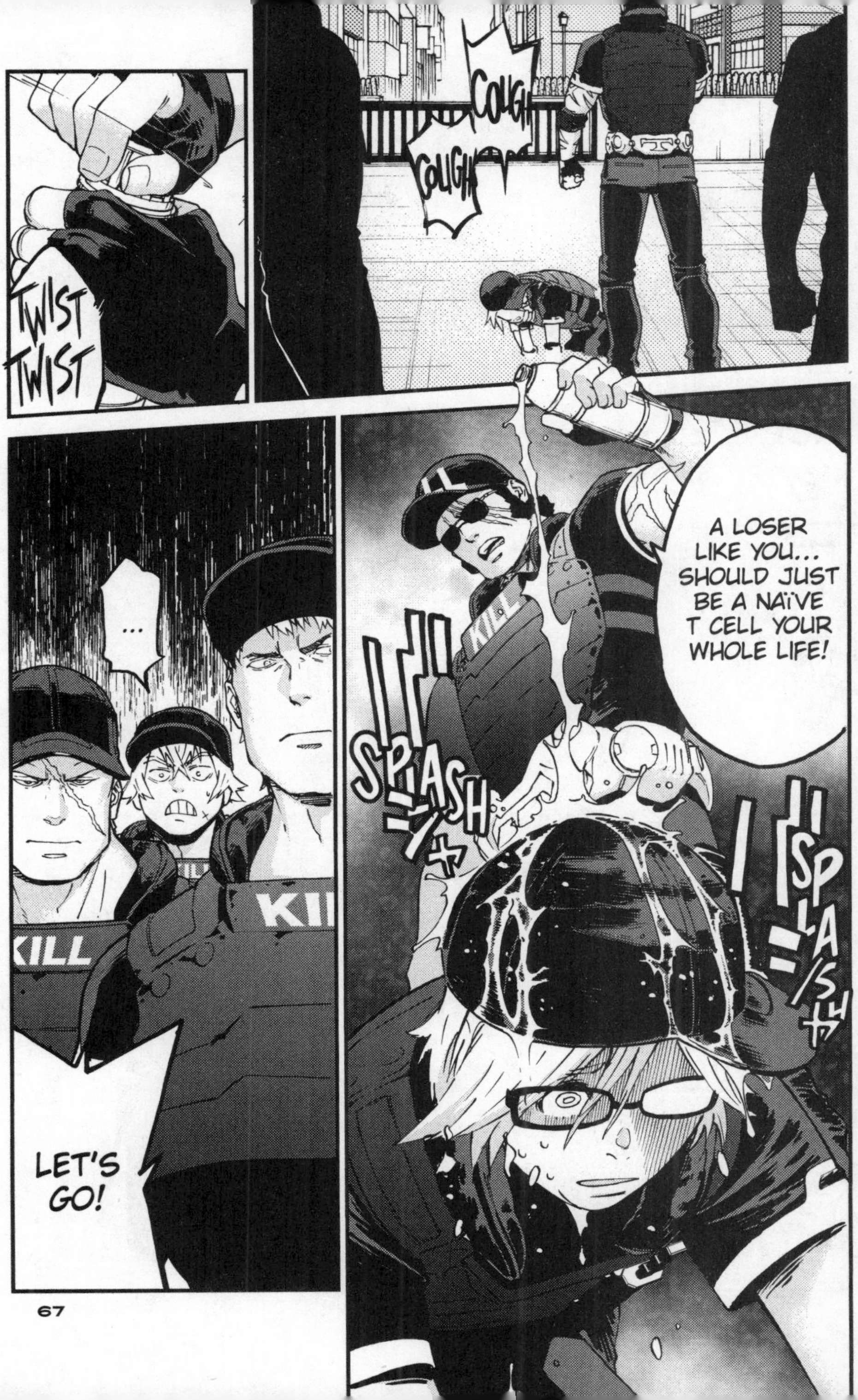
COUGH
COUGH
TWIST
TWIST
A LOSER LIKE YOU... SHOULD JUST BE A NAÏVE T CELL YOUR WHOLE LIFE!
SPLASH
SPLASH
...
LET'S GO!

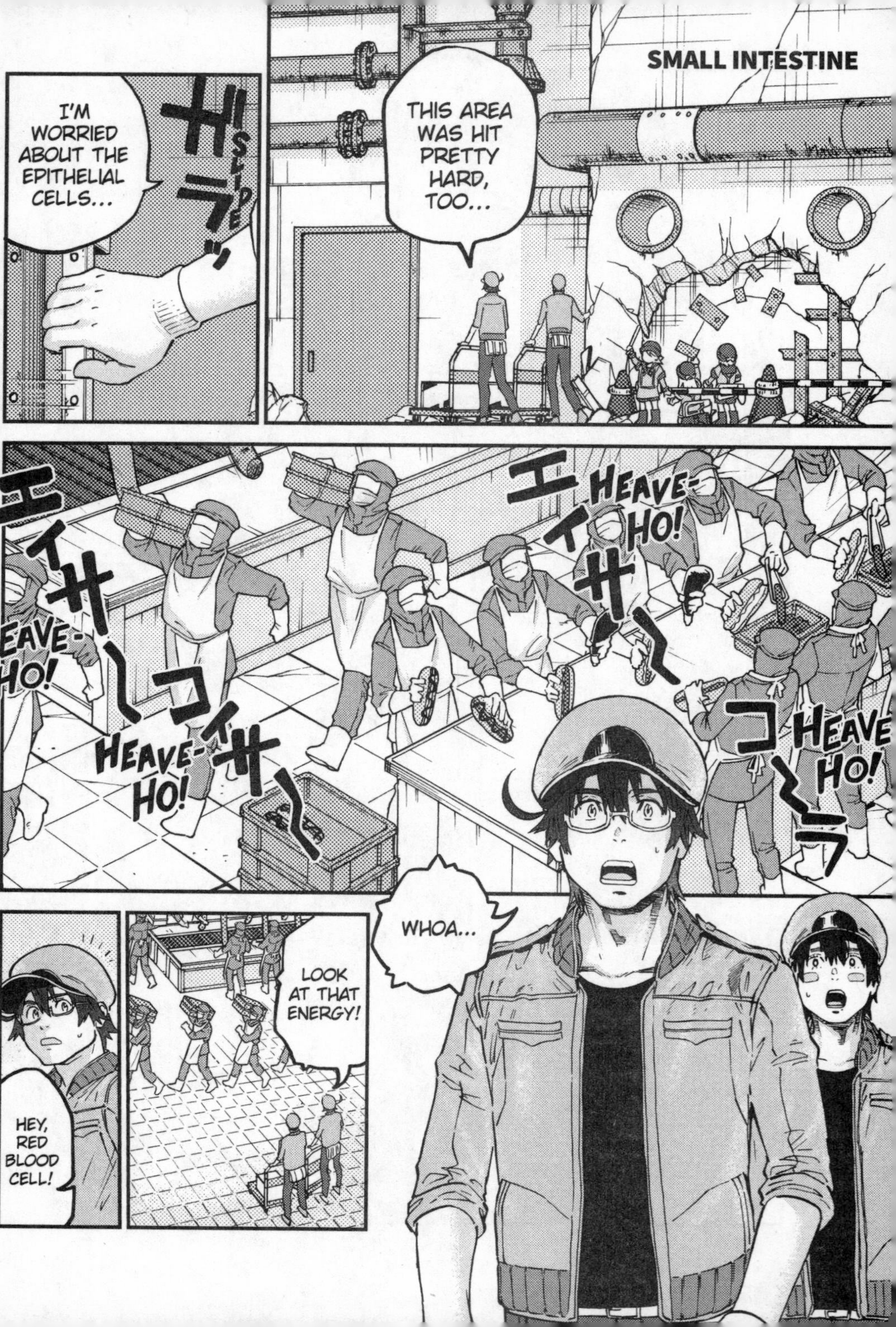
SMALL INTESTINE
THIS AREA WAS HIT PRETTY HARD, TOO…
I'M WORRIED ABOUT THE EPITHELIAL CELLS…
SLIDE
HEAVE-HO!
HEAVE-HO!
HEAVE-HO!
HEAVE-HO!
WHOA…
LOOK AT THAT ENERGY!
HEY, RED BLOOD CELL!

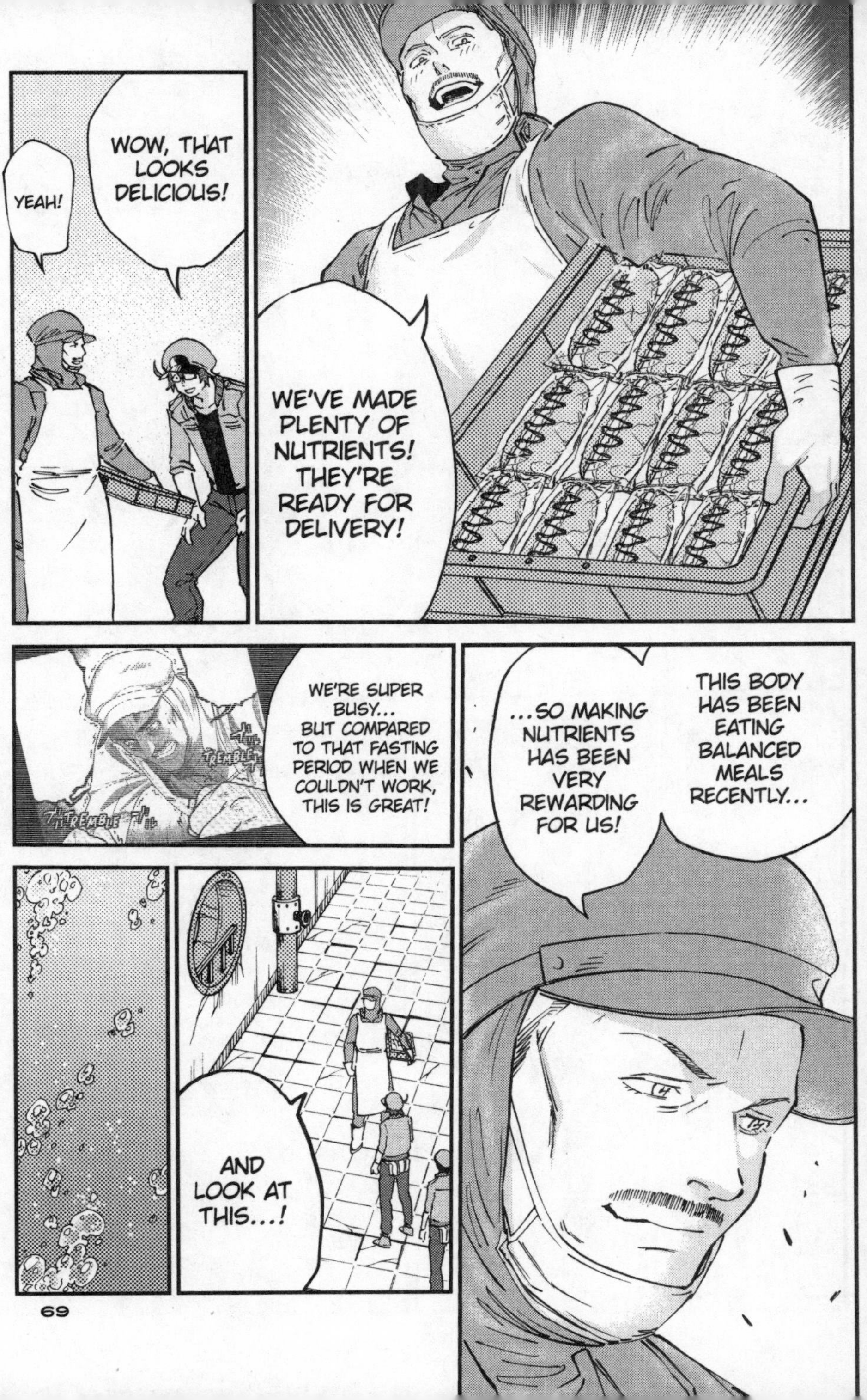

WE'VE MADE PLENTY OF NUTRIENTS! THEY'RE READY FOR DELIVERY!
WOW, THAT LOOKS DELICIOUS!
YEAH!
THIS BODY HAS BEEN EATING BALANCED MEALS RECENTLY...
...SO MAKING NUTRIENTS HAS BEEN VERY REWARDING FOR US!
WE'RE SUPER BUSY... BUT COMPARED TO THAT FASTING PERIOD WHEN WE COULDN'T WORK, THIS IS GREAT!
TREMBLE
TREMBLE
AND LOOK AT THIS...!

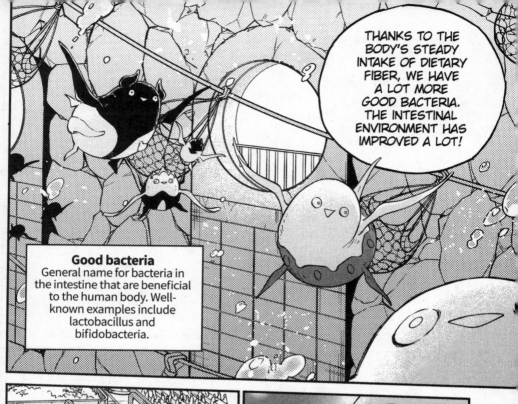

THANKS TO THE BODY'S STEADY INTAKE OF DIETARY FIBER, WE HAVE A LOT MORE GOOD BACTERIA. THE INTESTINAL ENVIRONMENT HAS IMPROVED A LOT!

**Good bacteria**
General name for bacteria in the intestine that are beneficial to the human body. Well-known examples include lactobacillus and bifidobacteria.

...

THIS BODY IS FINALLY TAKING CARE OF ITS OWN HEALTH!

SUCH POSITIVE ENERGY IS A GREAT INVESTMENT IN OUR COLLECTIVE FUTURE!

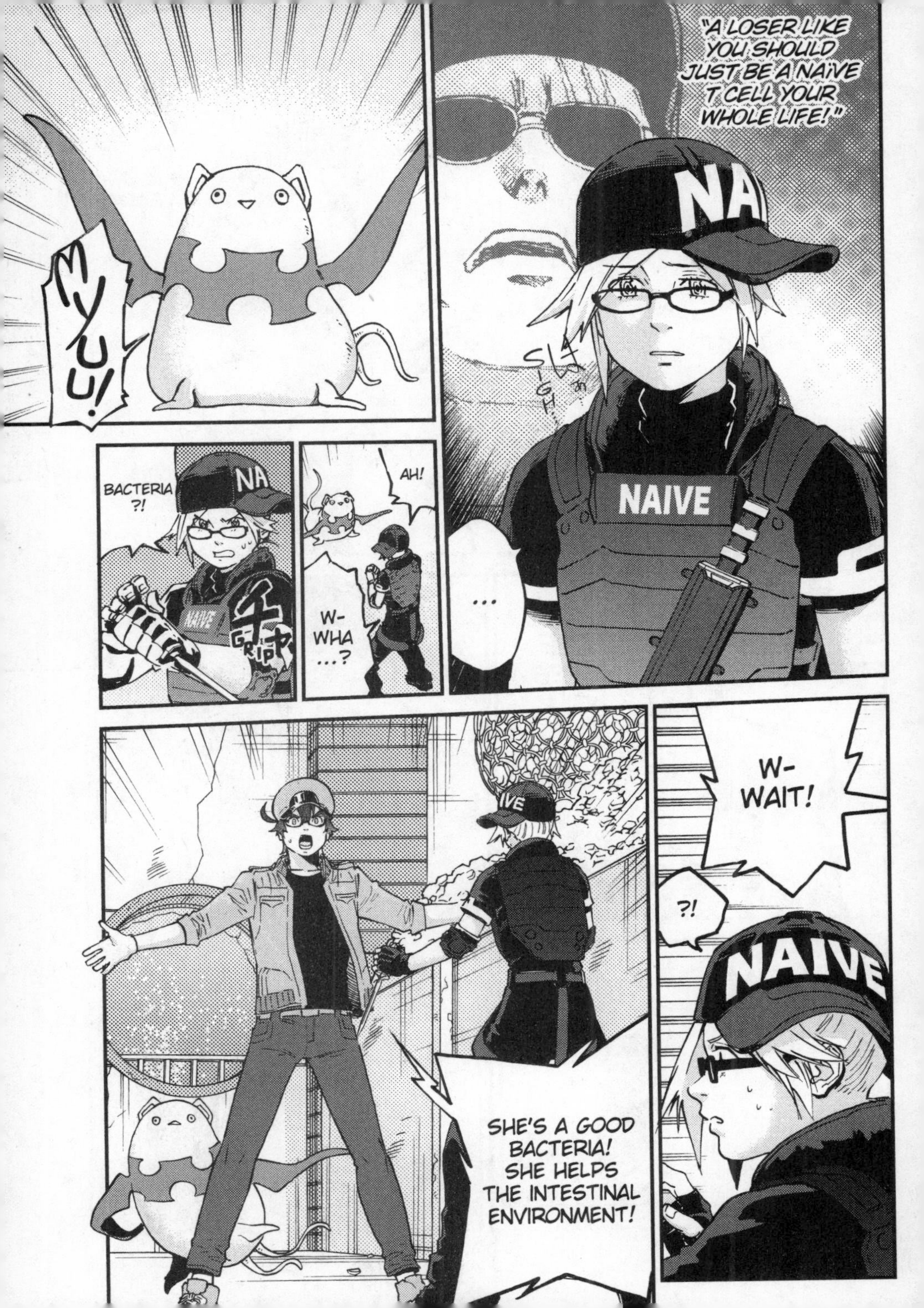
"A LOSER LIKE YOU SHOULD JUST BE A NAIVE T CELL YOUR WHOLE LIFE!"
NA
SIGH
NAIVE
...
MYUUU!
AH!
W-WHA...?
NA
BACTERIA?!
NAIVE
GRIP
W-WAIT!
?!
NAIVE
IVE
SHE'S A GOOD BACTERIA! SHE HELPS THE INTESTINAL ENVIRONMENT!

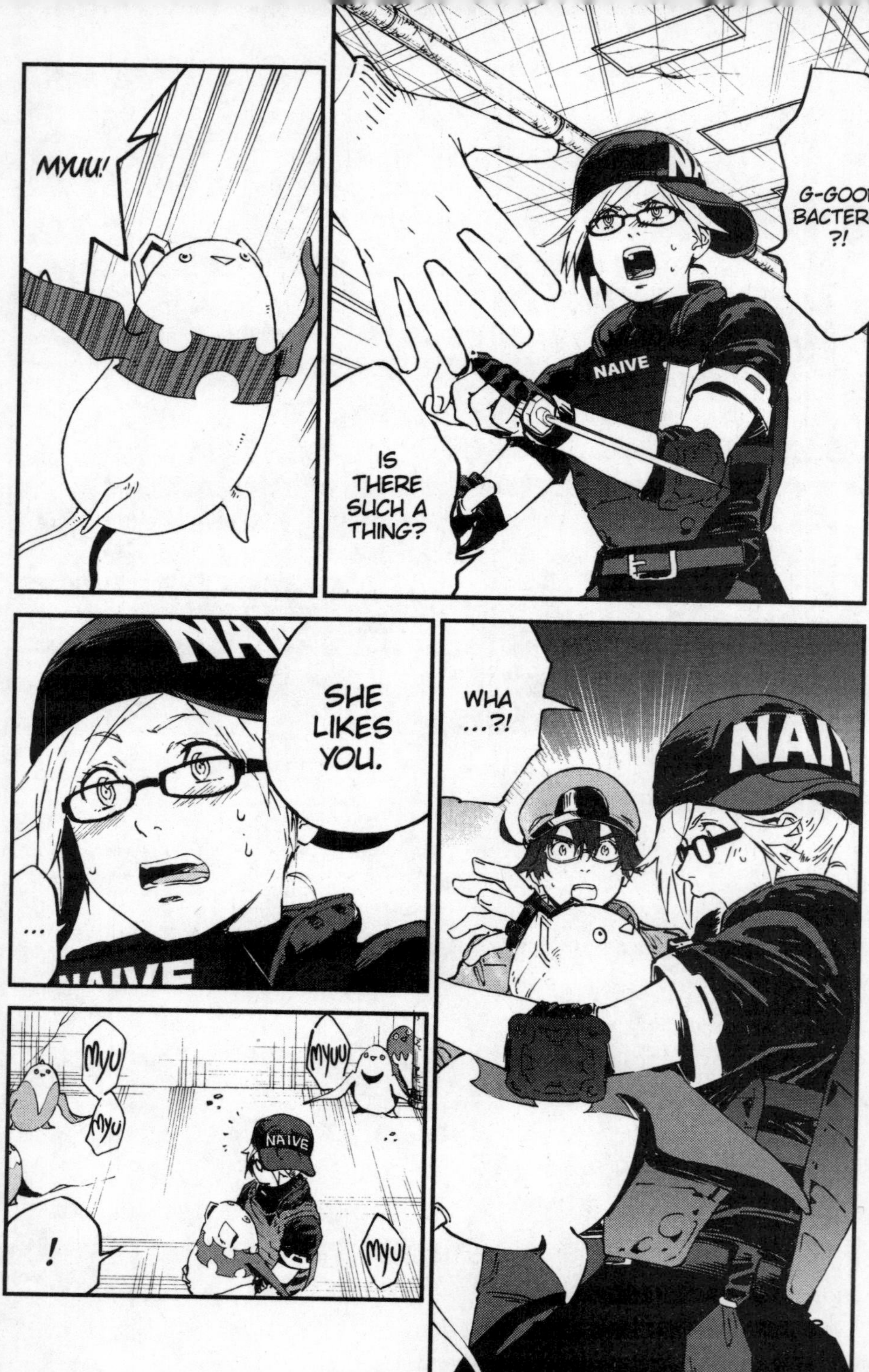
G-GOOD BACTERIA ?!
IS THERE SUCH A THING?
MYUU!
WHA ...?!
SHE LIKES YOU.
...
Myuu
Myu
Myu
Myu
!

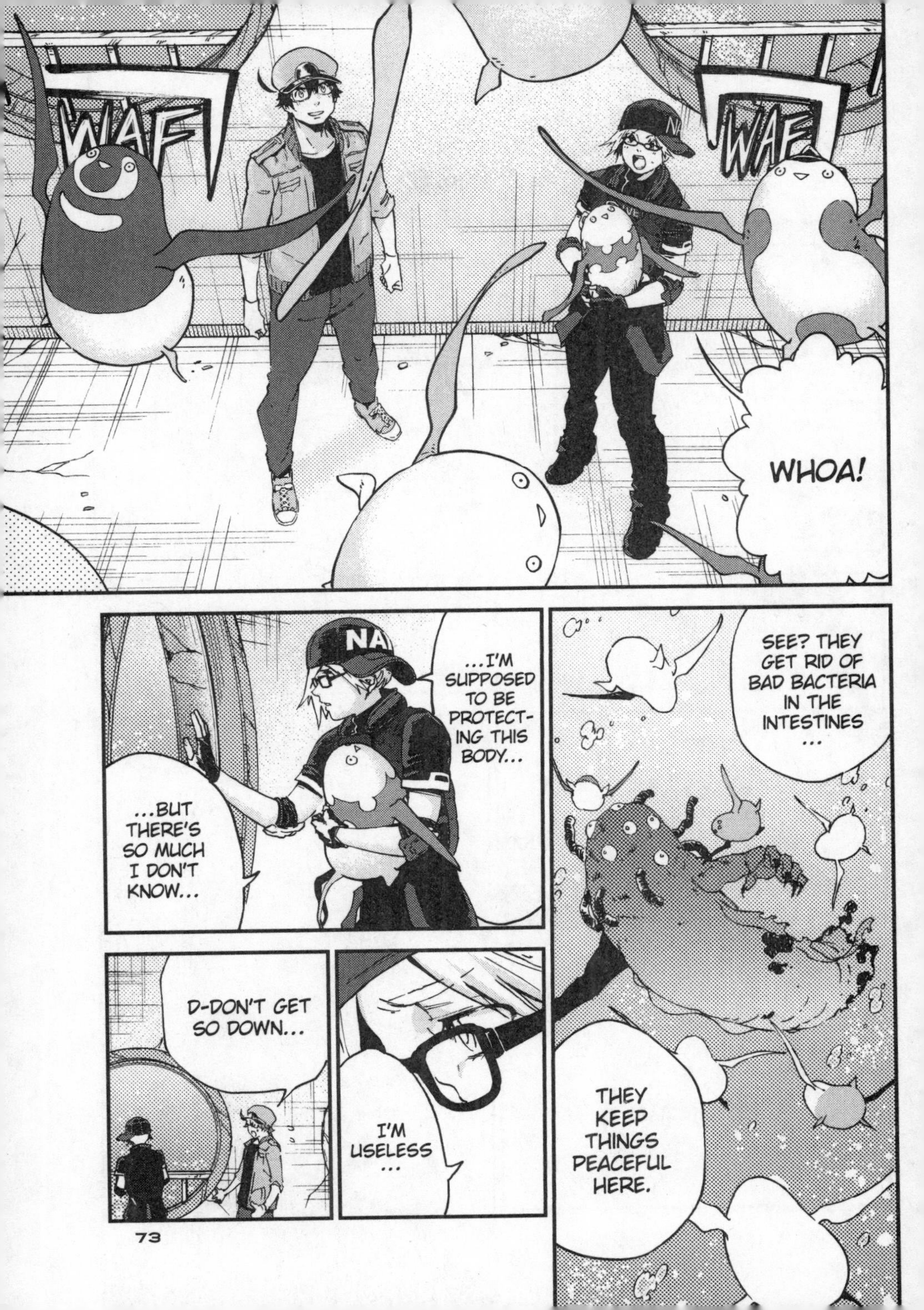

WAF
WAF
WHOA!
SEE? THEY GET RID OF BAD BACTERIA IN THE INTESTINES ...
THEY KEEP THINGS PEACEFUL HERE.
...I'M SUPPOSED TO BE PROTECT-ING THIS BODY...
...BUT THERE'S SO MUCH I DON'T KNOW...
I'M USELESS ...
D-DON'T GET SO DOWN...

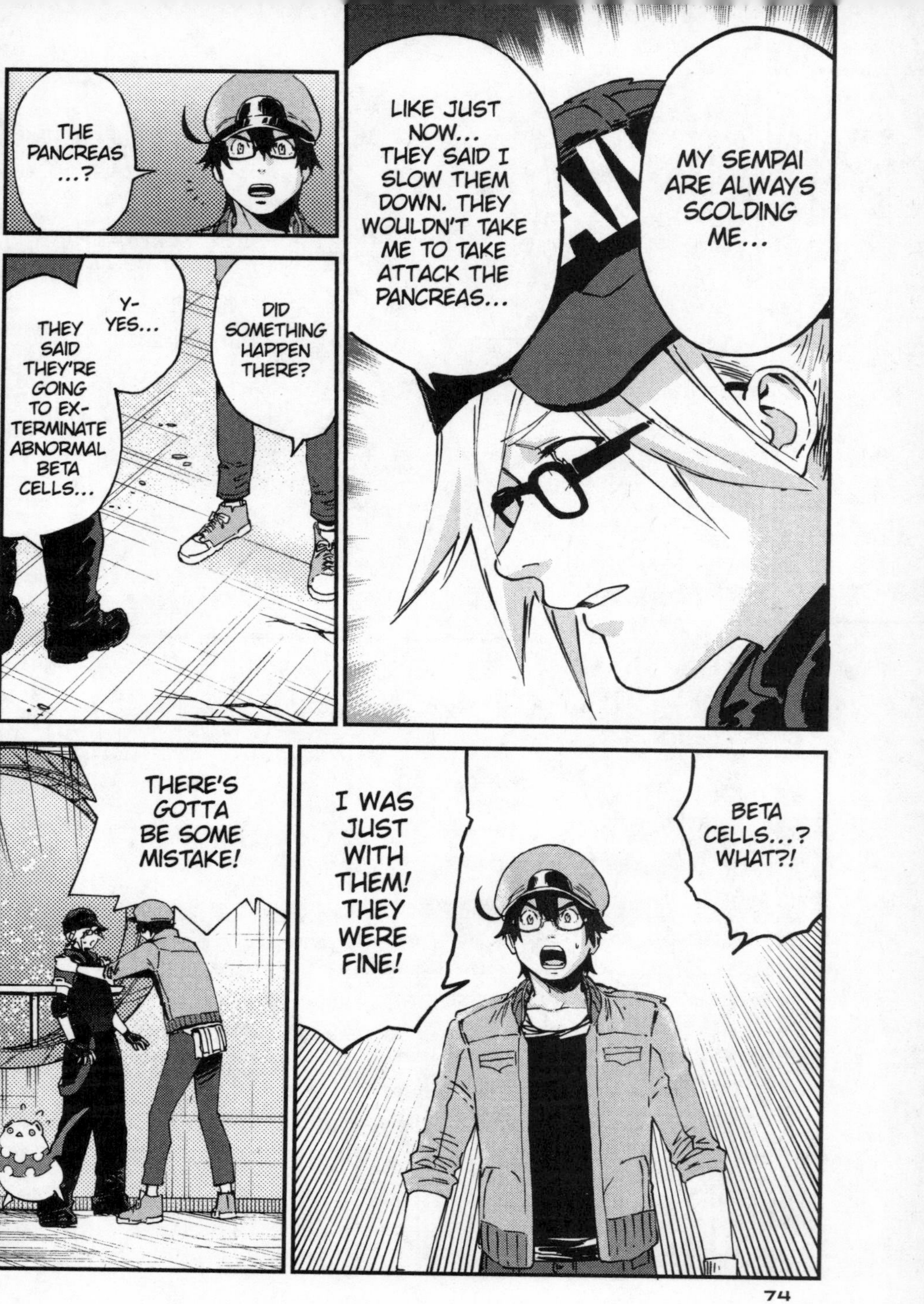
MY SEMPAI ARE ALWAYS SCOLDING ME...
LIKE JUST NOW... THEY SAID I SLOW THEM DOWN. THEY WOULDN'T TAKE ME TO TAKE ATTACK THE PANCREAS...
THE PANCREAS ...?
DID SOMETHING HAPPEN THERE?
Y- YES...
THEY SAID THEY'RE GOING TO EX-TERMINATE ABNORMAL BETA CELLS...
BETA CELLS...? WHAT?!
I WAS JUST WITH THEM! THEY WERE FINE!
THERE'S GOTTA BE SOME MISTAKE!

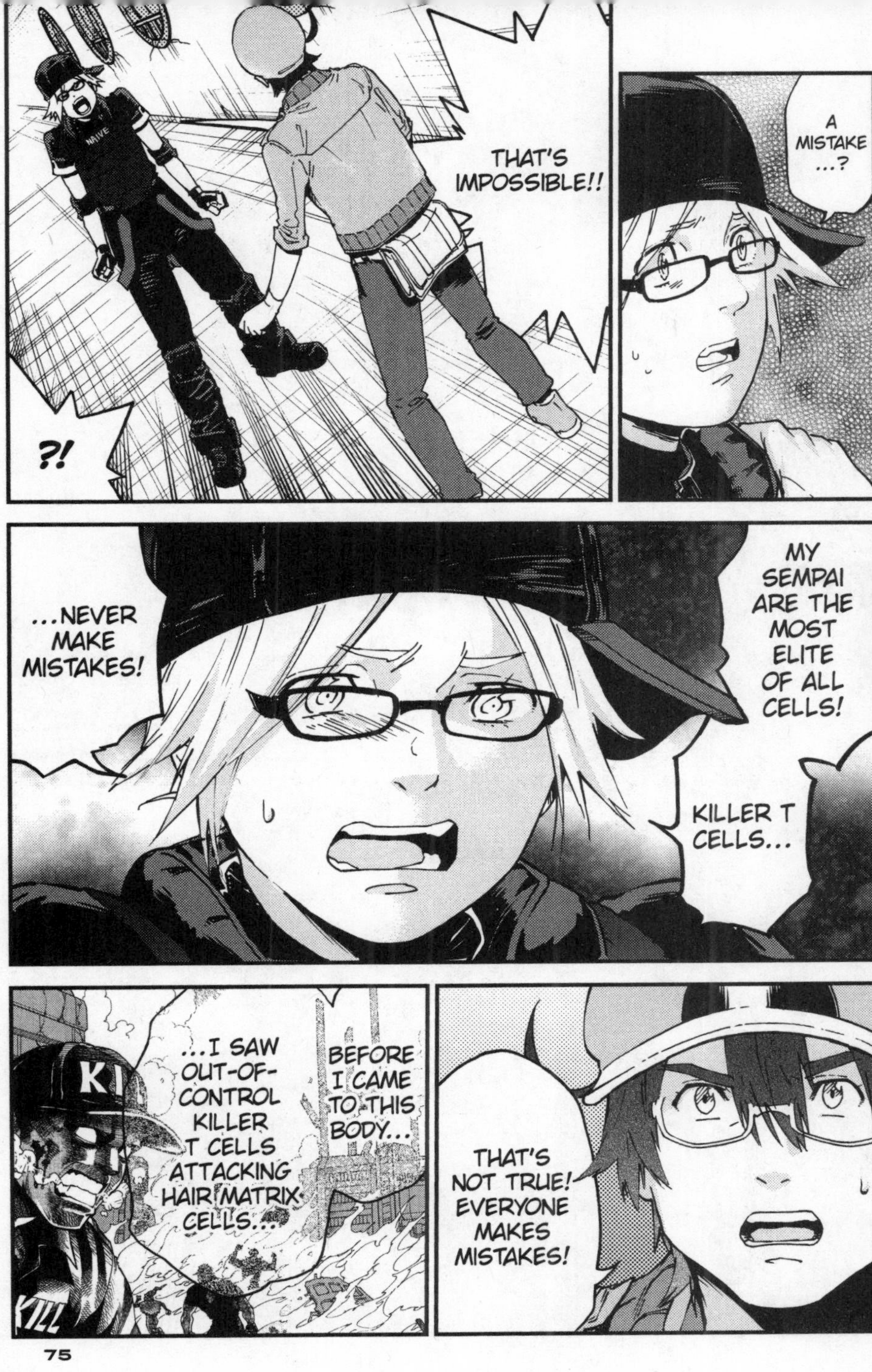
A MISTAKE ...?
THAT'S IMPOSSIBLE!!
?!
MY SEMPAI ARE THE MOST ELITE OF ALL CELLS!
KILLER T CELLS...
...NEVER MAKE MISTAKES!
THAT'S NOT TRUE! EVERYONE MAKES MISTAKES!
BEFORE I CAME TO THIS BODY...
...I SAW OUT-OF-CONTROL KILLER T CELLS ATTACKING HAIR MATRIX CELLS...

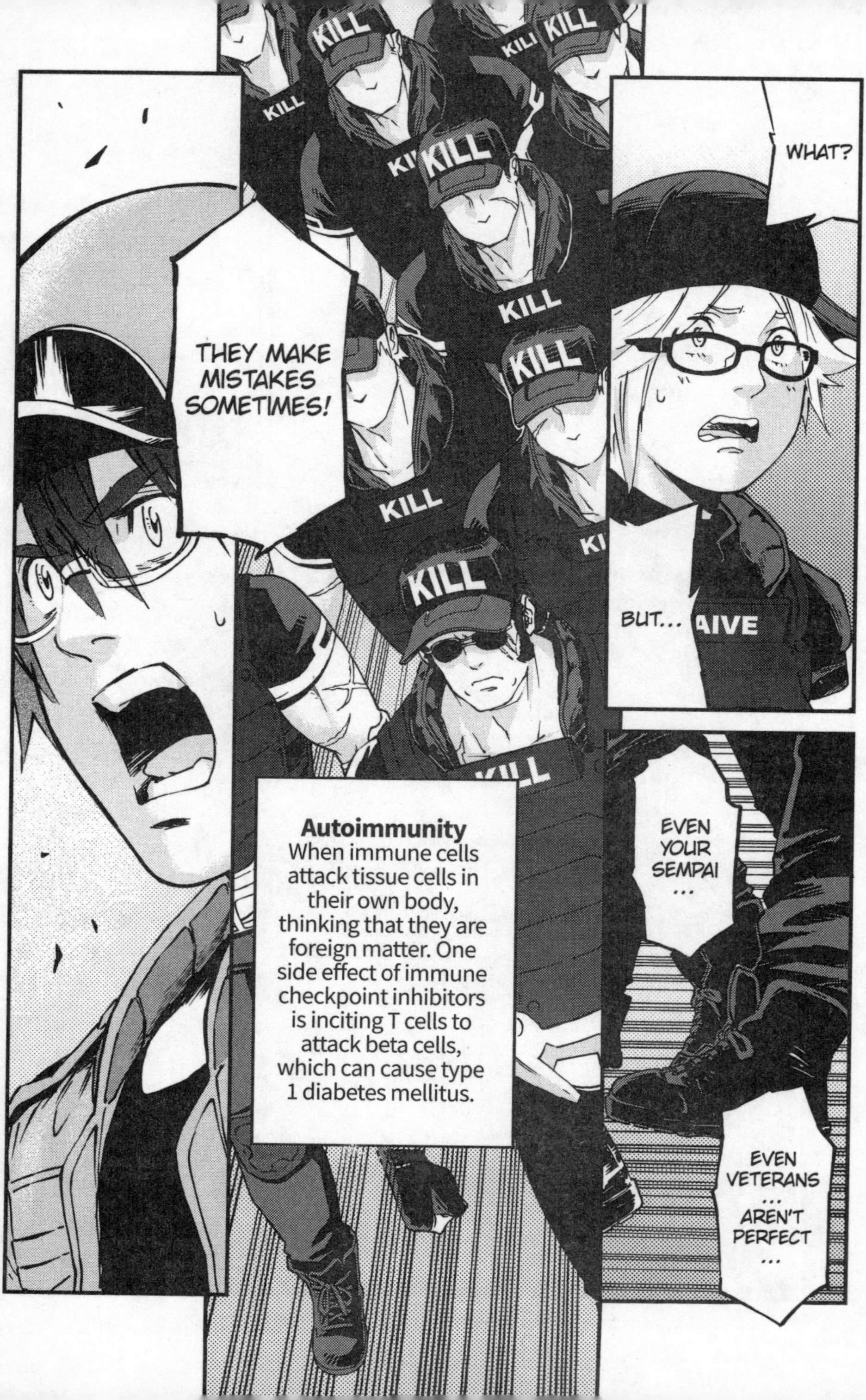
WHAT?
BUT...
EVEN YOUR SEMPAI ...
EVEN VETERANS ... AREN'T PERFECT ...
THEY MAKE MISTAKES SOMETIMES!
Autoimmunity
When immune cells attack tissue cells in their own body, thinking that they are foreign matter. One side effect of immune checkpoint inhibitors is inciting T cells to attack beta cells, which can cause type 1 diabetes mellitus.

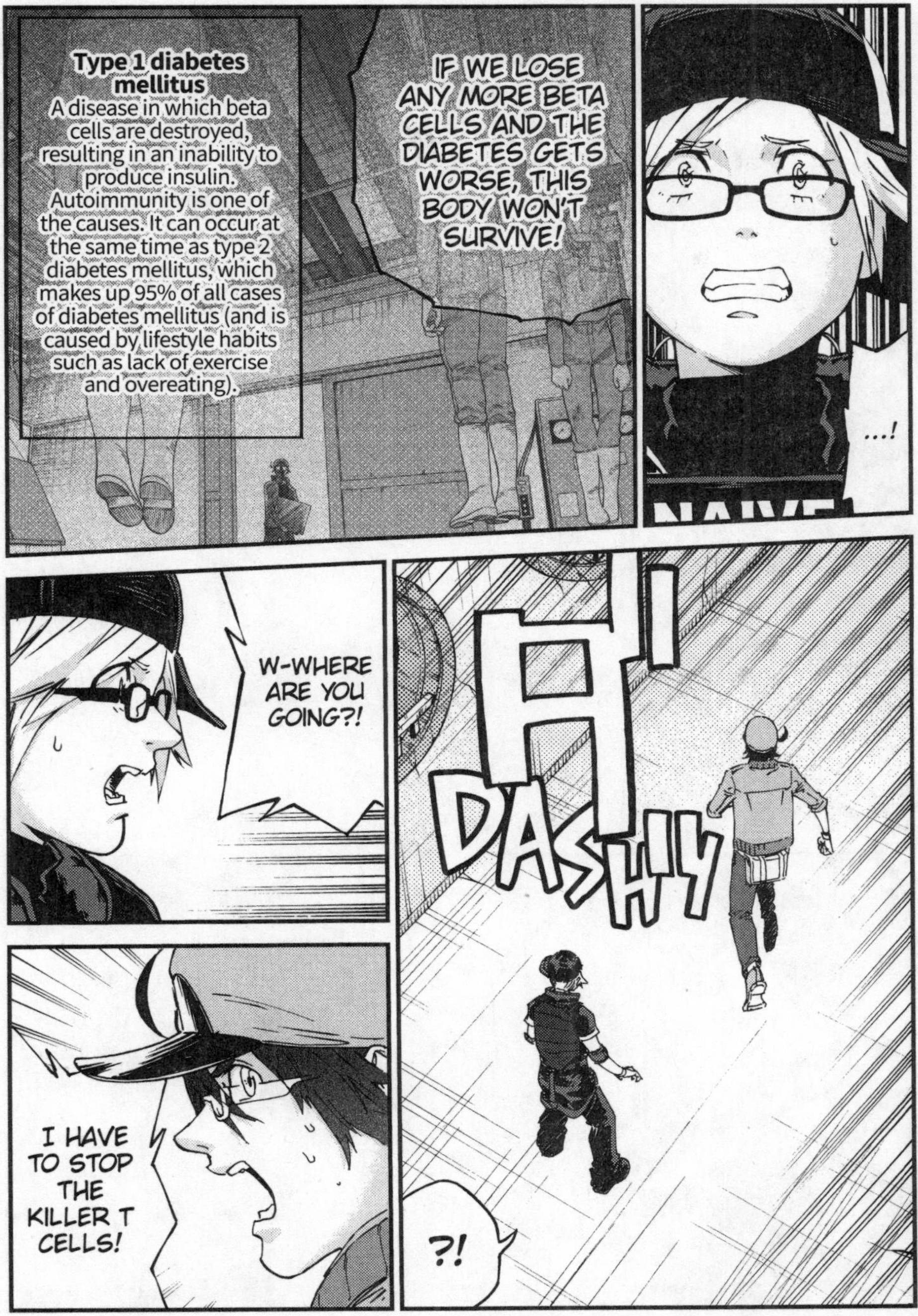
...!
IF WE LOSE ANY MORE BETA CELLS AND THE DIABETES GETS WORSE, THIS BODY WON'T SURVIVE!
**Type 1 diabetes mellitus**
A disease in which beta cells are destroyed, resulting in an inability to produce insulin. Autoimmunity is one of the causes. It can occur at the same time as type 2 diabetes mellitus, which makes up 95% of all cases of diabetes mellitus (and is caused by lifestyle habits such as lack of exercise and overeating).
DASH!
?!
W-WHERE ARE YOU GOING?!
I HAVE TO STOP THE KILLER T CELLS!

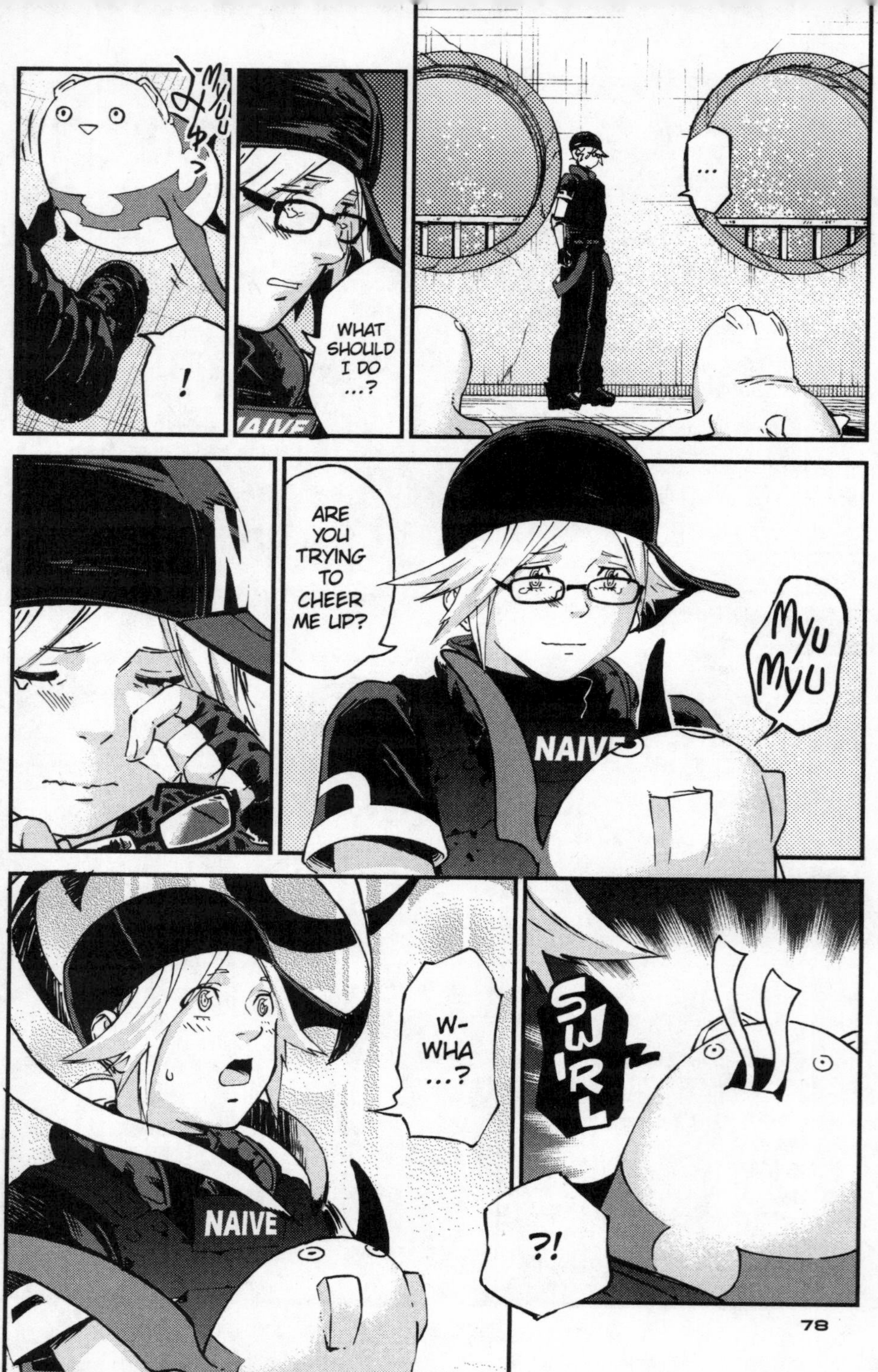
...
WHAT SHOULD I DO ...?
MYUU
!
ARE YOU TRYING TO CHEER ME UP?
MYU MYU
SWIRL
W-WHA ...?
?!

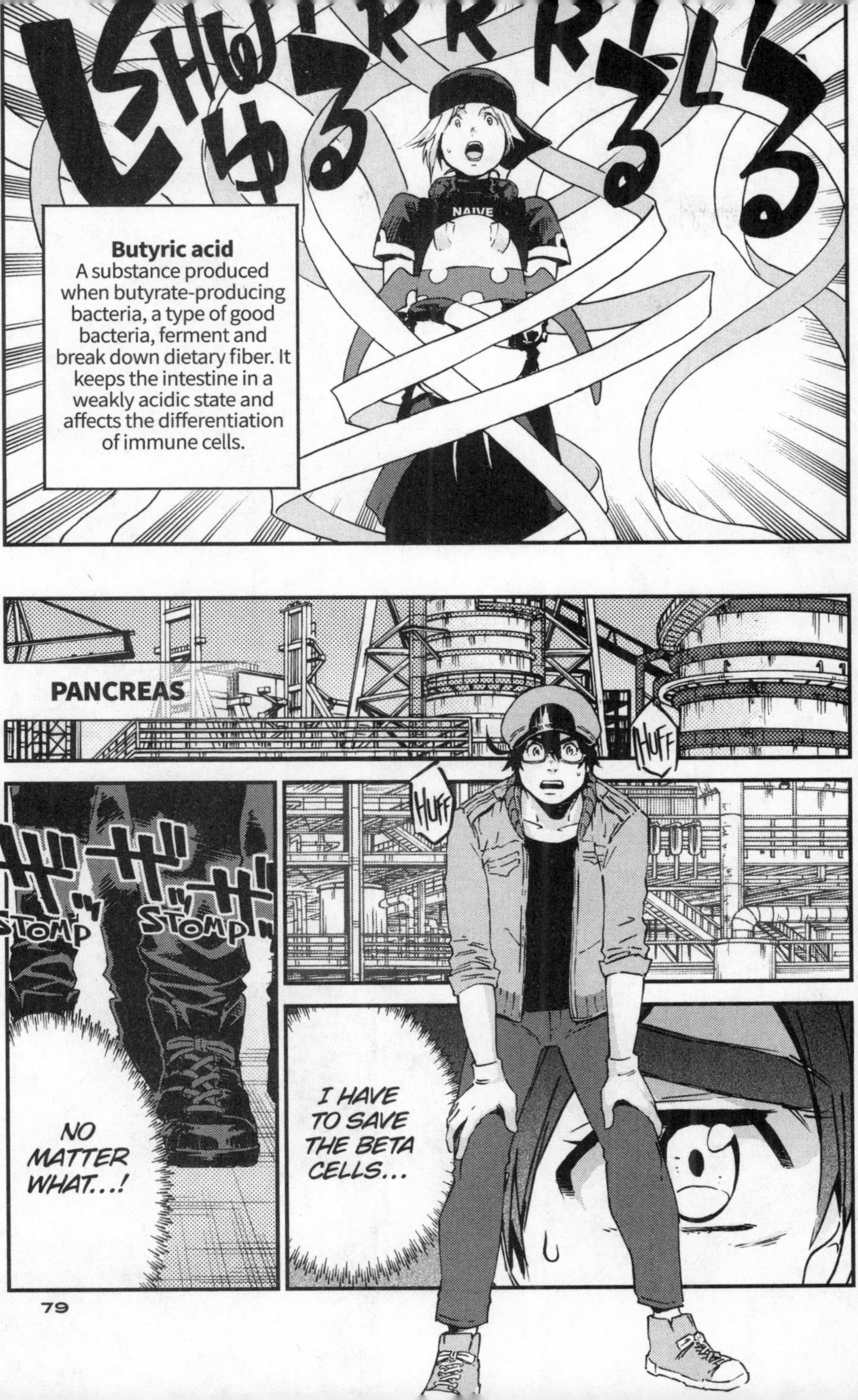
SHURRRL!
しゅるるる
Butyric acid
A substance produced when butyrate-producing bacteria, a type of good bacteria, ferment and break down dietary fiber. It keeps the intestine in a weakly acidic state and affects the differentiation of immune cells.
NAIVE
PANCREAS
HUFF
HUFF
I HAVE TO SAVE THE BETA CELLS...
ザッ ザッ ザッ
STOMP STOMP
NO MATTER WHAT...!

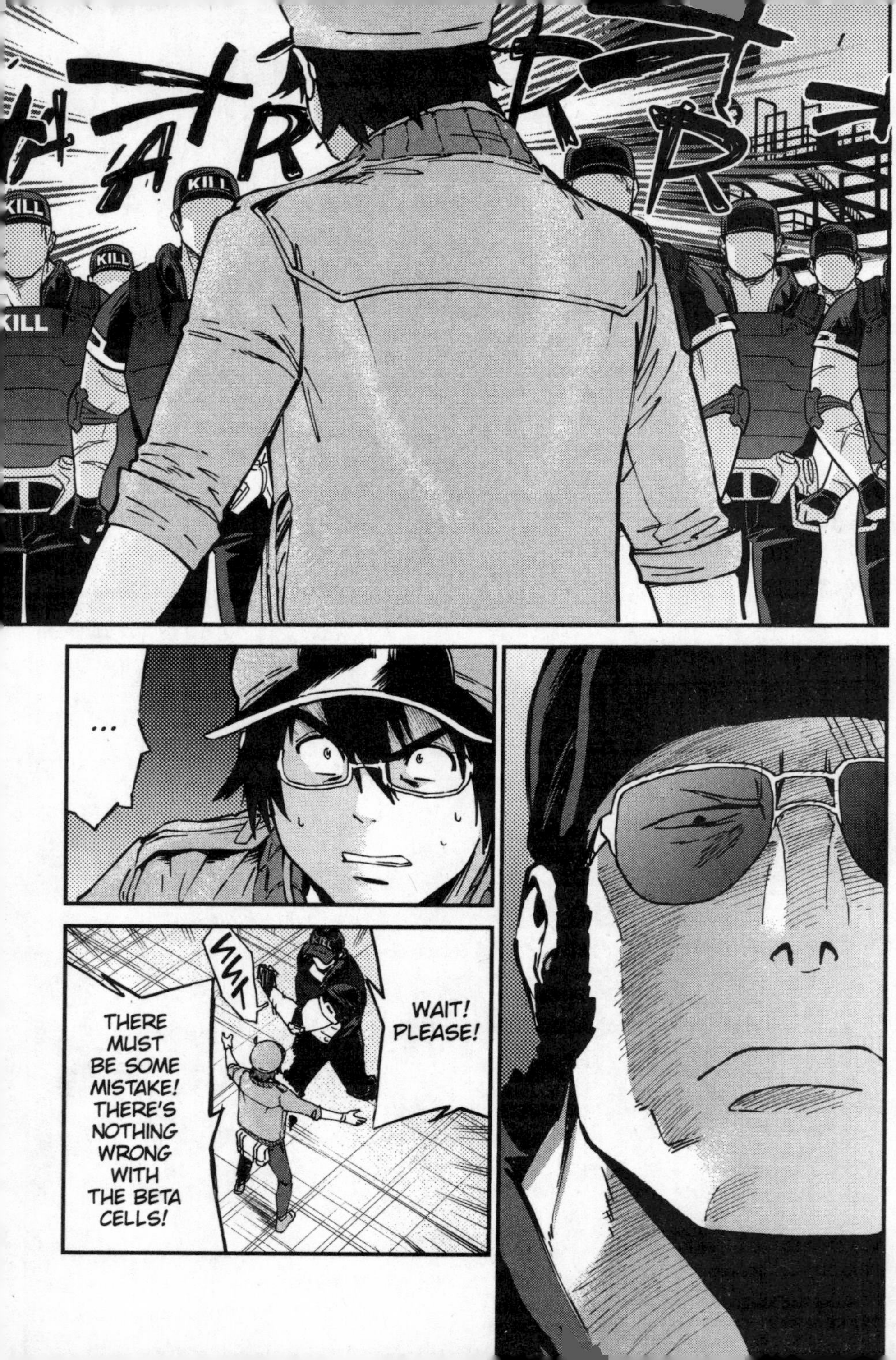
KILL
...
WAIT! PLEASE!
THERE MUST BE SOME MISTAKE! THERE'S NOTHING WRONG WITH THE BETA CELLS!

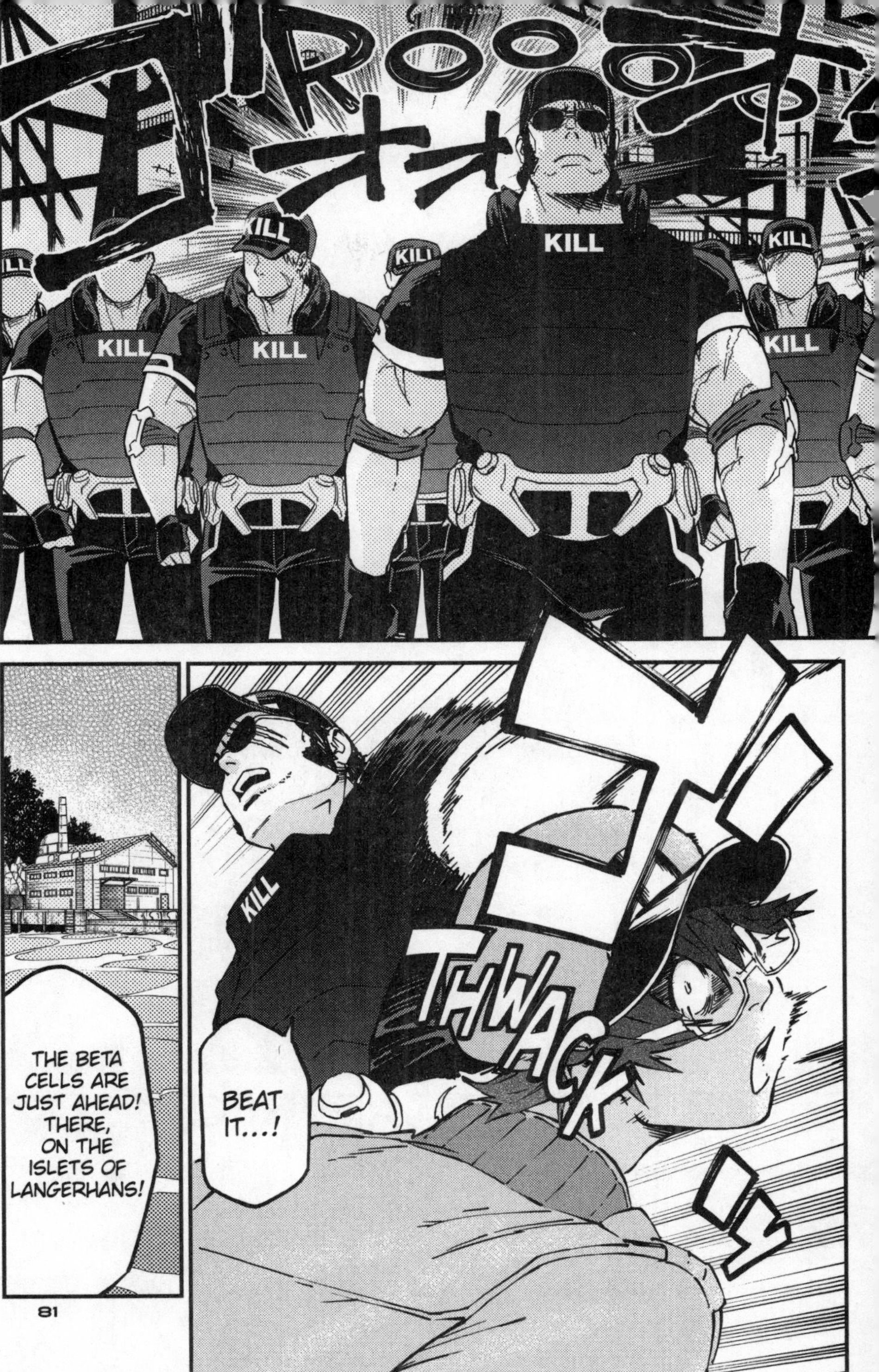
KILL
KILL
KILL
KILL
KILL
KILL
KILL
KILL
THWACK
BEAT IT...!
KILL
THE BETA CELLS ARE JUST AHEAD! THERE, ON THE ISLETS OF LANGERHANS!

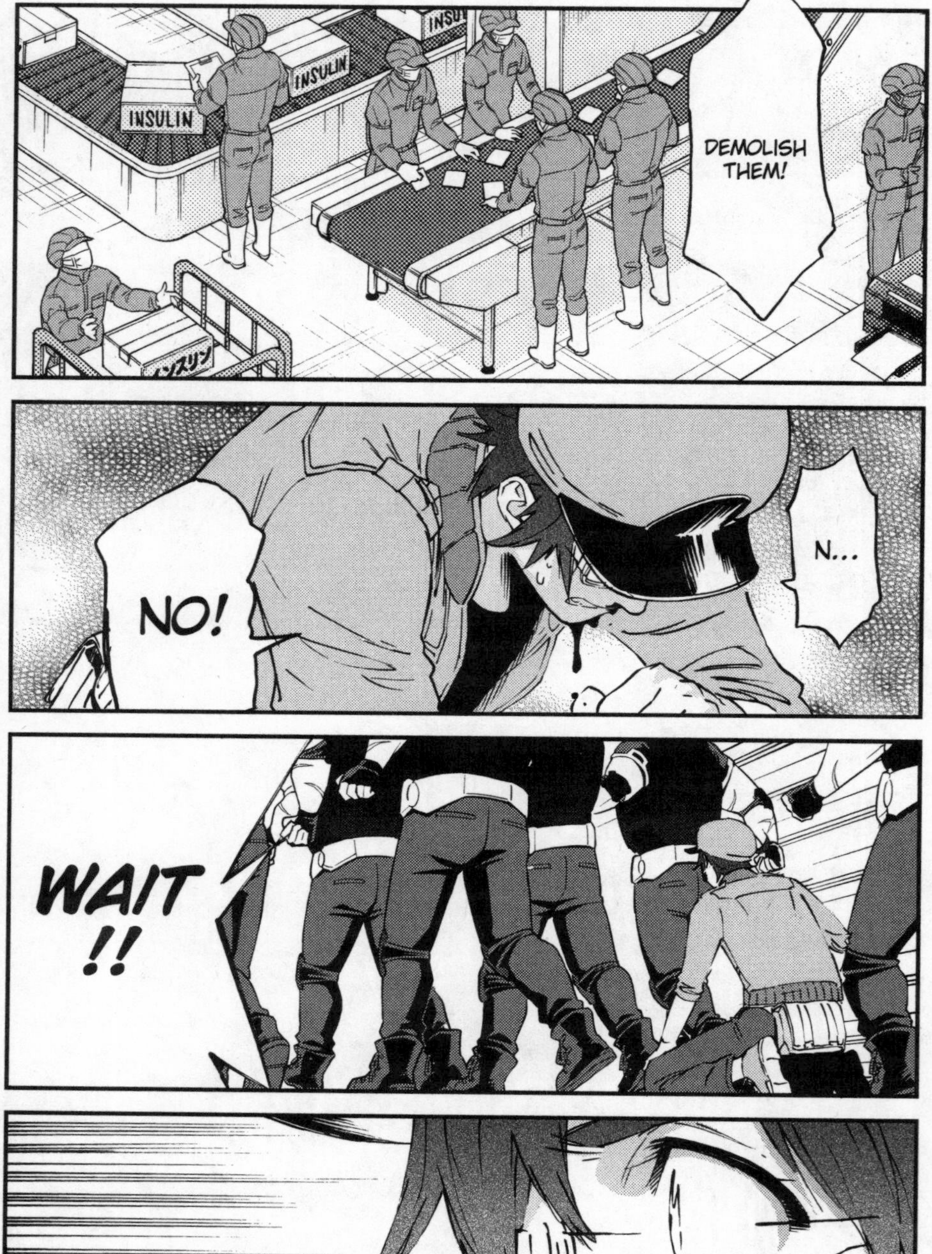
DEMOLISH THEM!
INSULIN
INSULIN
N...
NO!
WAIT !!

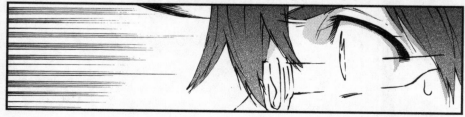

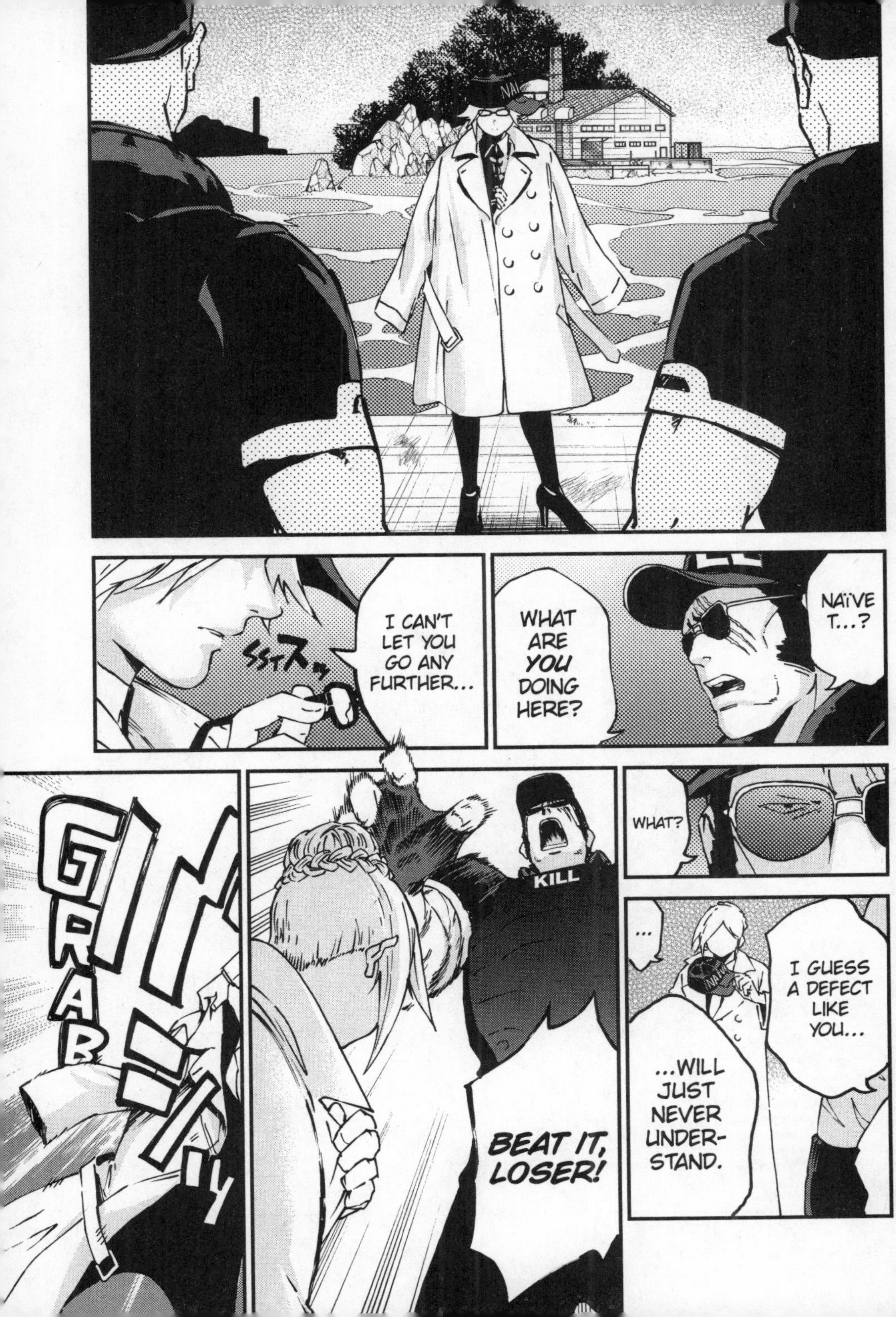
NAÏVE T...?
WHAT ARE *YOU* DOING HERE?
I CAN'T LET YOU GO ANY FURTHER...
WHAT?
I GUESS A DEFECT LIKE YOU...
...
...WILL JUST NEVER UNDER-STAND.
KILL
BEAT IT, LOSER!
GRAB

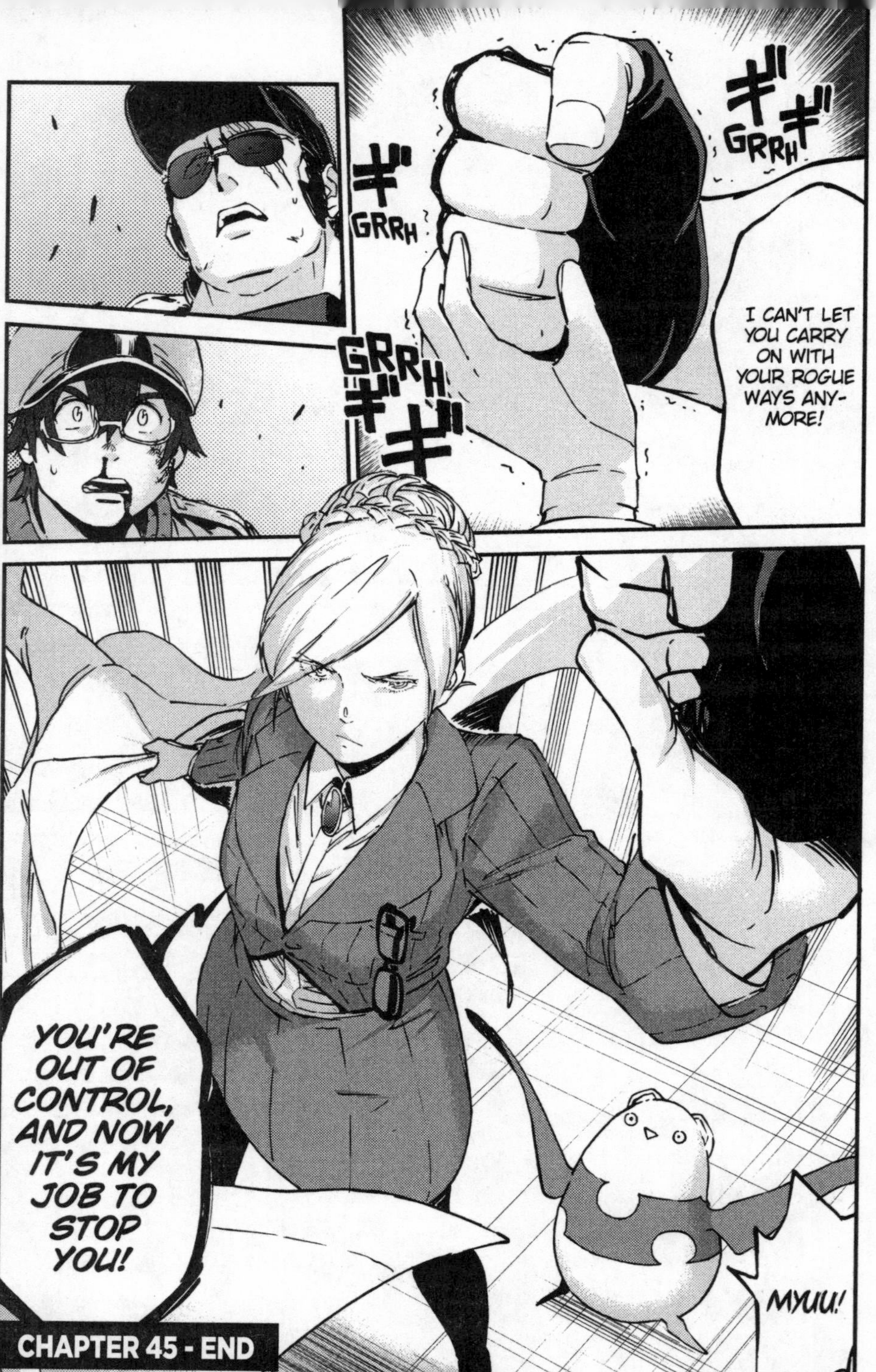
ギギ
GRRH
ギ
GRRH
I CAN'T LET YOU CARRY ON WITH YOUR ROGUE WAYS ANY-MORE!
GRRH
ギギ
YOU'RE OUT OF CONTROL, AND NOW IT'S MY JOB TO STOP YOU!
MYUU!

CHAPTER 45 - END

Cells at Work!
はたらく細胞
CODE BLACK

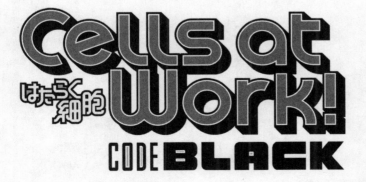

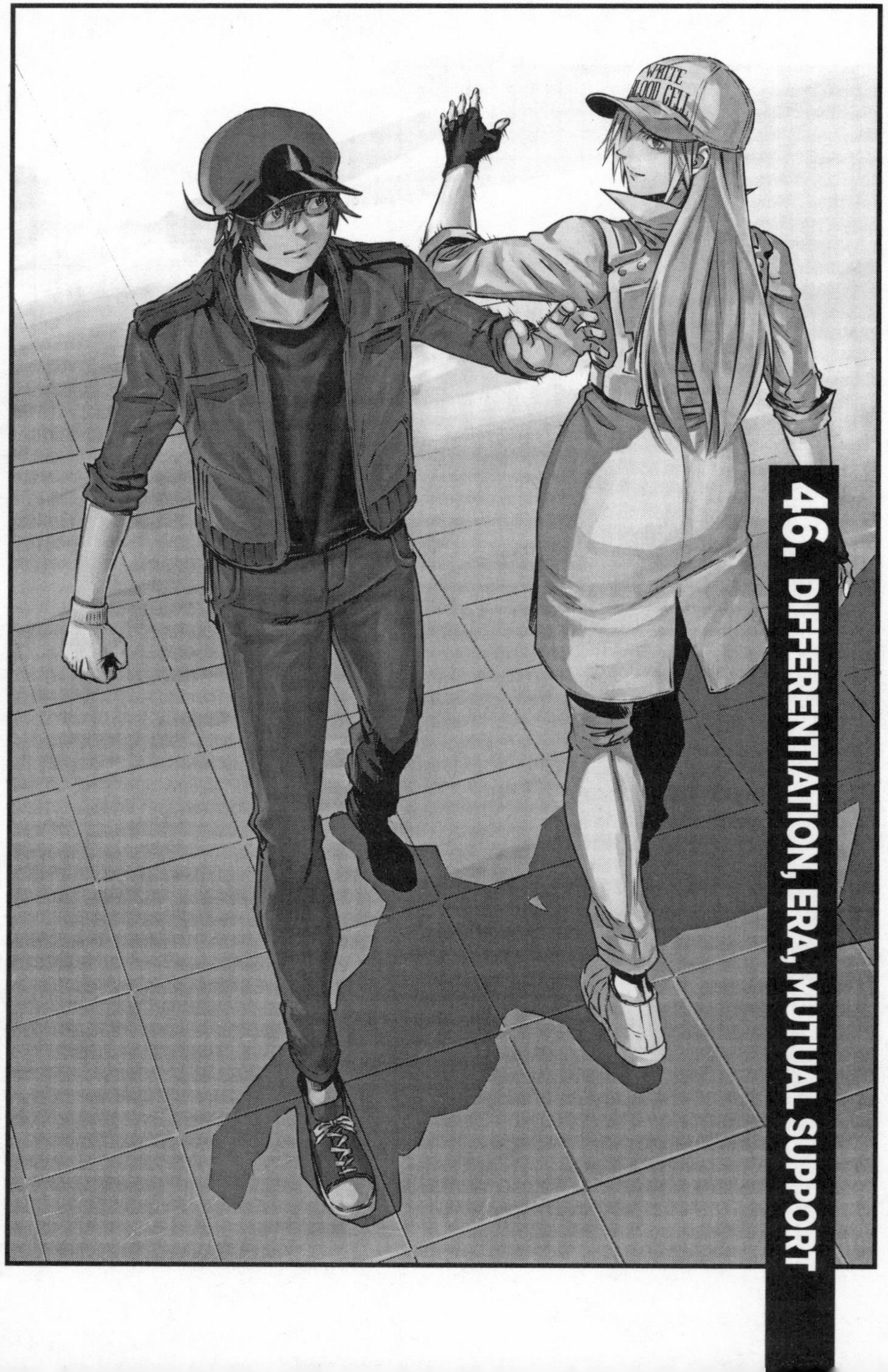
WHITE BLOOD CELL

# 46. DIFFERENTIATION, ERA, MUTUAL SUPPORT

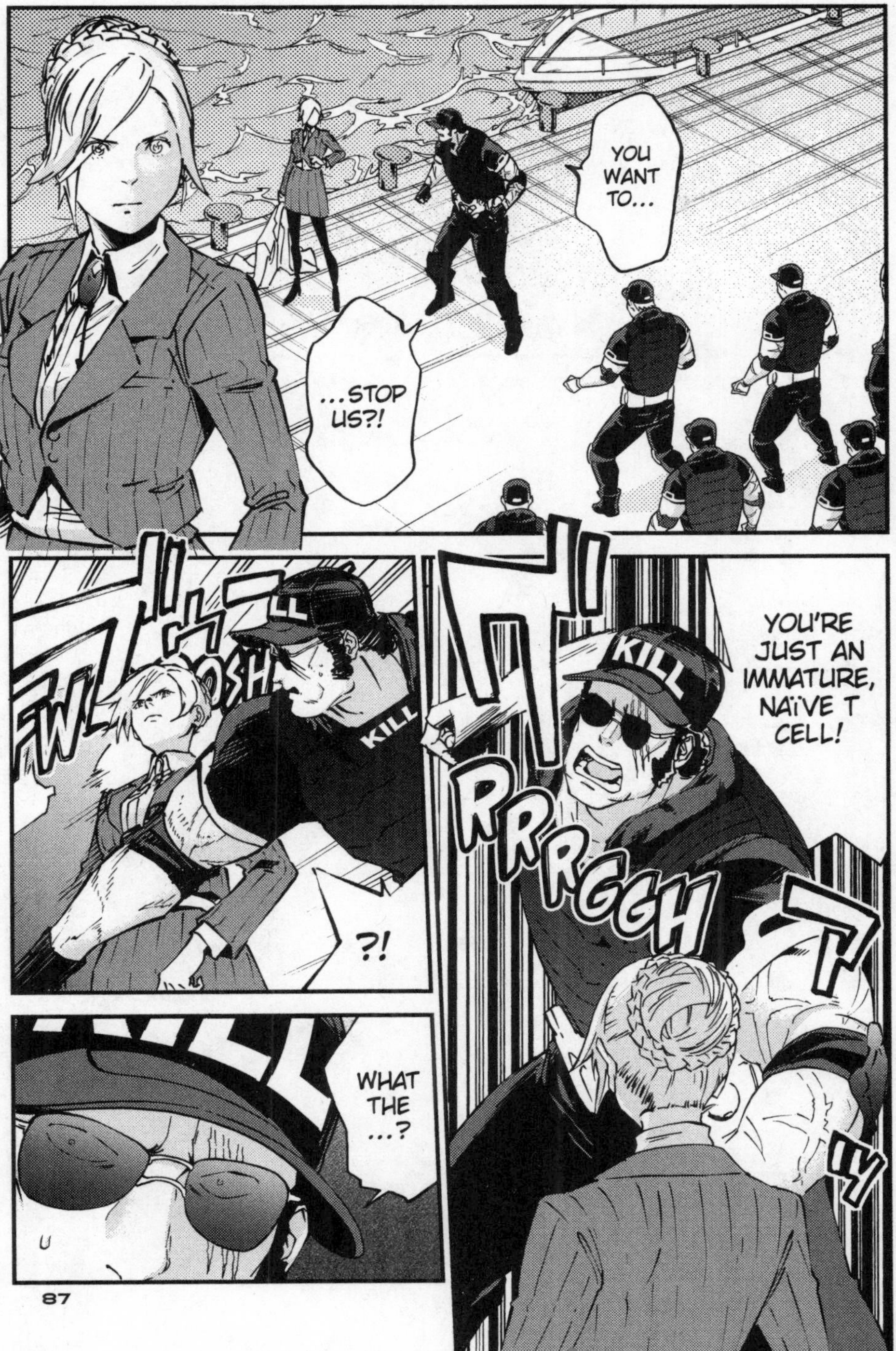
YOU WANT TO...
...STOP US?!
YOU'RE JUST AN IMMATURE, NAÏVE T CELL!
RRRGGH
?!
WHAT THE ...?

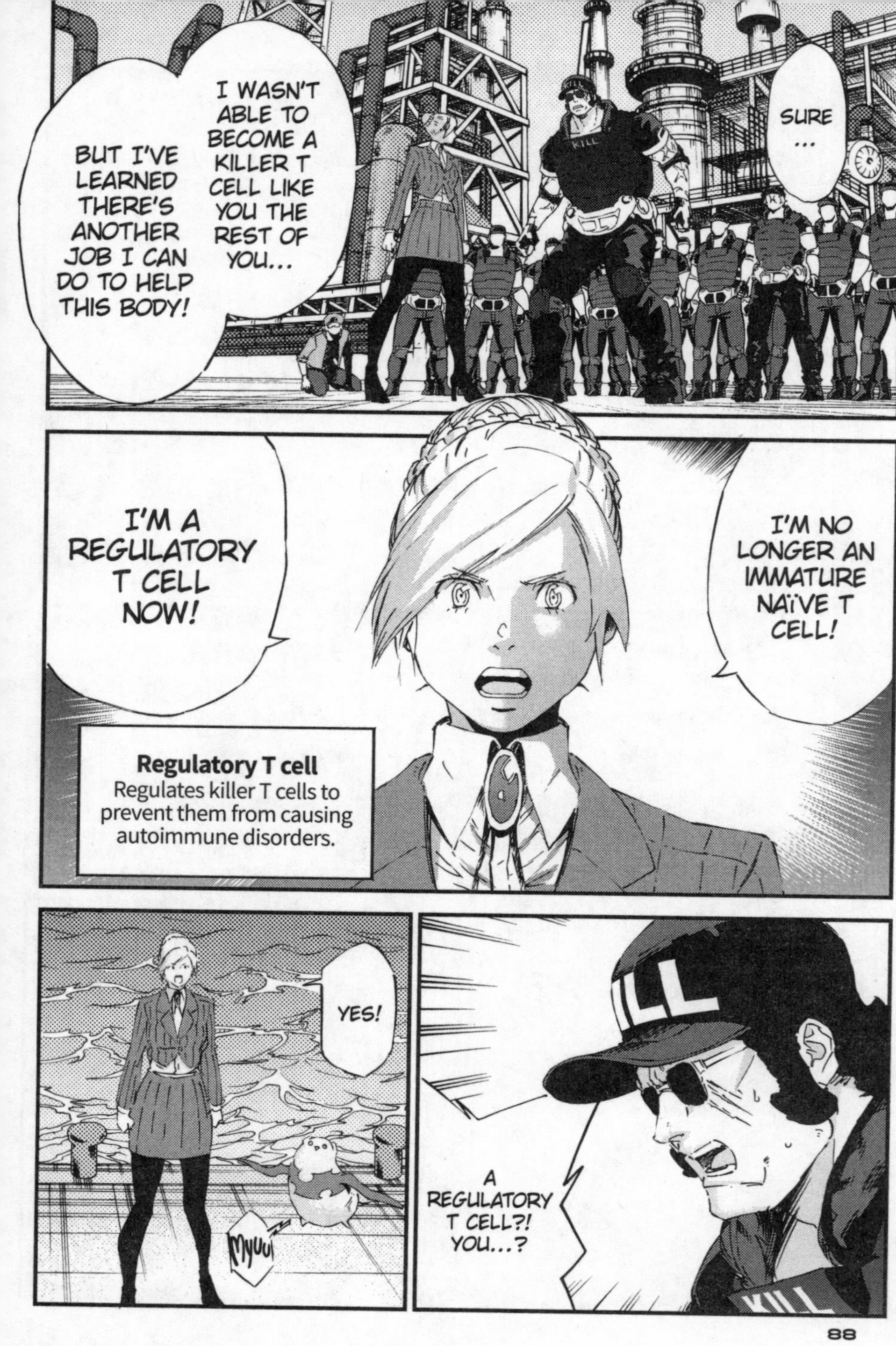
SURE ...
I WASN'T ABLE TO BECOME A KILLER T CELL LIKE YOU THE REST OF YOU...
BUT I'VE LEARNED THERE'S ANOTHER JOB I CAN DO TO HELP THIS BODY!
I'M NO LONGER AN IMMATURE NAïVE T CELL!
I'M A REGULATORY T CELL NOW!
Regulatory T cell
Regulates killer T cells to prevent them from causing autoimmune disorders.
A REGULATORY T CELL?! YOU...?
YES!
MYUU

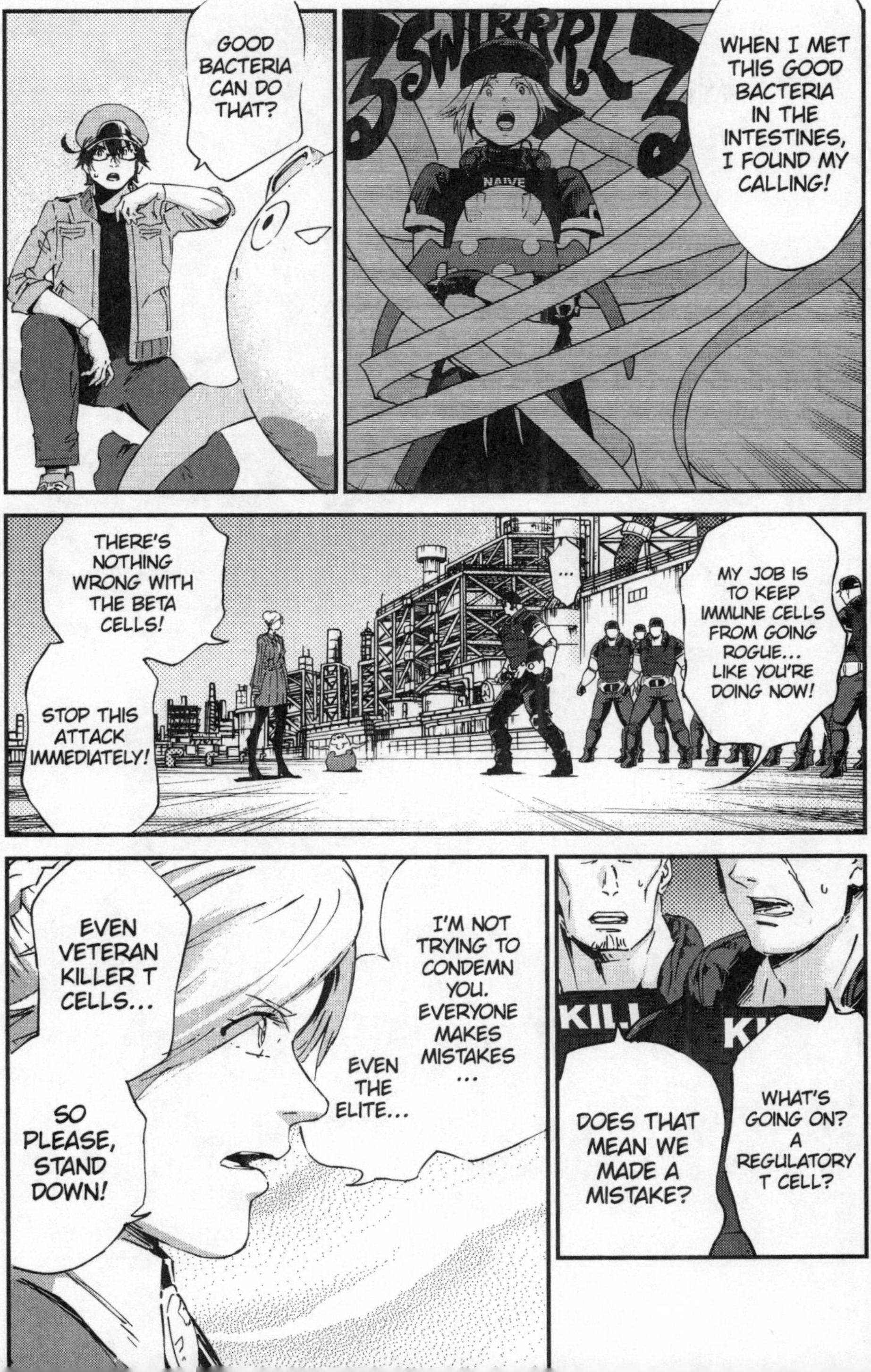
SWIRRRL
WHEN I MET THIS GOOD BACTERIA IN THE INTESTINES, I FOUND MY CALLING!
GOOD BACTERIA CAN DO THAT?
MY JOB IS TO KEEP IMMUNE CELLS FROM GOING ROGUE... LIKE YOU'RE DOING NOW!
...
THERE'S NOTHING WRONG WITH THE BETA CELLS!
STOP THIS ATTACK IMMEDIATELY!
WHAT'S GOING ON? A REGULATORY T CELL?
DOES THAT MEAN WE MADE A MISTAKE?
I'M NOT TRYING TO CONDEMN YOU. EVERYONE MAKES MISTAKES...
EVEN THE ELITE...
EVEN VETERAN KILLER T CELLS...
SO PLEASE, STAND DOWN!

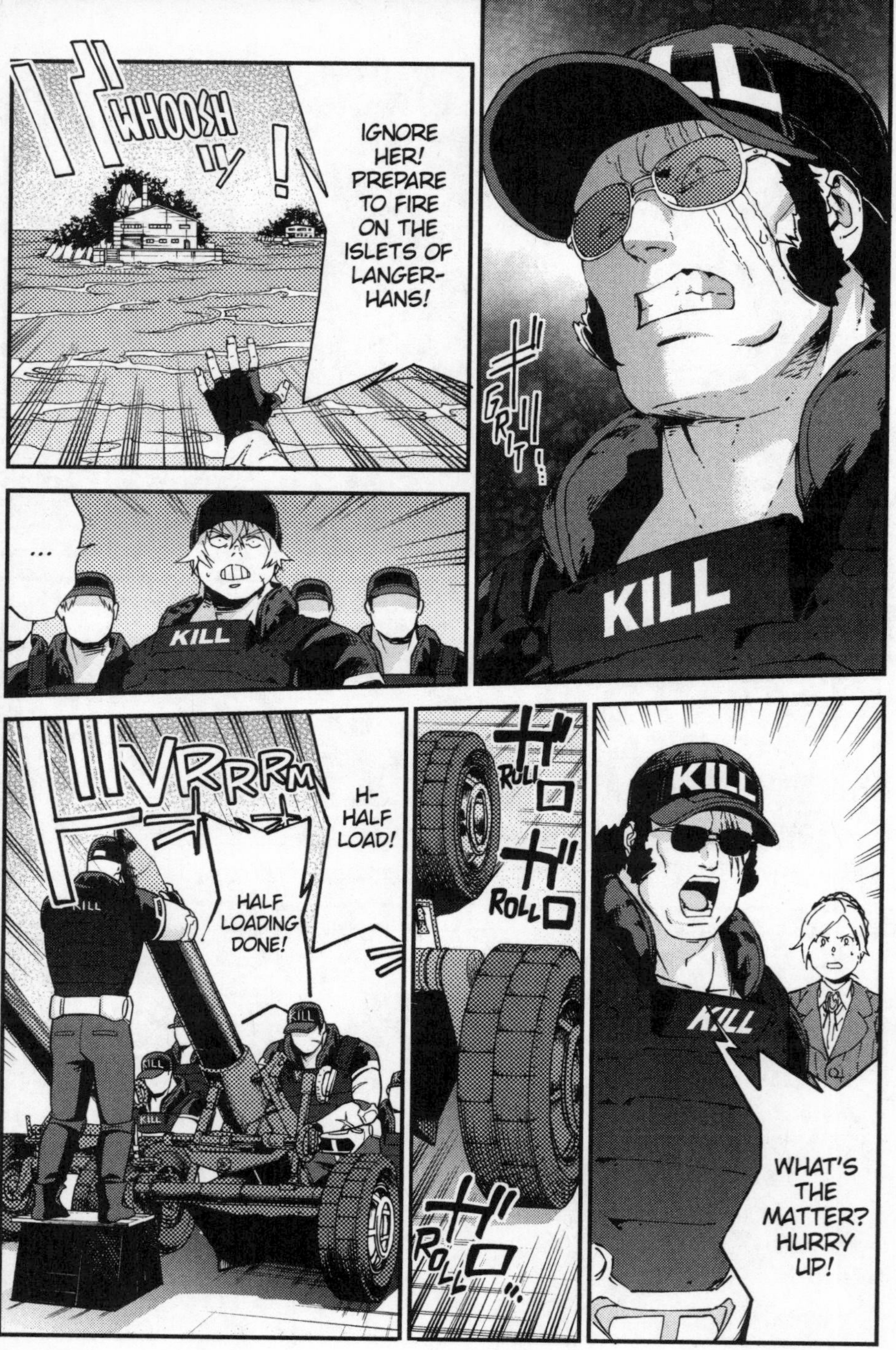
GRIT...
WHOOSH
!
IGNORE HER! PREPARE TO FIRE ON THE ISLETS OF LANGER-HANS!
...
KILL
WHAT'S THE MATTER? HURRY UP!
ROLL
ROLL
ROLL
VRRRM
H-HALF LOAD!
HALF LOADING DONE!

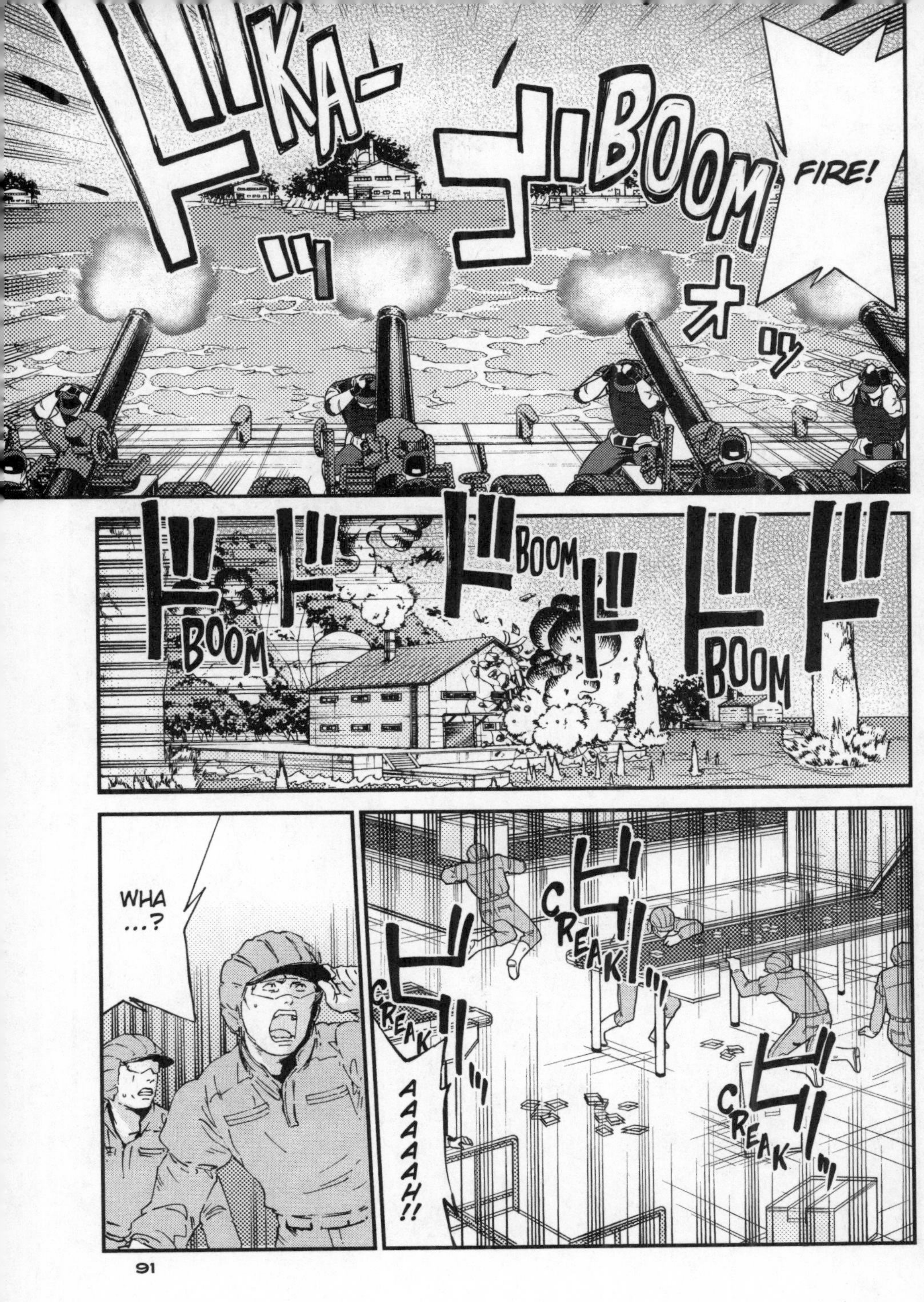
FIRE!
KA-BOOM
BOOM
BOOM
BOOM
CREAK
CREAK
CREAK
AAAAAAH!!
WHA ...?

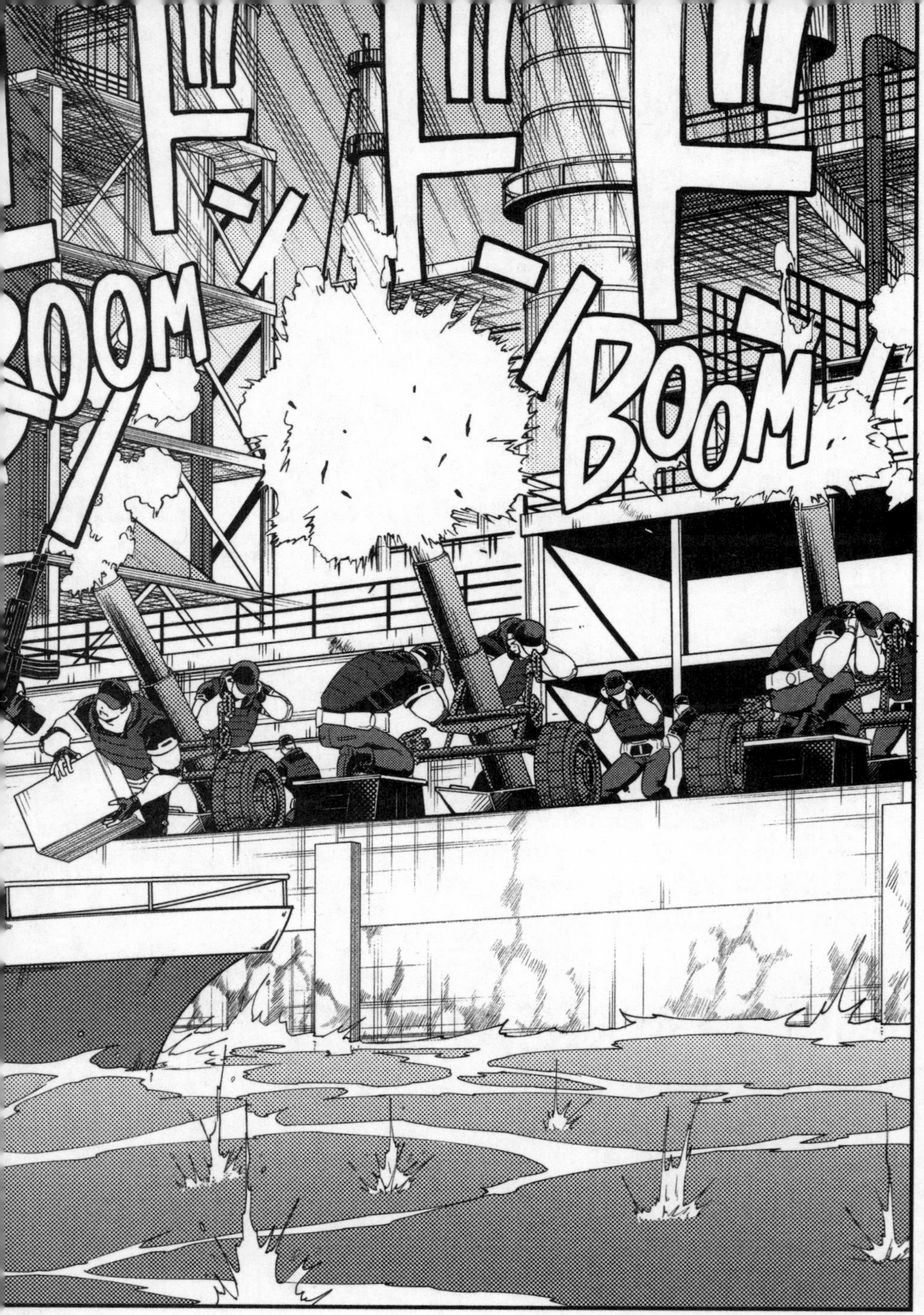
BOOM
ROOM

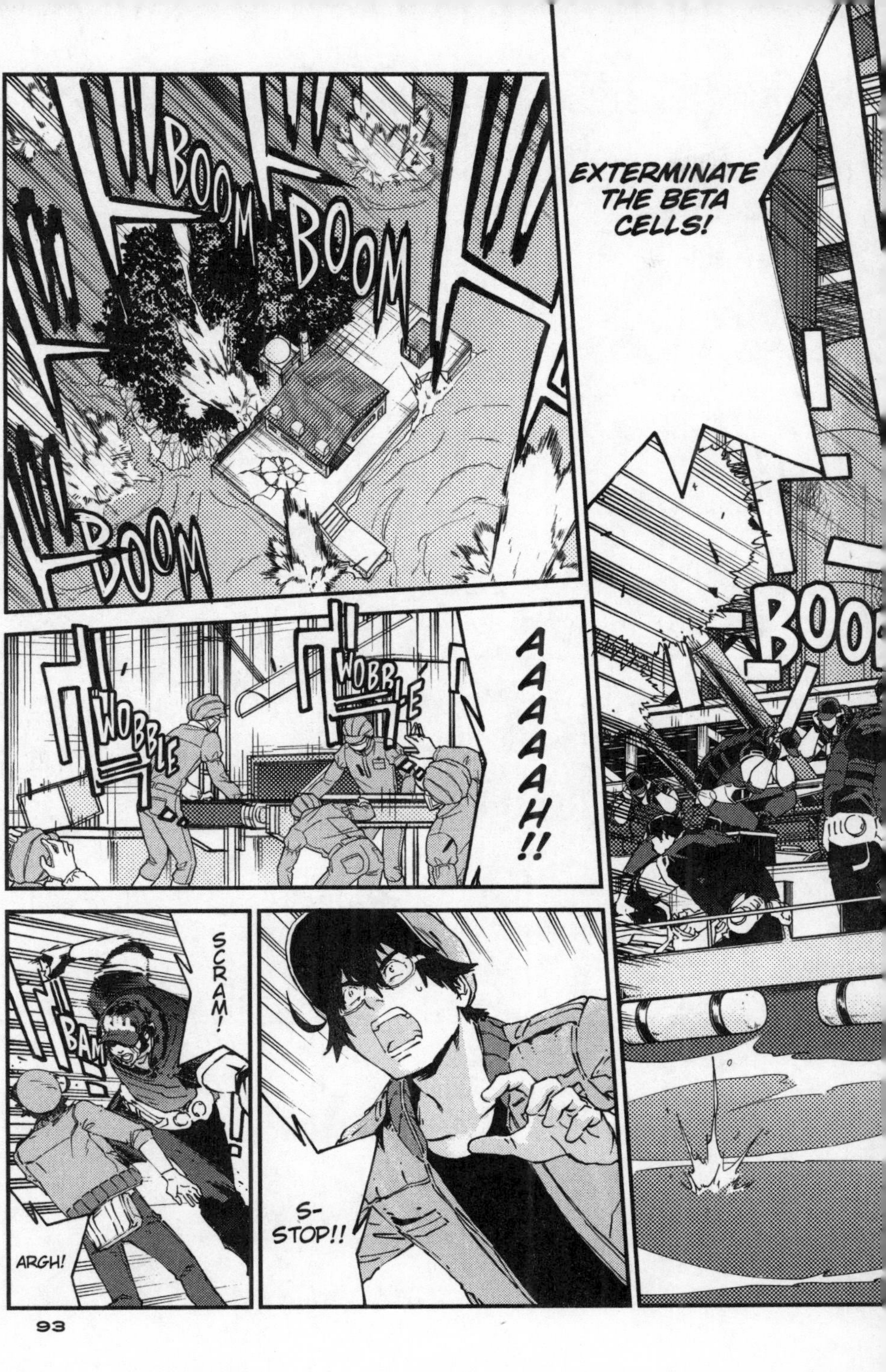
EXTERMINATE THE BETA CELLS!
BOO
BOOM
BOOM
BOOM
AAAAAAH!!
WOBBLE
WOBBLE
S- STOP!!
SCRAM!
BAM
ARGH!

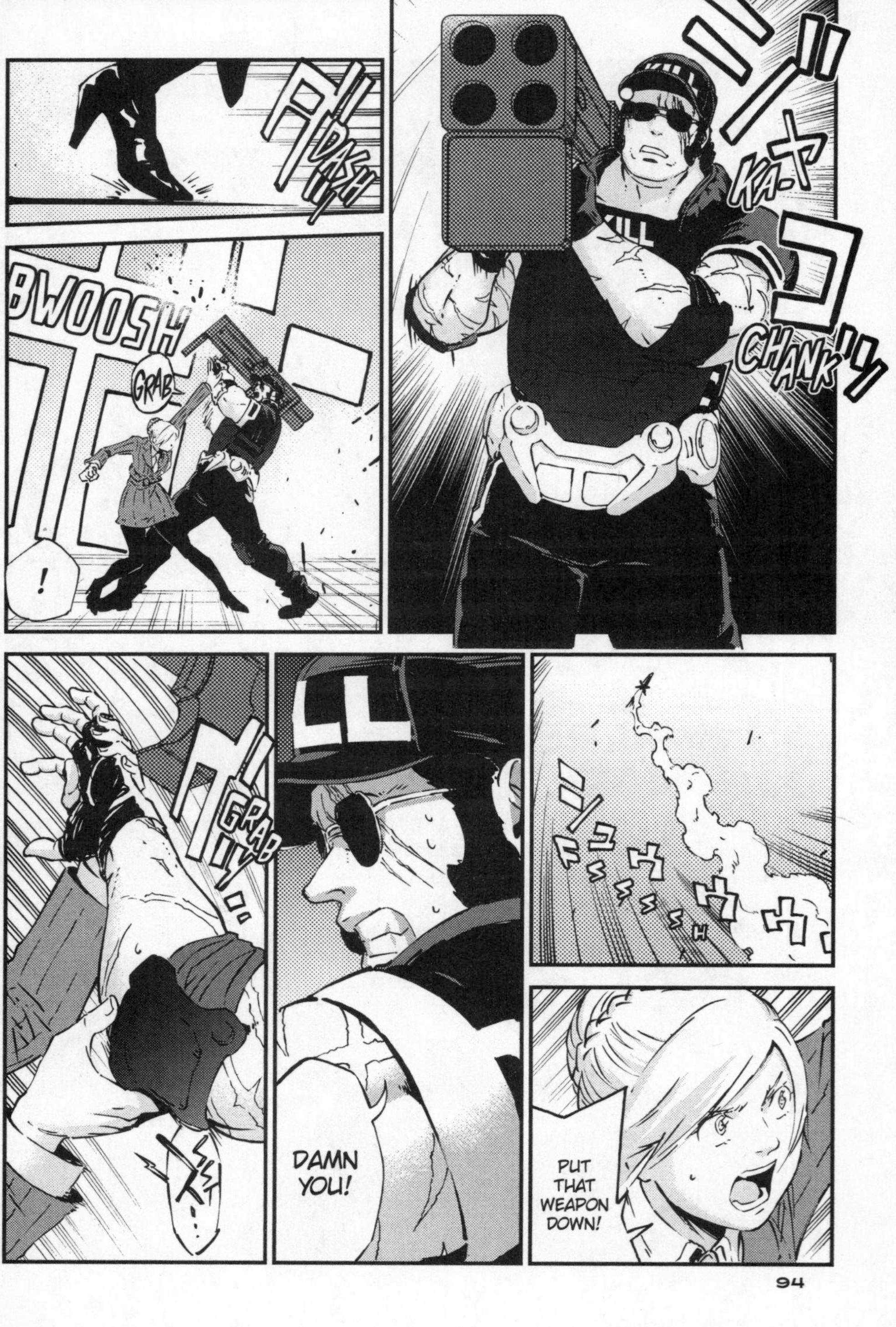
KA-
CHANK
DASH
BWOOSH
GRAB
!
FSSSSSH
PUT THAT WEAPON DOWN!
DAMN YOU!
GRAB

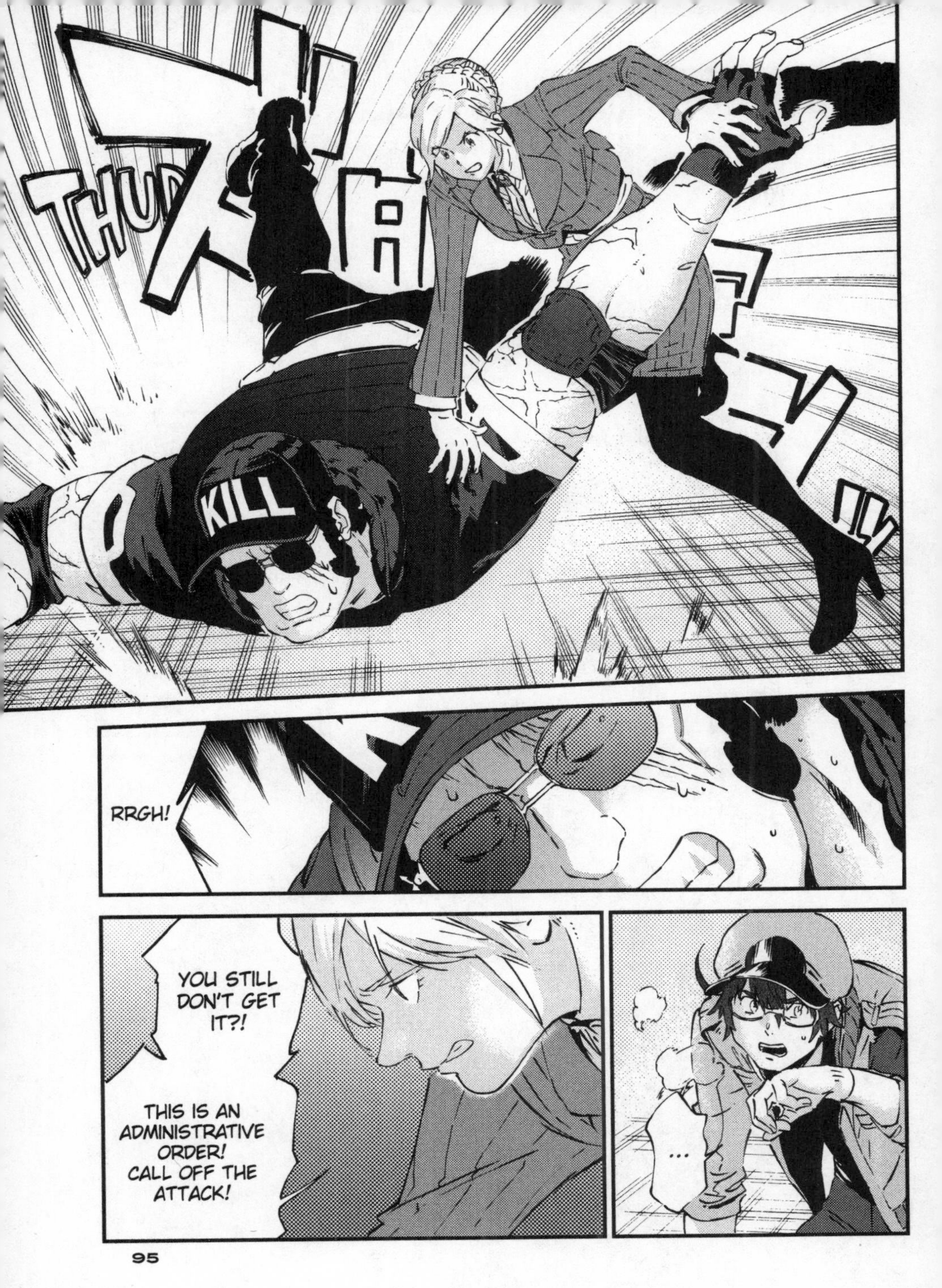
THUD
RRGH!
...
YOU STILL DON'T GET IT?!
THIS IS AN ADMINISTRATIVE ORDER! CALL OFF THE ATTACK!

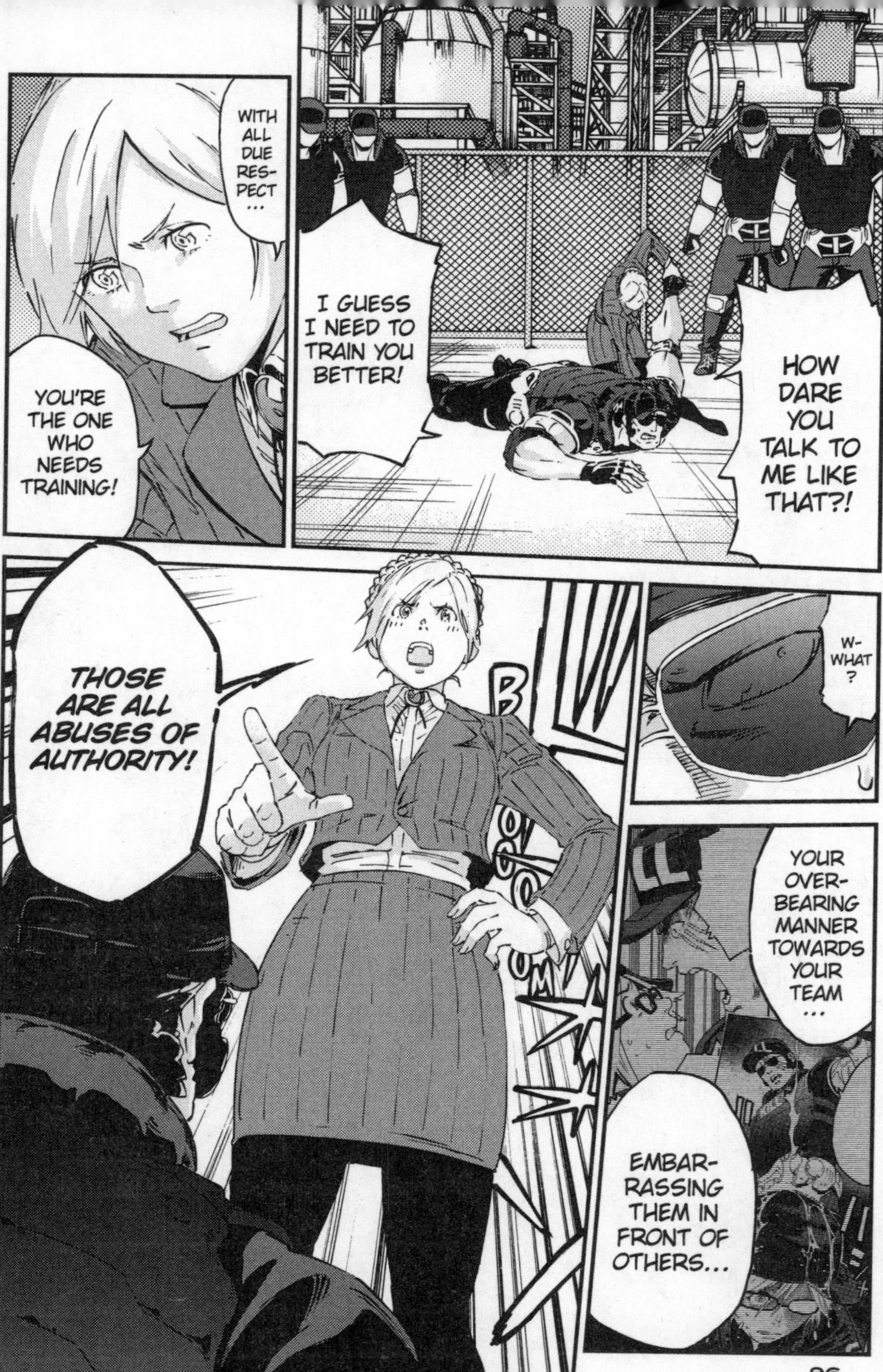
HOW DARE YOU TALK TO ME LIKE THAT?!
I GUESS I NEED TO TRAIN YOU BETTER!
WITH ALL DUE RES-PECT...
YOU'RE THE ONE WHO NEEDS TRAINING!
W-WHAT?
YOUR OVER-BEARING MANNER TOWARDS YOUR TEAM...
EMBAR-RASSING THEM IN FRONT OF OTHERS...
BOOOOM
THOSE ARE ALL ABUSES OF AUTHORITY!

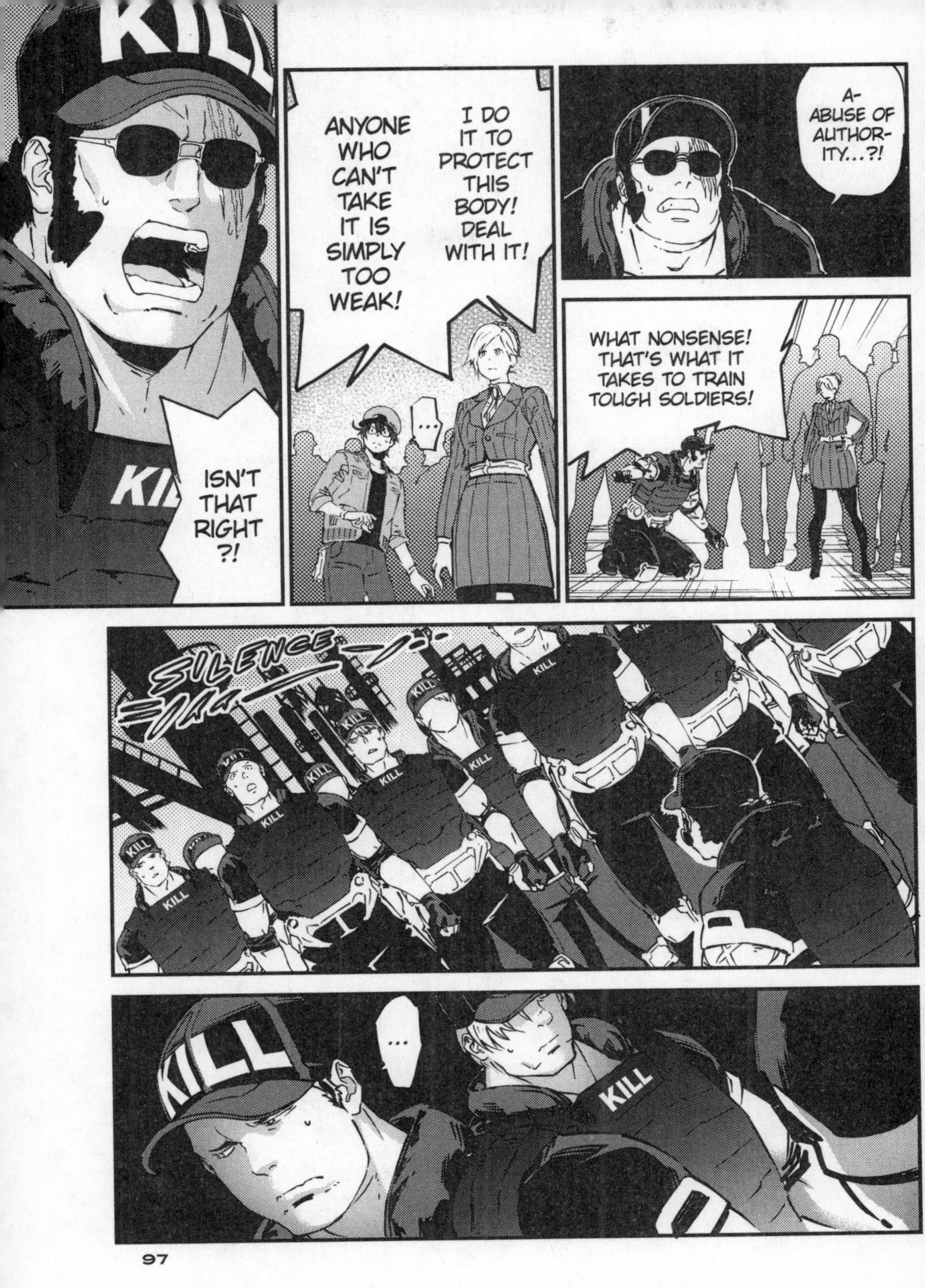
A-ABUSE OF AUTHOR-ITY...?!
WHAT NONSENSE! THAT'S WHAT IT TAKES TO TRAIN TOUGH SOLDIERS!
I DO IT TO PROTECT THIS BODY! DEAL WITH IT!
ANYONE WHO CAN'T TAKE IT IS SIMPLY TOO WEAK!
...
ISN'T THAT RIGHT?!
SILENCE---!!
...

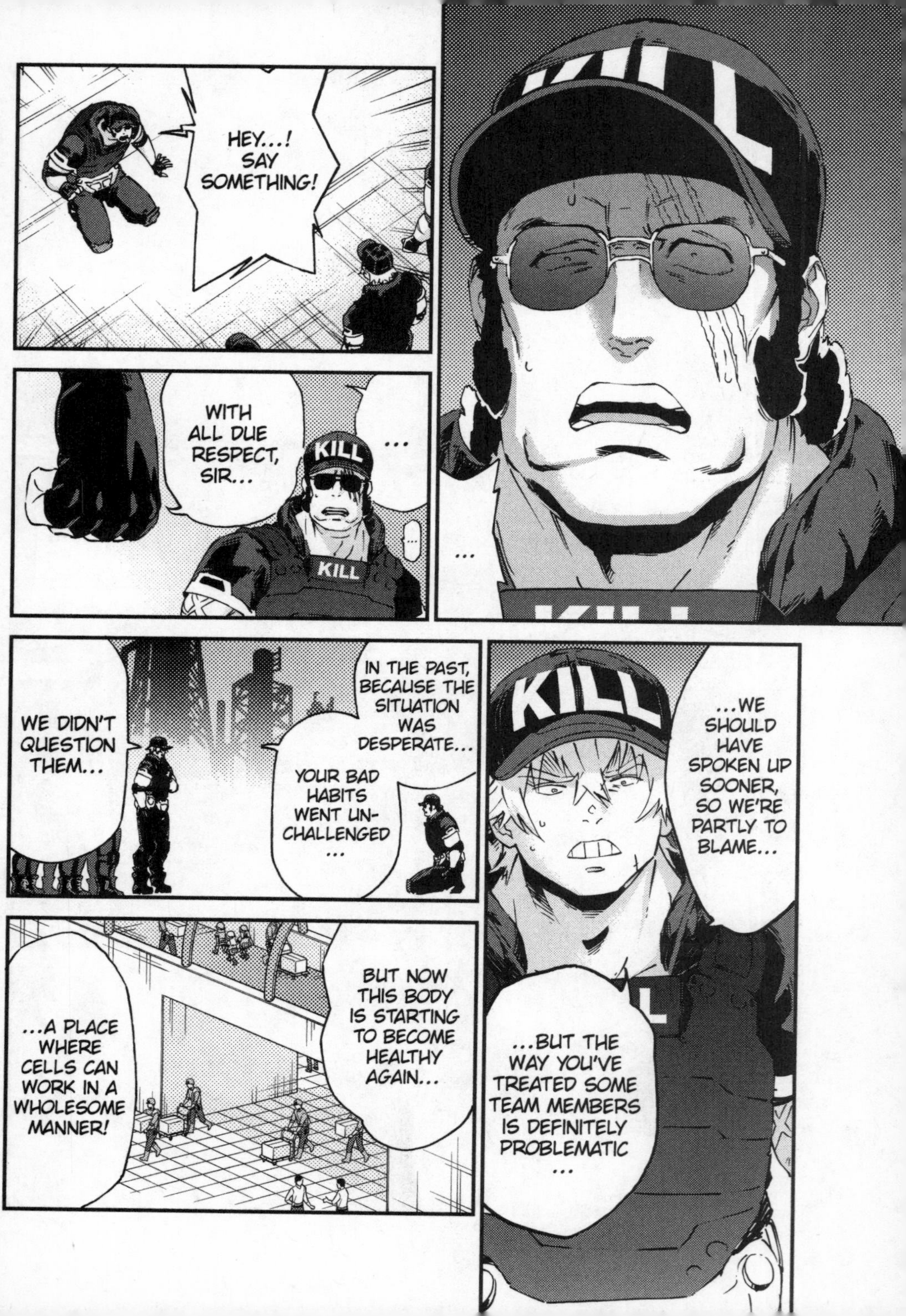
...
HEY...! SAY SOMETHING!
...
WITH ALL DUE RESPECT, SIR...
...
...WE SHOULD HAVE SPOKEN UP SOONER, SO WE'RE PARTLY TO BLAME...
...BUT THE WAY YOU'VE TREATED SOME TEAM MEMBERS IS DEFINITELY PROBLEMATIC...
IN THE PAST, BECAUSE THE SITUATION WAS DESPERATE...
YOUR BAD HABITS WENT UN-CHALLENGED...
WE DIDN'T QUESTION THEM...
BUT NOW THIS BODY IS STARTING TO BECOME HEALTHY AGAIN...
...A PLACE WHERE CELLS CAN WORK IN A WHOLESOME MANNER!

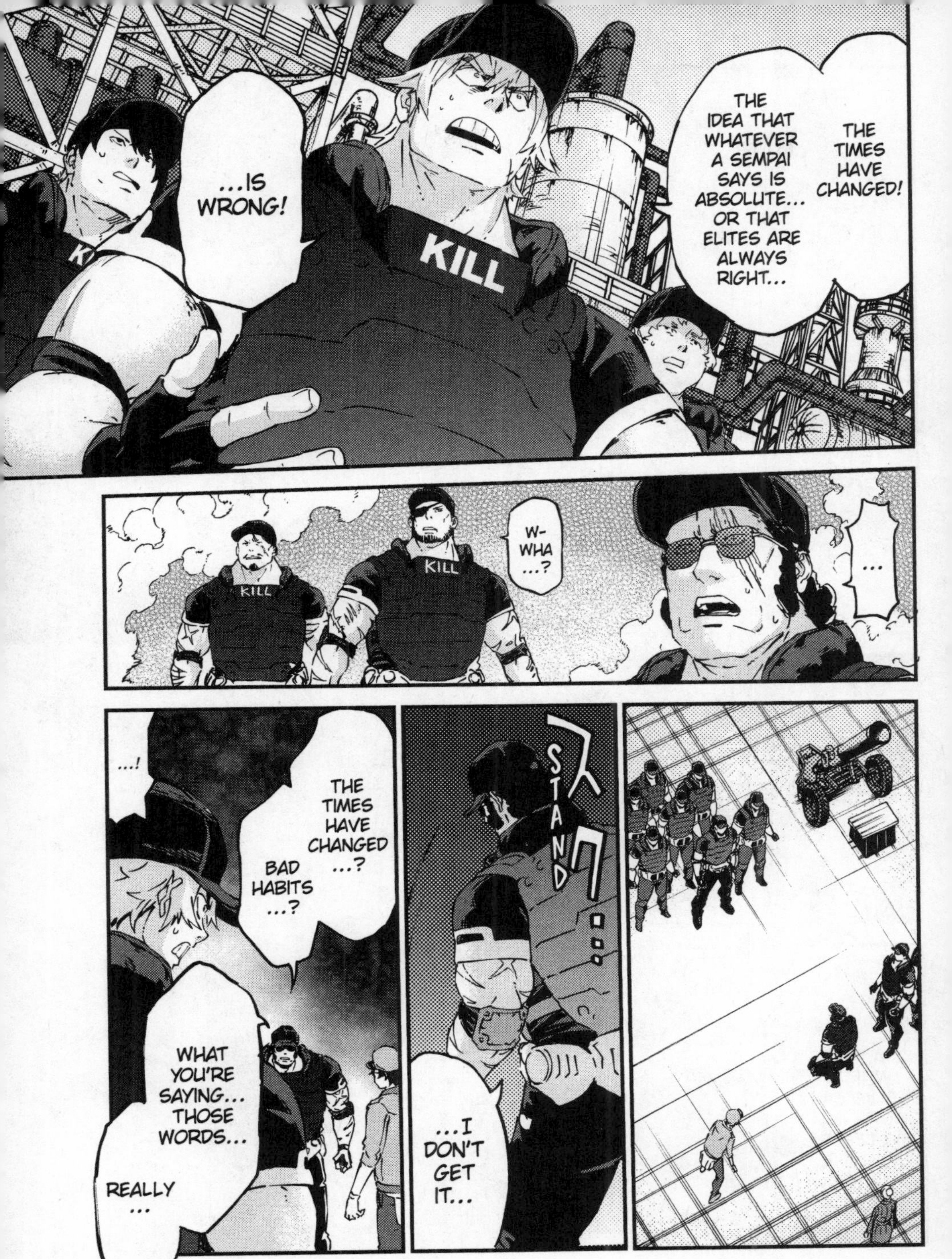
THE TIMES HAVE CHANGED!
THE IDEA THAT WHATEVER A SEMPAI SAYS IS ABSOLUTE... OR THAT ELITES ARE ALWAYS RIGHT...
...IS WRONG!
...
W-WHA...?
STAND
...I DON'T GET IT...
...!
THE TIMES HAVE CHANGED...?
BAD HABITS...?
WHAT YOU'RE SAYING... THOSE WORDS...
REALLY...

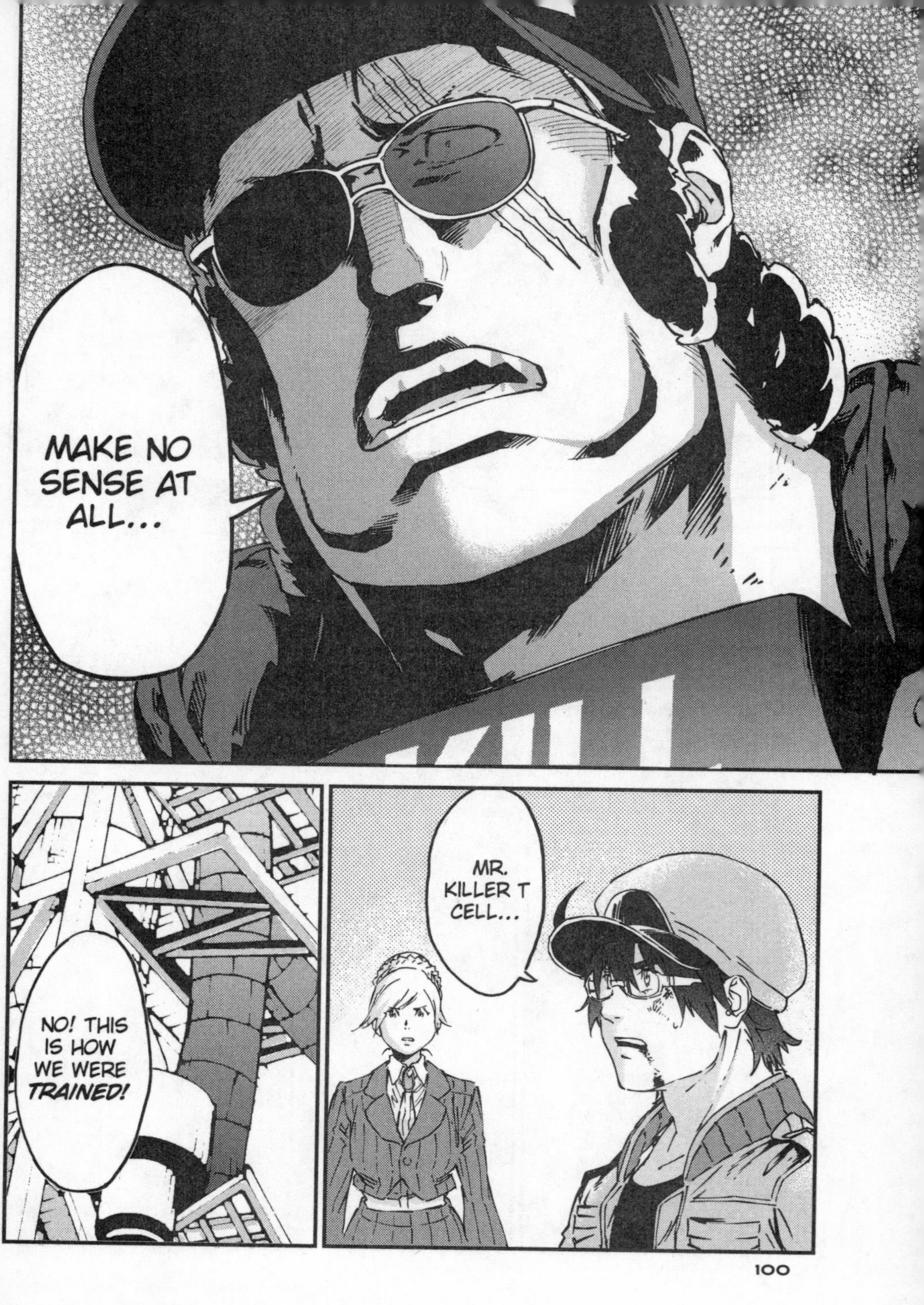
MAKE NO SENSE AT ALL...
MR. KILLER T CELL...
NO! THIS IS HOW WE WERE *TRAINED!*

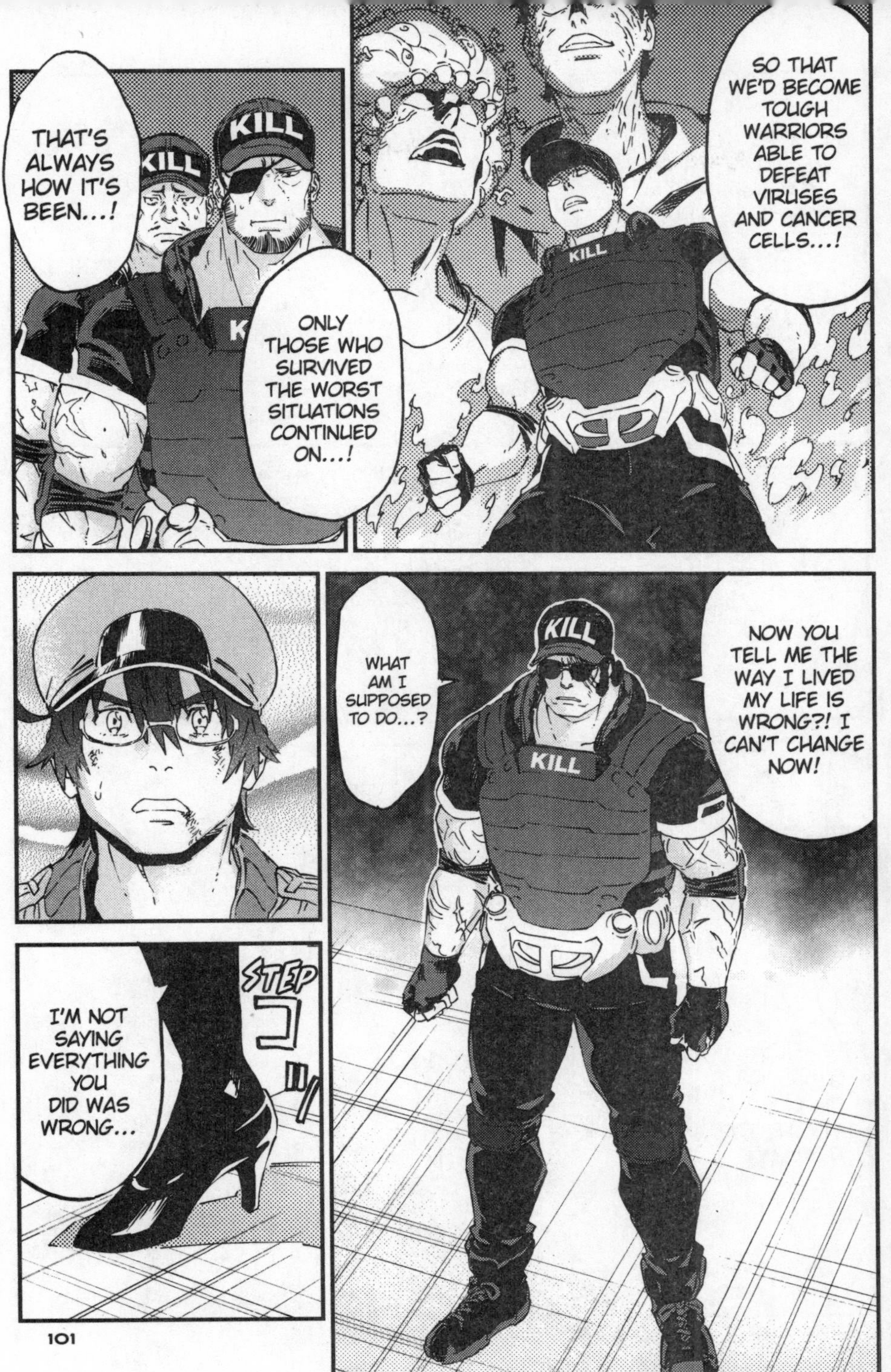
SO THAT WE'D BECOME TOUGH WARRIORS ABLE TO DEFEAT VIRUSES AND CANCER CELLS...!
THAT'S ALWAYS HOW IT'S BEEN...!
ONLY THOSE WHO SURVIVED THE WORST SITUATIONS CONTINUED ON...!
NOW YOU TELL ME THE WAY I LIVED MY LIFE IS WRONG?! I CAN'T CHANGE NOW!
WHAT AM I SUPPOSED TO DO...?
STEP
I'M NOT SAYING EVERYTHING YOU DID WAS WRONG...

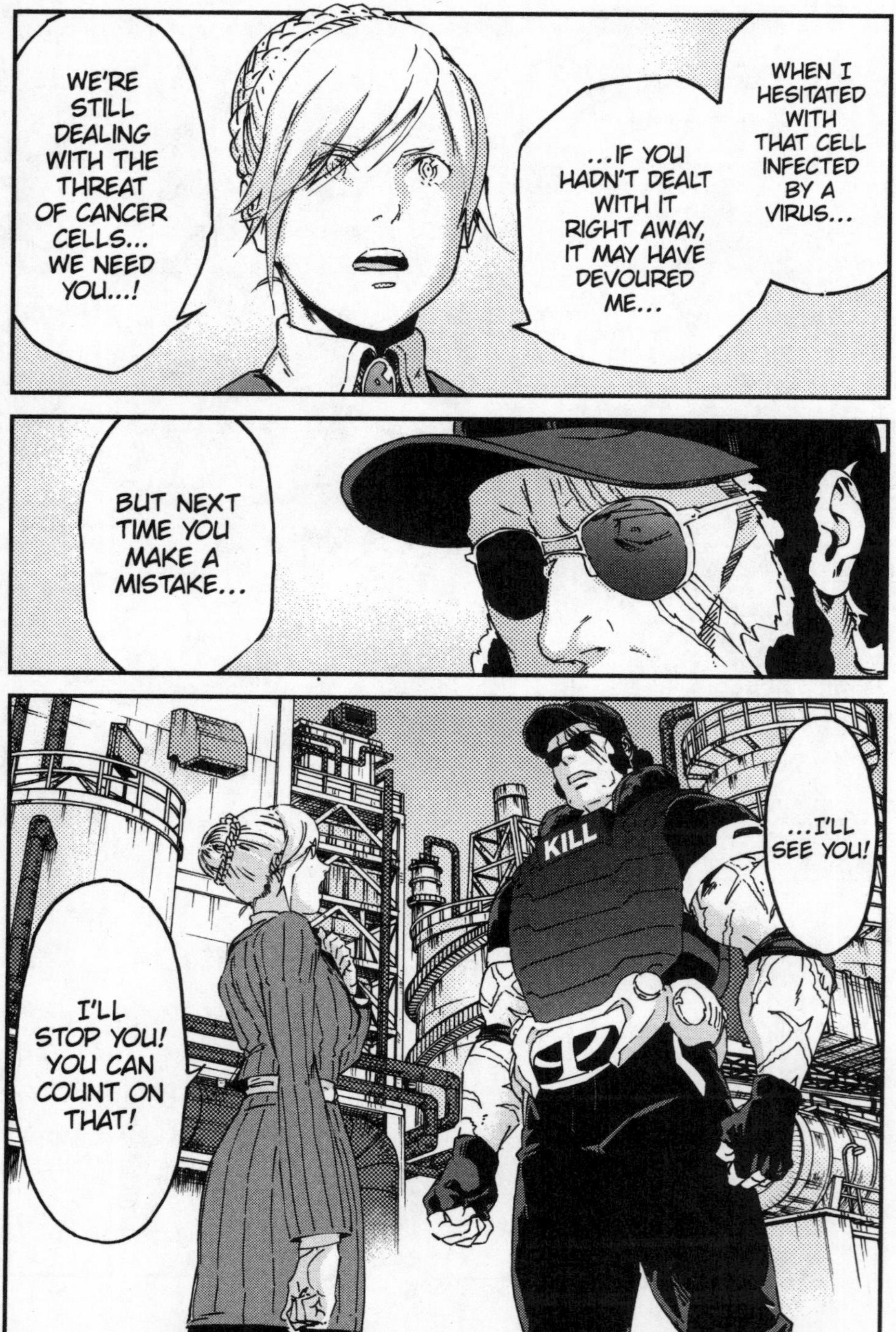
WHEN I HESITATED WITH THAT CELL INFECTED BY A VIRUS...
...IF YOU HADN'T DEALT WITH IT RIGHT AWAY, IT MAY HAVE DEVOURED ME...
WE'RE STILL DEALING WITH THE THREAT OF CANCER CELLS... WE NEED YOU...!
BUT NEXT TIME YOU MAKE A MISTAKE...
...I'LL SEE YOU!
KILL
I'LL STOP YOU! YOU CAN COUNT ON THAT!

KILL

THE ATTACK IS OFF ...

KILL
KILL
KILL
KILL
KILL

KILL

PULL OUT!

SEMPAI ...!

WHIRL

HOW ARE THE BETA CELLS ...?!

103

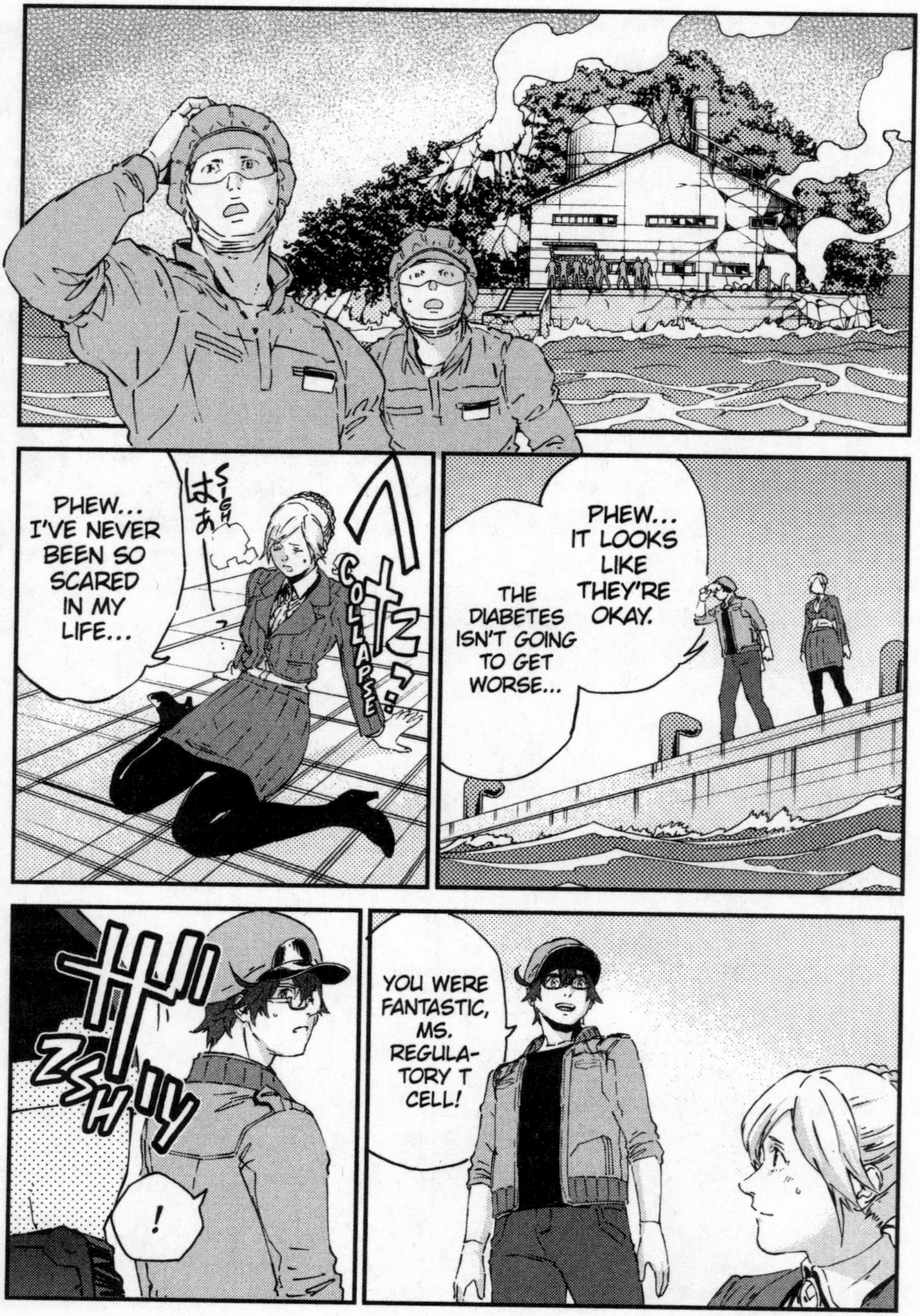
PHEW... IT LOOKS LIKE THEY'RE OKAY.
THE DIABETES ISN'T GOING TO GET WORSE...
はぁ SIGH
PHEW... I'VE NEVER BEEN SO SCARED IN MY LIFE...
COLLAPSE
YOU WERE FANTASTIC, MS. REGULATORY T CELL!
ZSHH
!

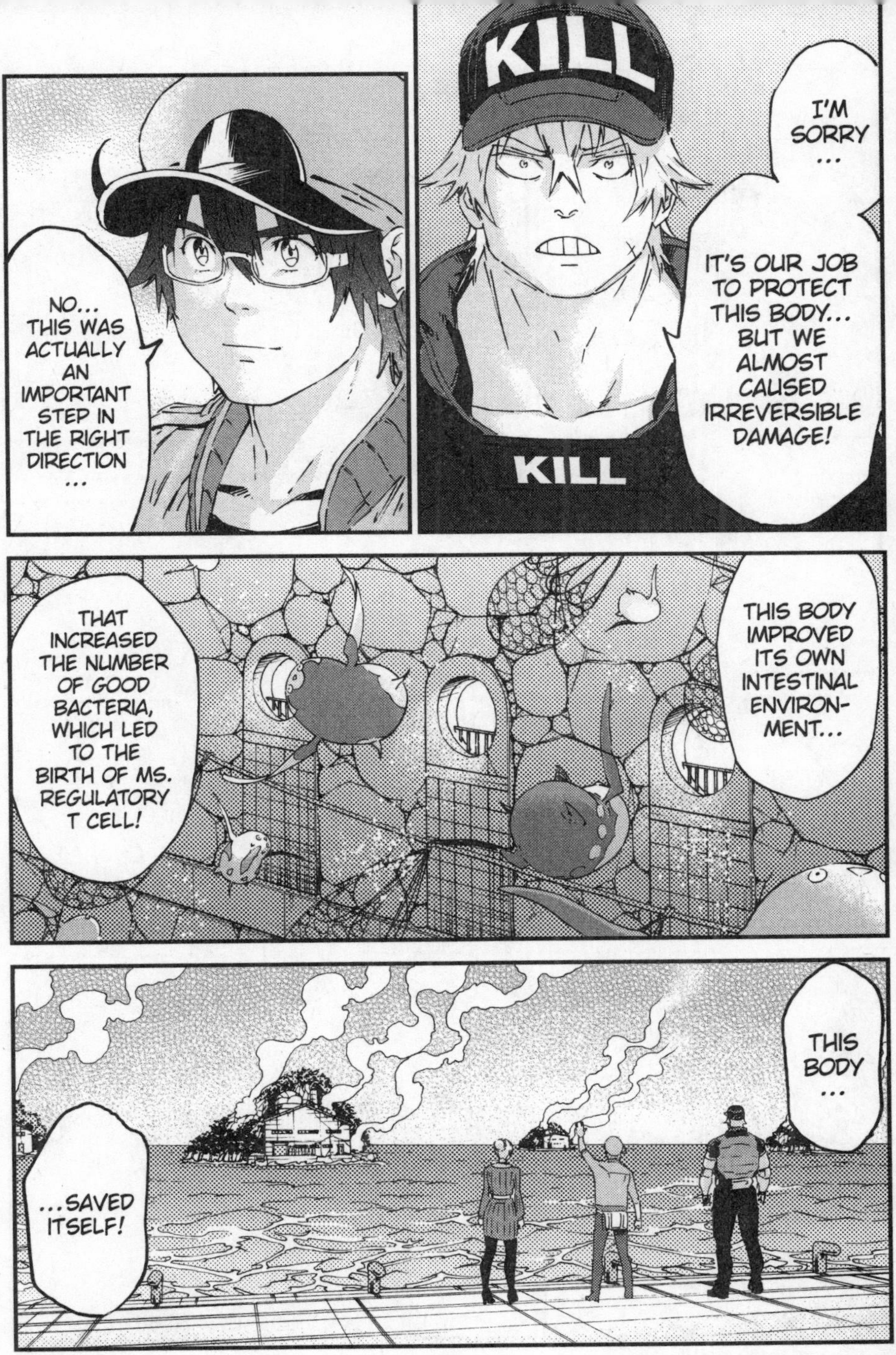
KILL
I'M SORRY ...
IT'S OUR JOB TO PROTECT THIS BODY... BUT WE ALMOST CAUSED IRREVERSIBLE DAMAGE!
KILL
NO... THIS WAS ACTUALLY AN IMPORTANT STEP IN THE RIGHT DIRECTION ...
THIS BODY IMPROVED ITS OWN INTESTINAL ENVIRON-MENT...
THAT INCREASED THE NUMBER OF GOOD BACTERIA, WHICH LED TO THE BIRTH OF MS. REGULATORY T CELL!
THIS BODY ...
...SAVED ITSELF!

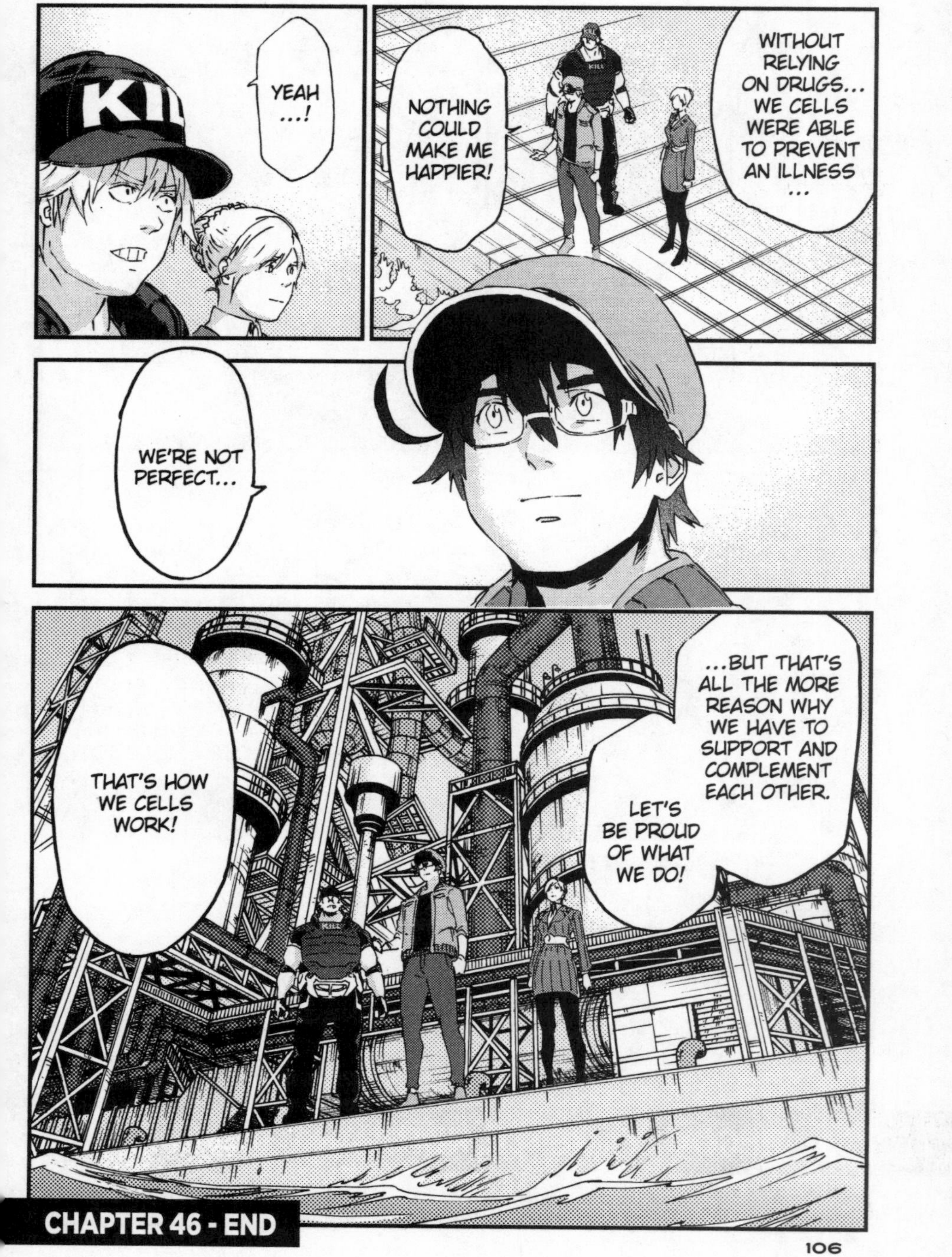
WITHOUT RELYING ON DRUGS... WE CELLS WERE ABLE TO PREVENT AN ILLNESS...
NOTHING COULD MAKE ME HAPPIER!
YEAH ...!
WE'RE NOT PERFECT...
...BUT THAT'S ALL THE MORE REASON WHY WE HAVE TO SUPPORT AND COMPLEMENT EACH OTHER.
LET'S BE PROUD OF WHAT WE DO!
THAT'S HOW WE CELLS WORK!
CHAPTER 46 - END

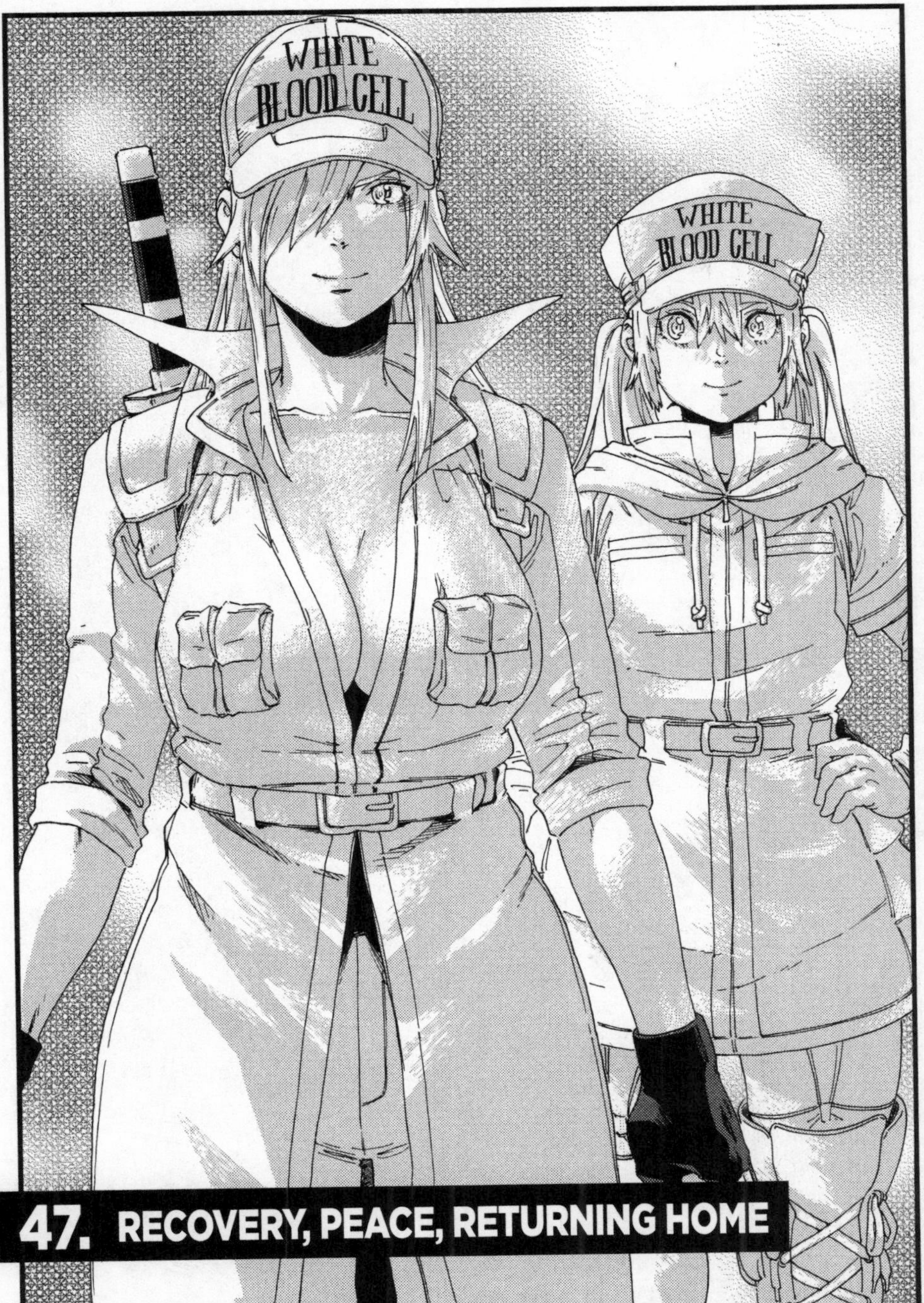
WHITE BLOOD CELL
WHITE BLOOD CELL

# 47. RECOVERY, PEACE, RETURNING HOME

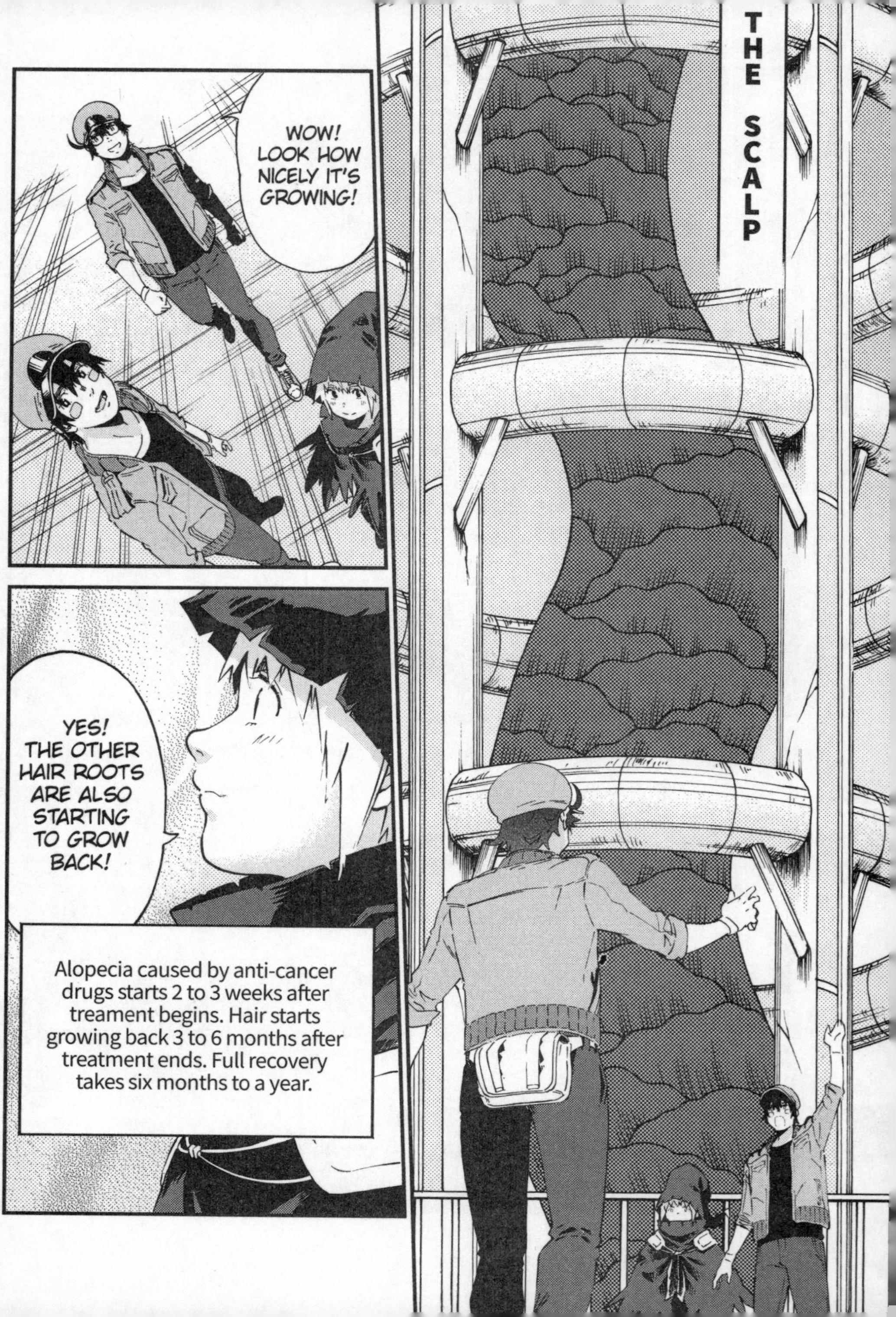
THE SCALP
WOW! LOOK HOW NICELY IT'S GROWING!
YES! THE OTHER HAIR ROOTS ARE ALSO STARTING TO GROW BACK!
Alopecia caused by anti-cancer drugs starts 2 to 3 weeks after treament begins. Hair starts growing back 3 to 6 months after treatment ends. Full recovery takes six months to a year.

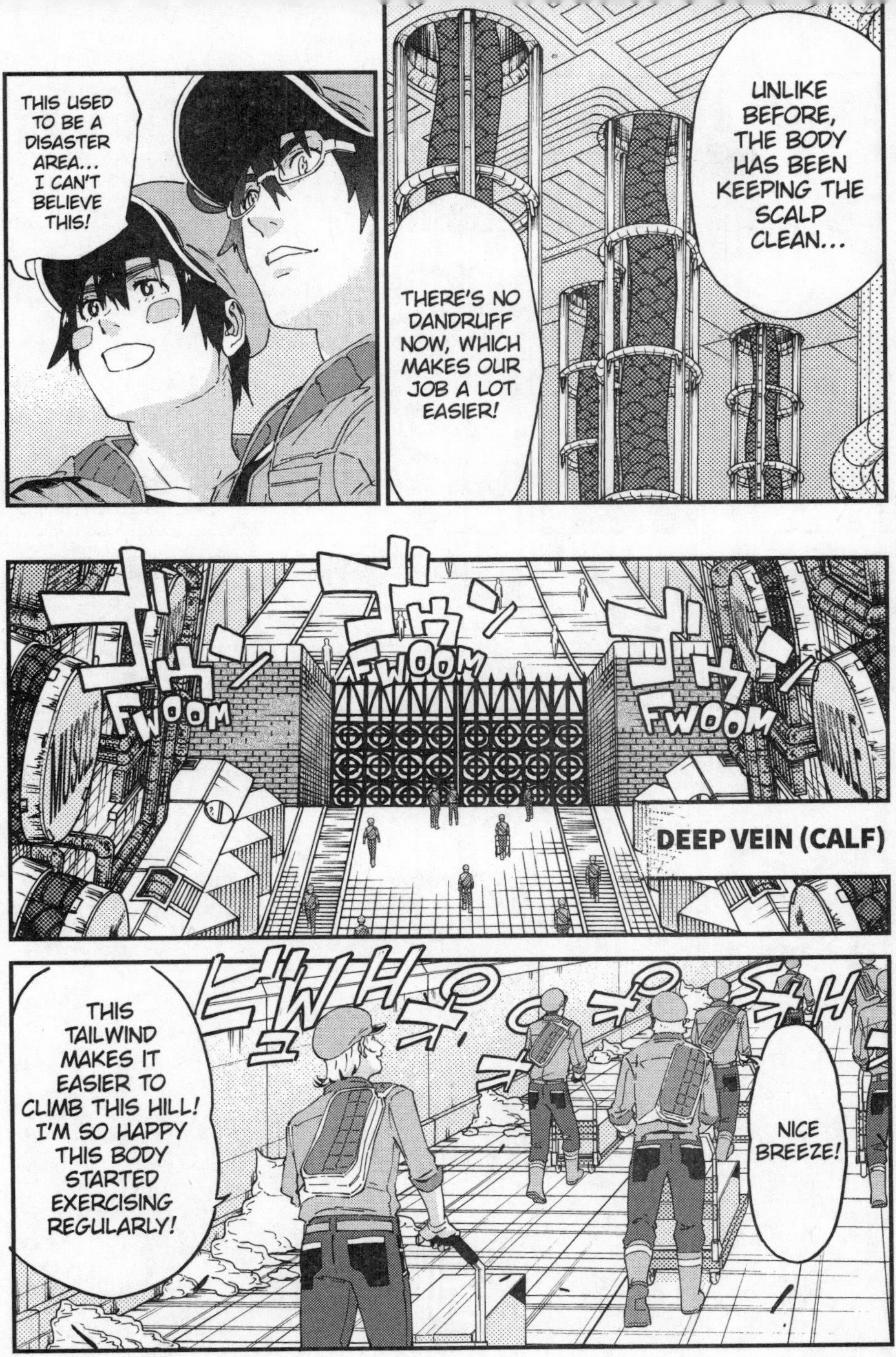
UNLIKE BEFORE, THE BODY HAS BEEN KEEPING THE SCALP CLEAN...
THERE'S NO DANDRUFF NOW, WHICH MAKES OUR JOB A LOT EASIER!
THIS USED TO BE A DISASTER AREA... I CAN'T BELIEVE THIS!
FWOOM
FWOOM
FWOOM
DEEP VEIN (CALF)
WHOOSH
NICE BREEZE!
THIS TAILWIND MAKES IT EASIER TO CLIMB THIS HILL! I'M SO HAPPY THIS BODY STARTED EXERCISING REGULARLY!

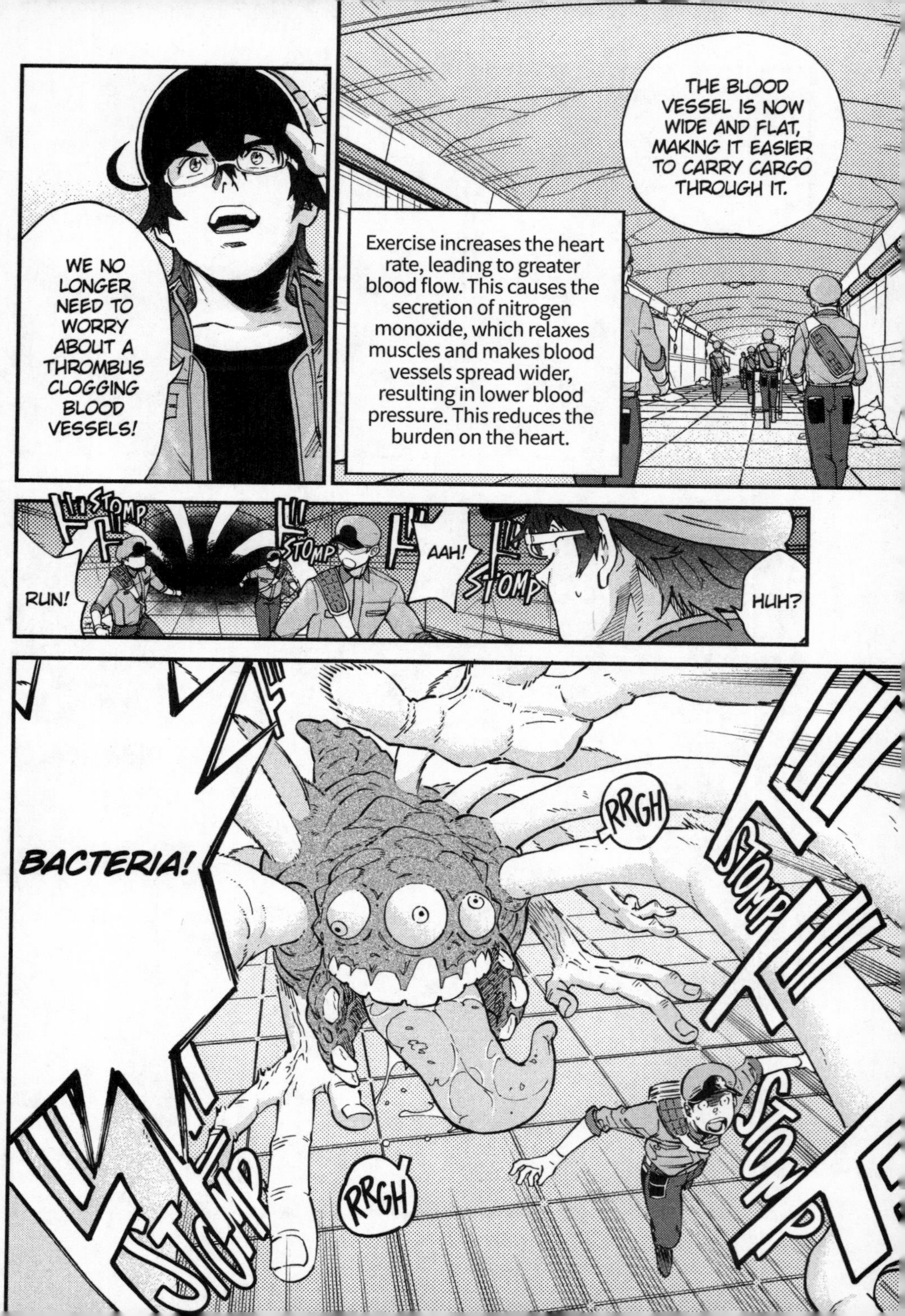
THE BLOOD VESSEL IS NOW WIDE AND FLAT, MAKING IT EASIER TO CARRY CARGO THROUGH IT.
Exercise increases the heart rate, leading to greater blood flow. This causes the secretion of nitrogen monoxide, which relaxes muscles and makes blood vessels spread wider, resulting in lower blood pressure. This reduces the burden on the heart.
WE NO LONGER NEED TO WORRY ABOUT A THROMBUS CLOGGING BLOOD VESSELS!
HUH?
STOMP
AAH!
STOMP
STOMP
RUN!
RRGH
STOMP
BACTERIA!
STOMP
RRGH
STOMP

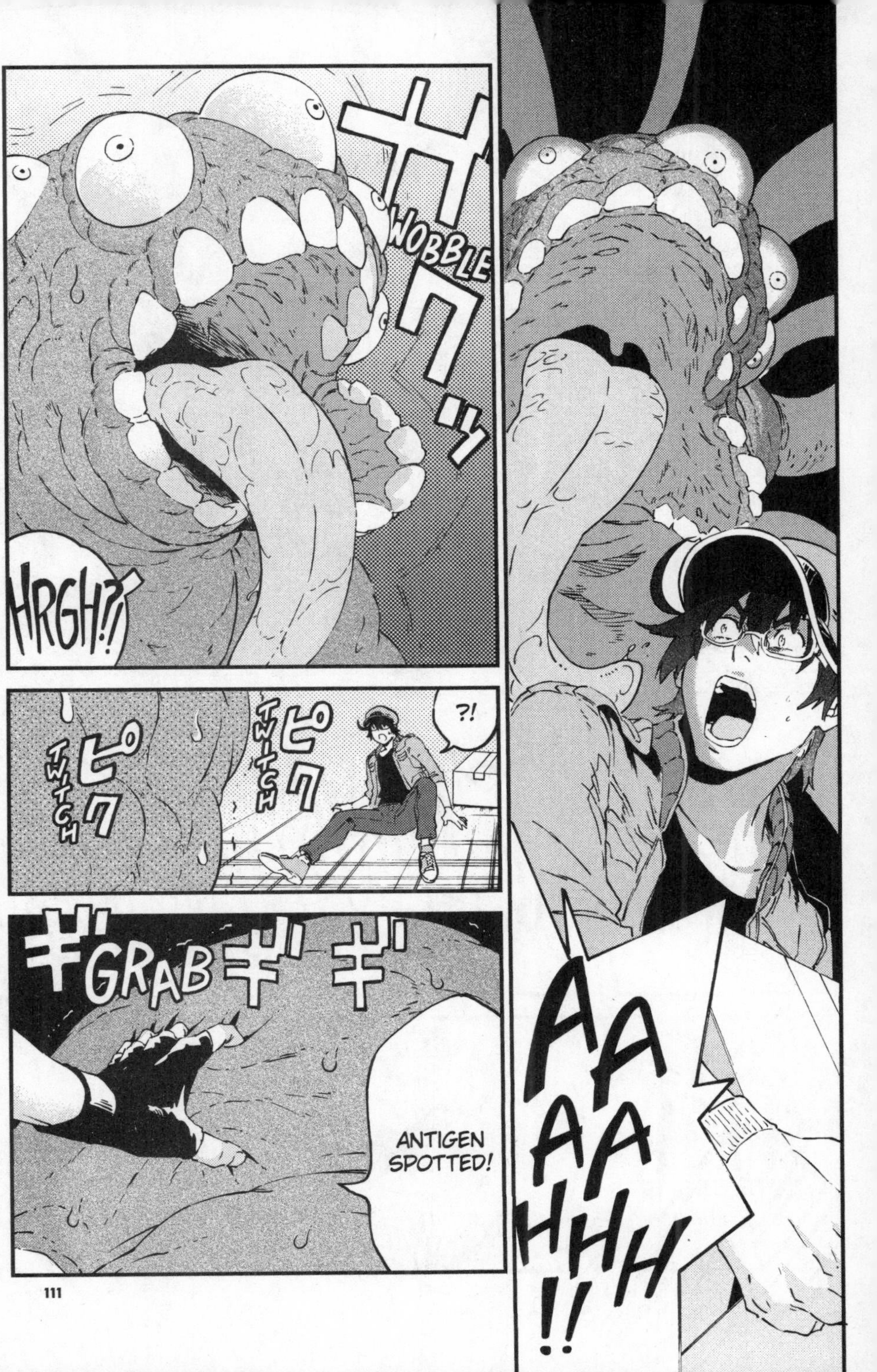
AAAAAHHHH!!
ガ
WOBBLE
クッ
HRGH?!
ピク
TWITCH
?!
ピク
TWITCH
ギ
GRAB
ギ
ギ
ANTIGEN SPOTTED!

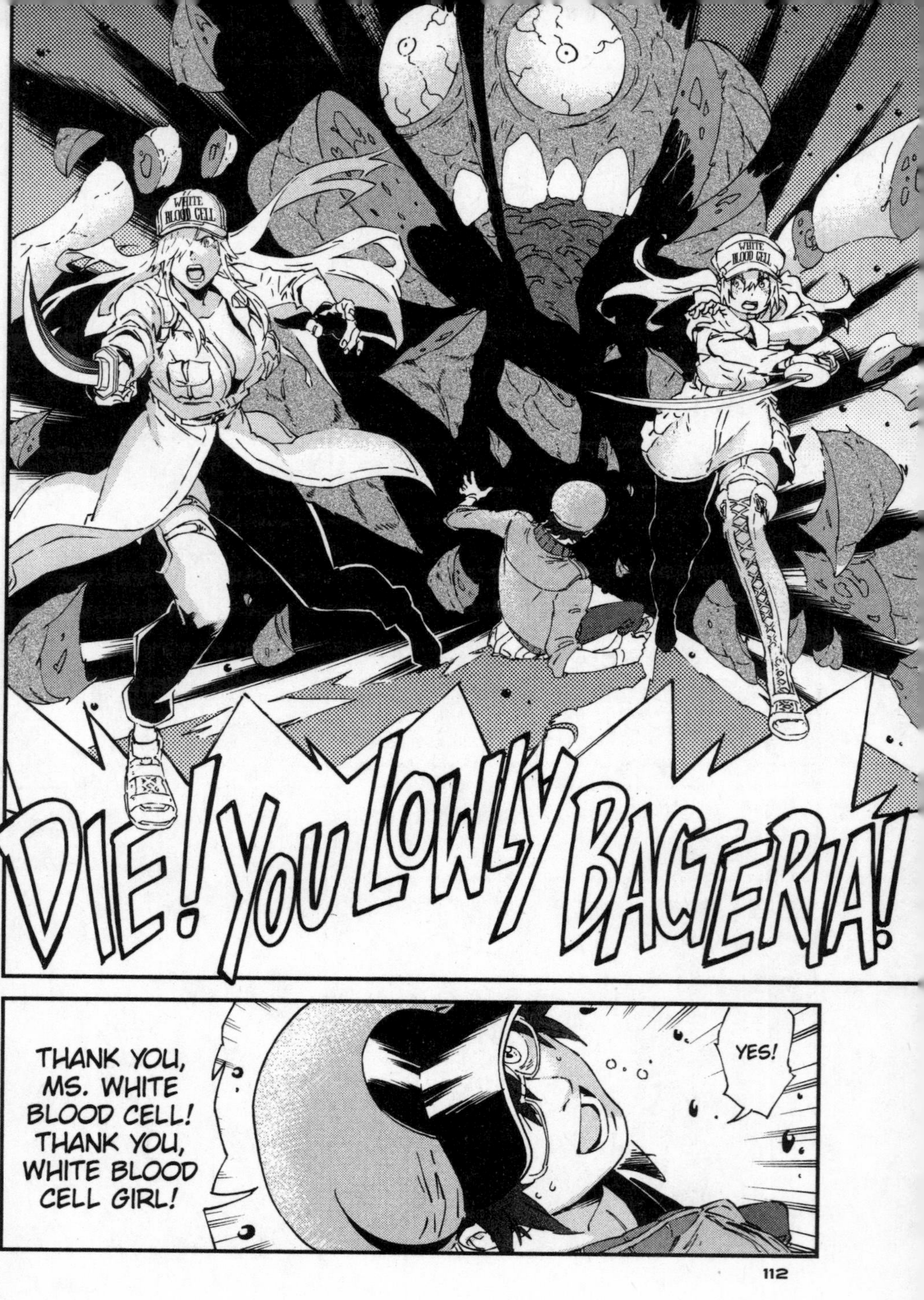
WHITE BLOOD CELL
WHITE BLOOD CELL
DIE! YOU LOWLY BACTERIA!
YES!
THANK YOU, MS. WHITE BLOOD CELL! THANK YOU, WHITE BLOOD CELL GIRL!

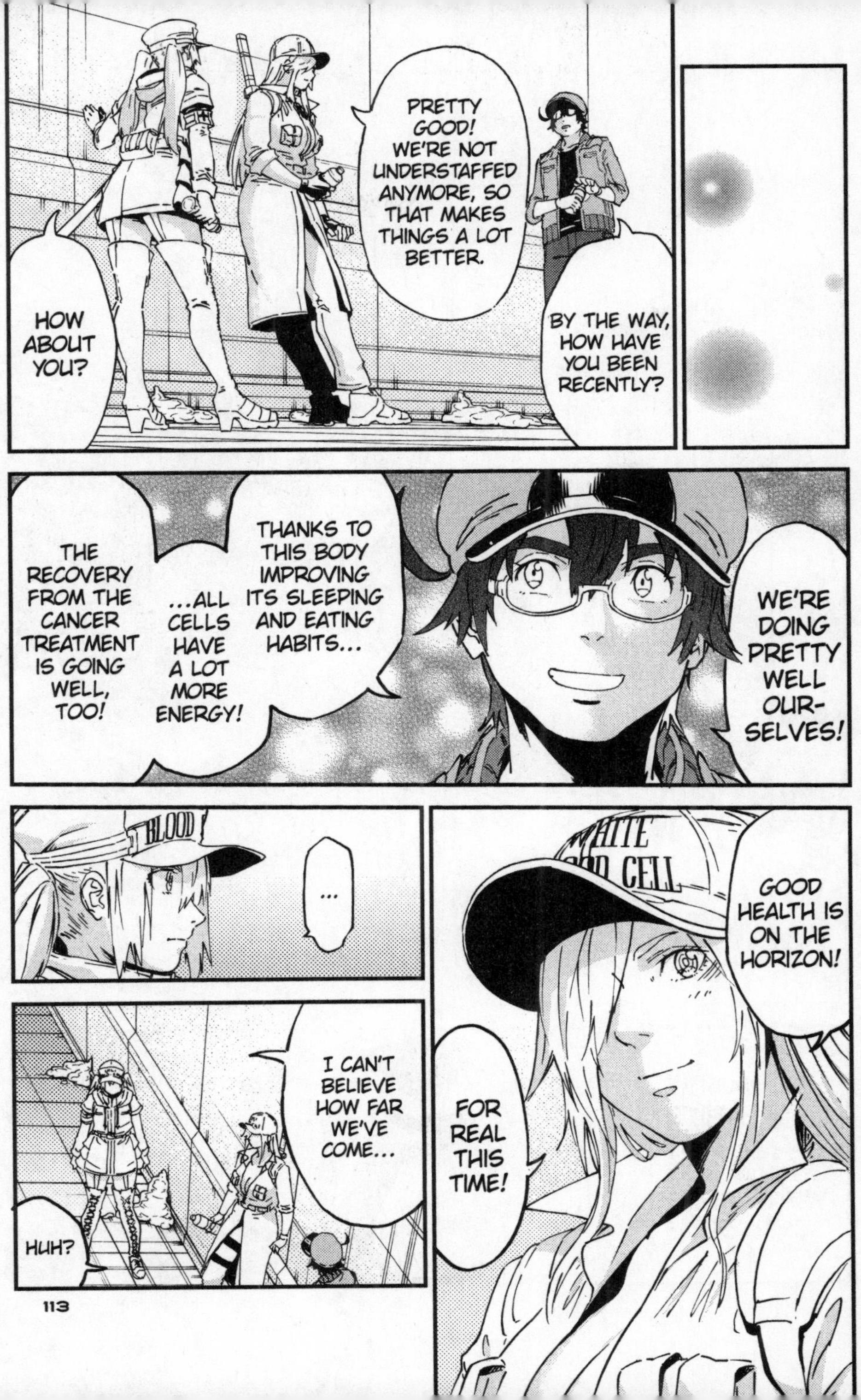
BY THE WAY, HOW HAVE YOU BEEN RECENTLY?
PRETTY GOOD! WE'RE NOT UNDERSTAFFED ANYMORE, SO THAT MAKES THINGS A LOT BETTER.
HOW ABOUT YOU?
WE'RE DOING PRETTY WELL OUR-SELVES!
THANKS TO THIS BODY IMPROVING ITS SLEEPING AND EATING HABITS...
...ALL CELLS HAVE A LOT MORE ENERGY!
THE RECOVERY FROM THE CANCER TREATMENT IS GOING WELL, TOO!
GOOD HEALTH IS ON THE HORIZON!
FOR REAL THIS TIME!
...
I CAN'T BELIEVE HOW FAR WE'VE COME...
HUH?

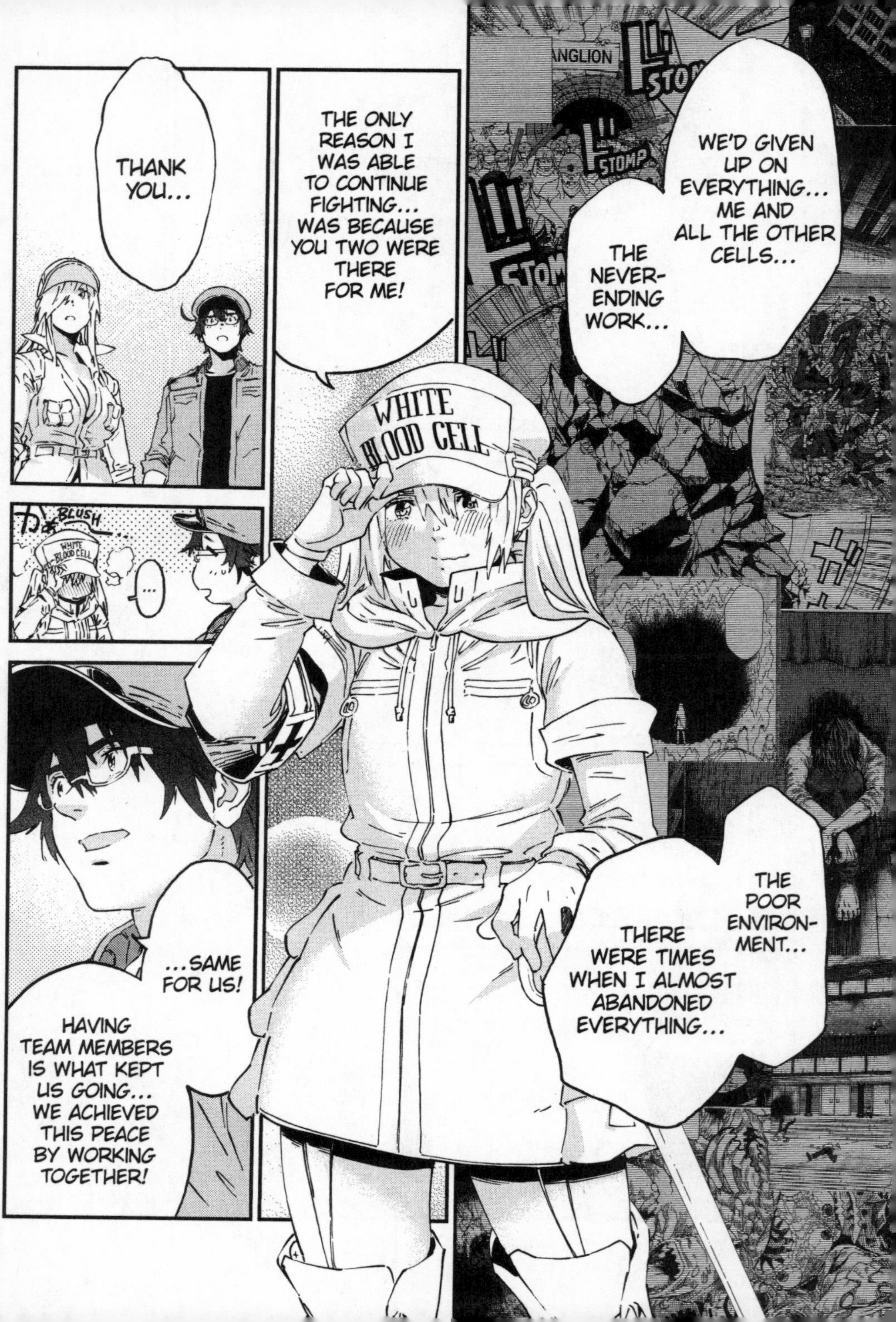

ANGLION
STOMP
STOMP
WE'D GIVEN UP ON EVERYTHING... ME AND ALL THE OTHER CELLS...
THE NEVER-ENDING WORK...
STOMP
THE POOR ENVIRONMENT...
THERE WERE TIMES WHEN I ALMOST ABANDONED EVERYTHING...
THE ONLY REASON I WAS ABLE TO CONTINUE FIGHTING... WAS BECAUSE YOU TWO WERE THERE FOR ME!
WHITE BLOOD CELL
THANK YOU...
BLUSH
WHITE BLOOD CELL
...
...SAME FOR US!
HAVING TEAM MEMBERS IS WHAT KEPT US GOING... WE ACHIEVED THIS PEACE BY WORKING TOGETHER!

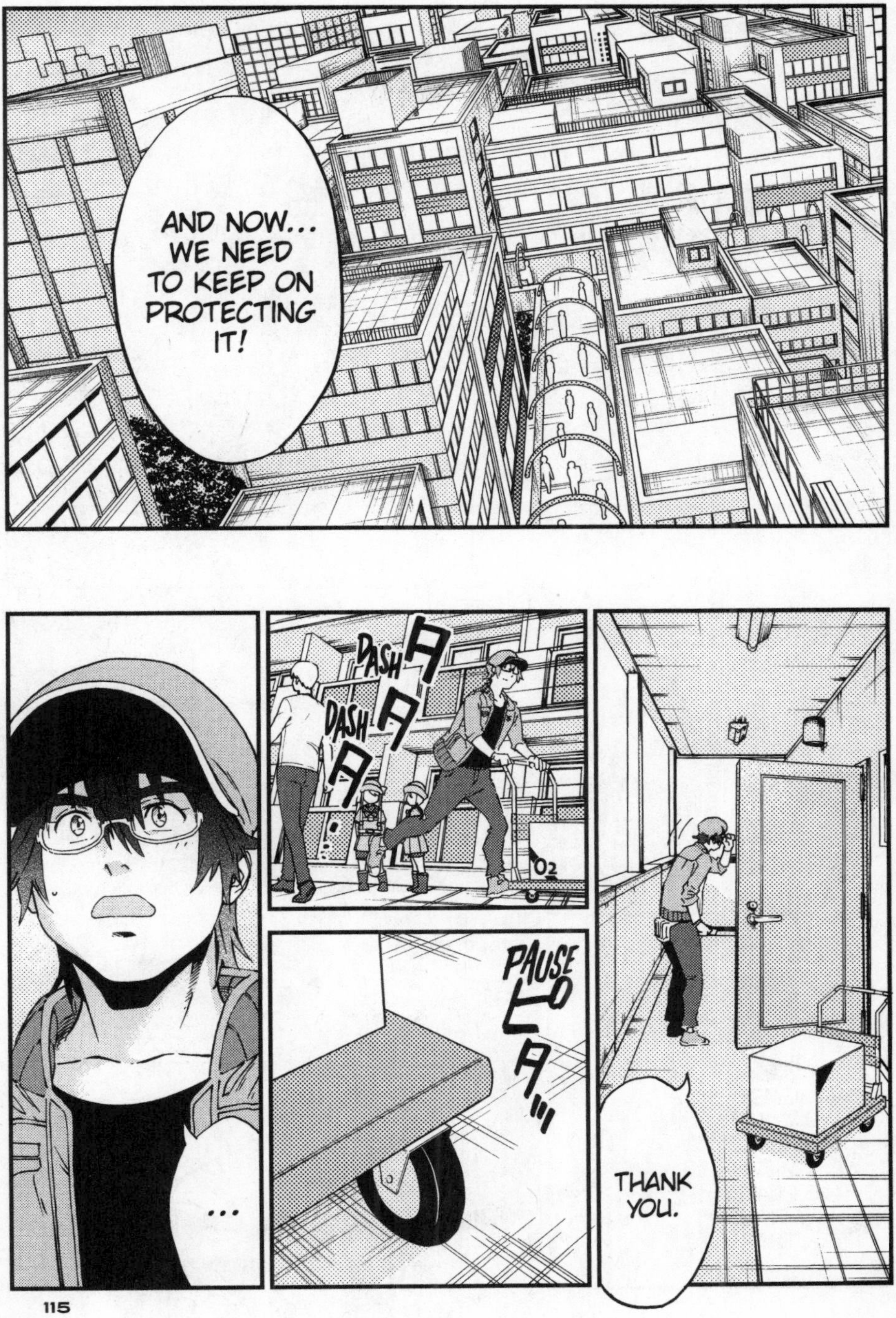
AND NOW... WE NEED TO KEEP ON PROTECTING IT!
THANK YOU.
DASH
DASH
PAUSE
...

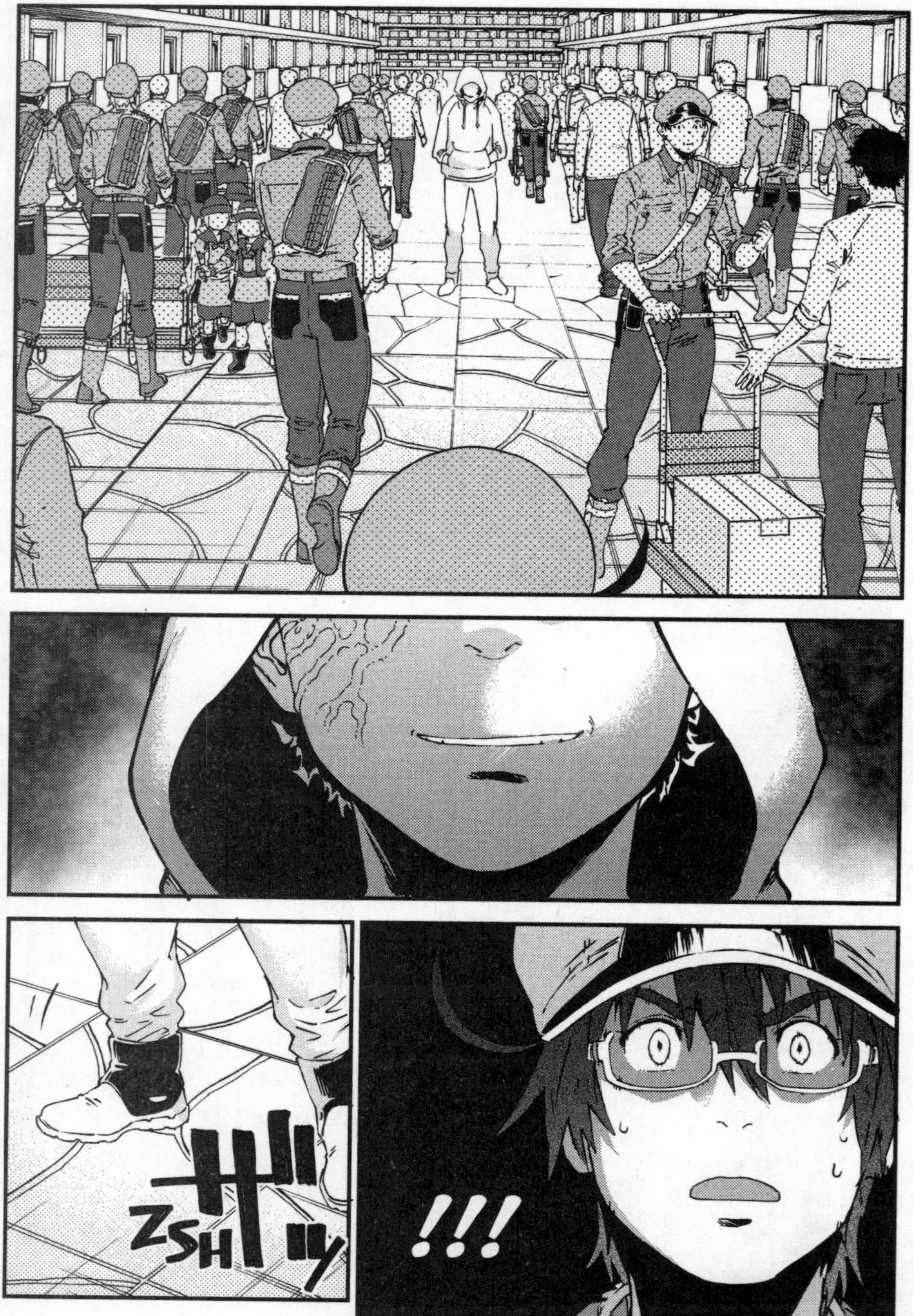
!!!
ZSH

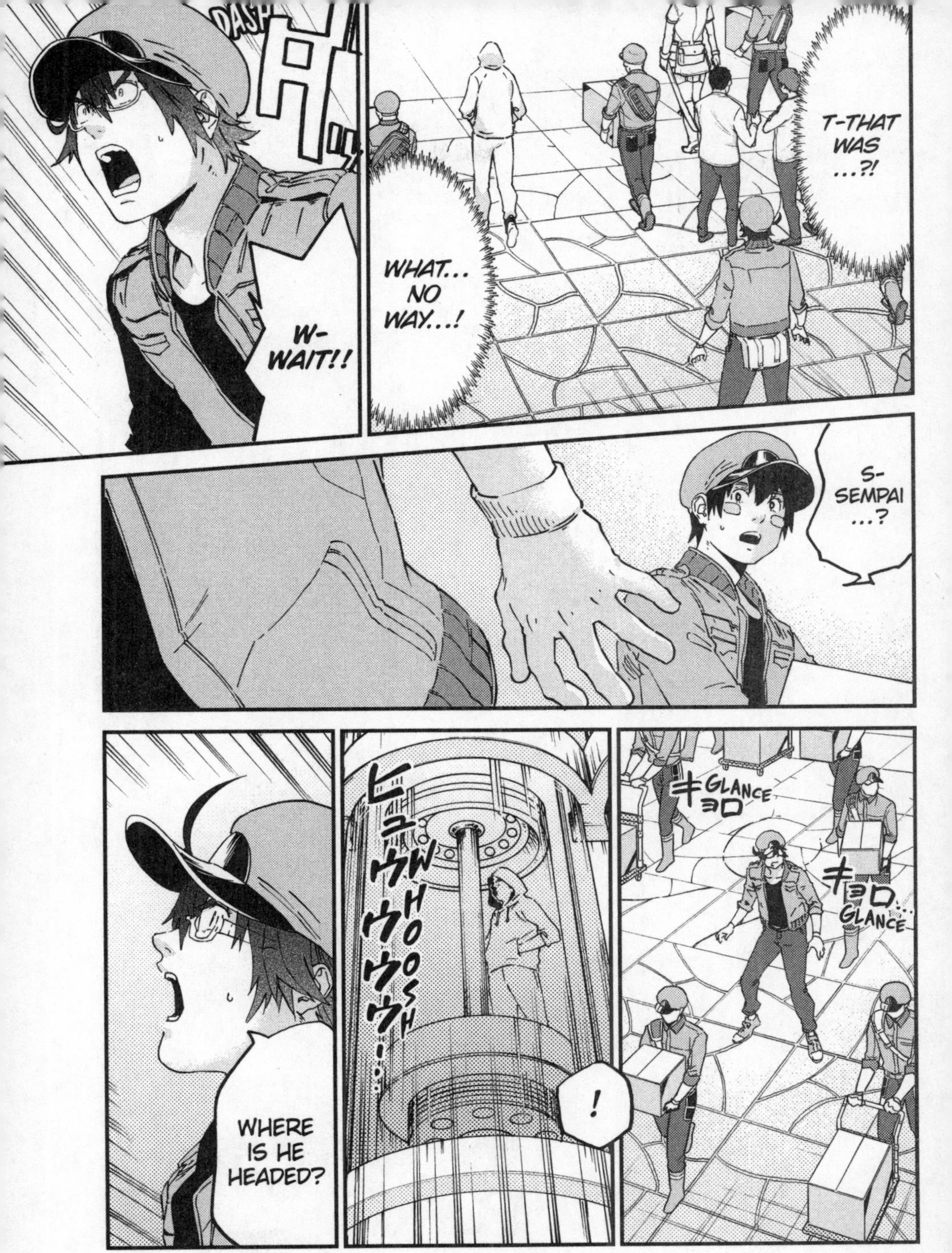
T-THAT WAS ...?!
WHAT... NO WAY...!
DASH
W-WAIT!!
S-SEMPAI ...?
キョロ GLANCE
キョロ... GLANCE
ヒュウウウウ...
WHOOSH
!
WHERE IS HE HEADED?

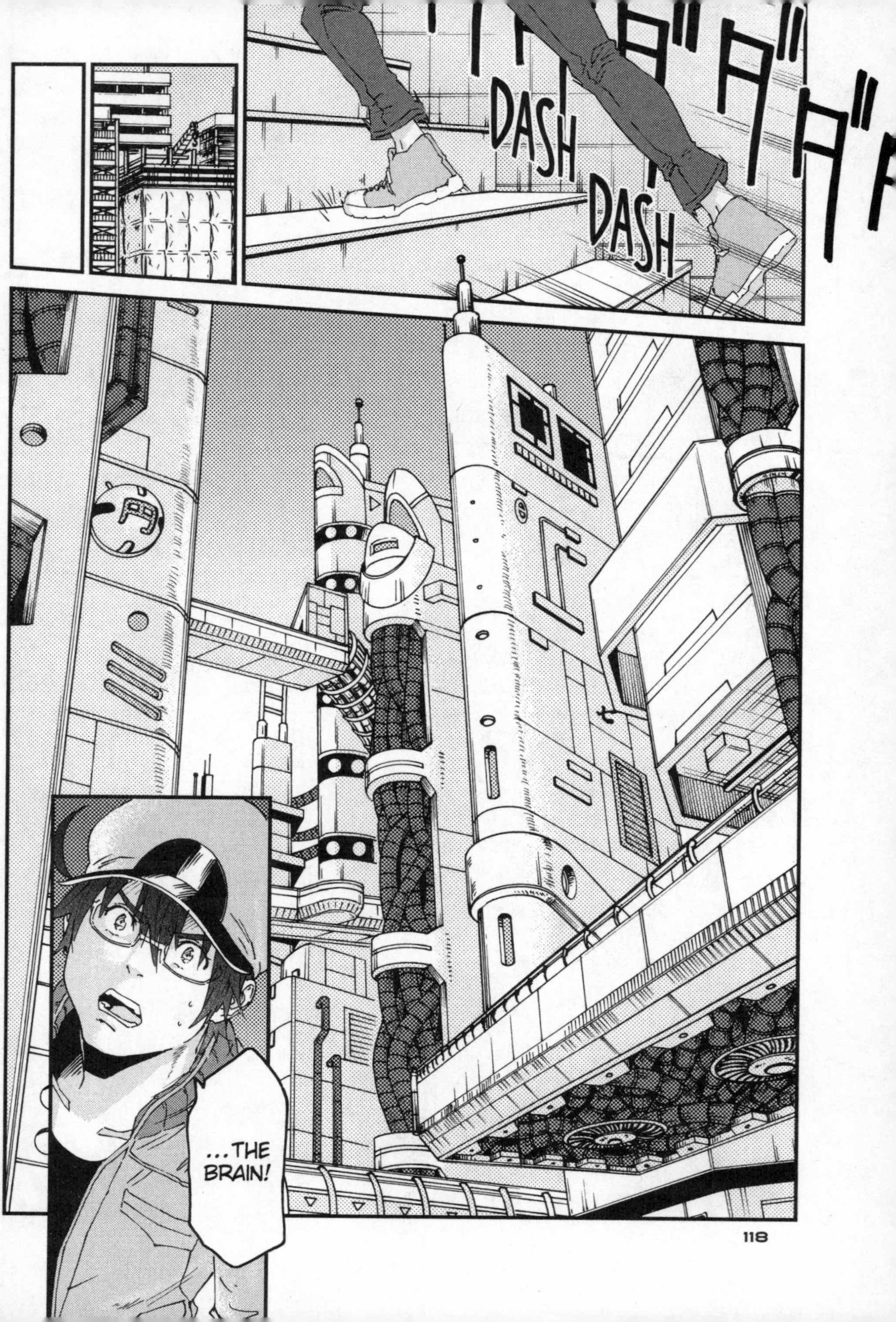
DASH
DASH
...THE BRAIN!

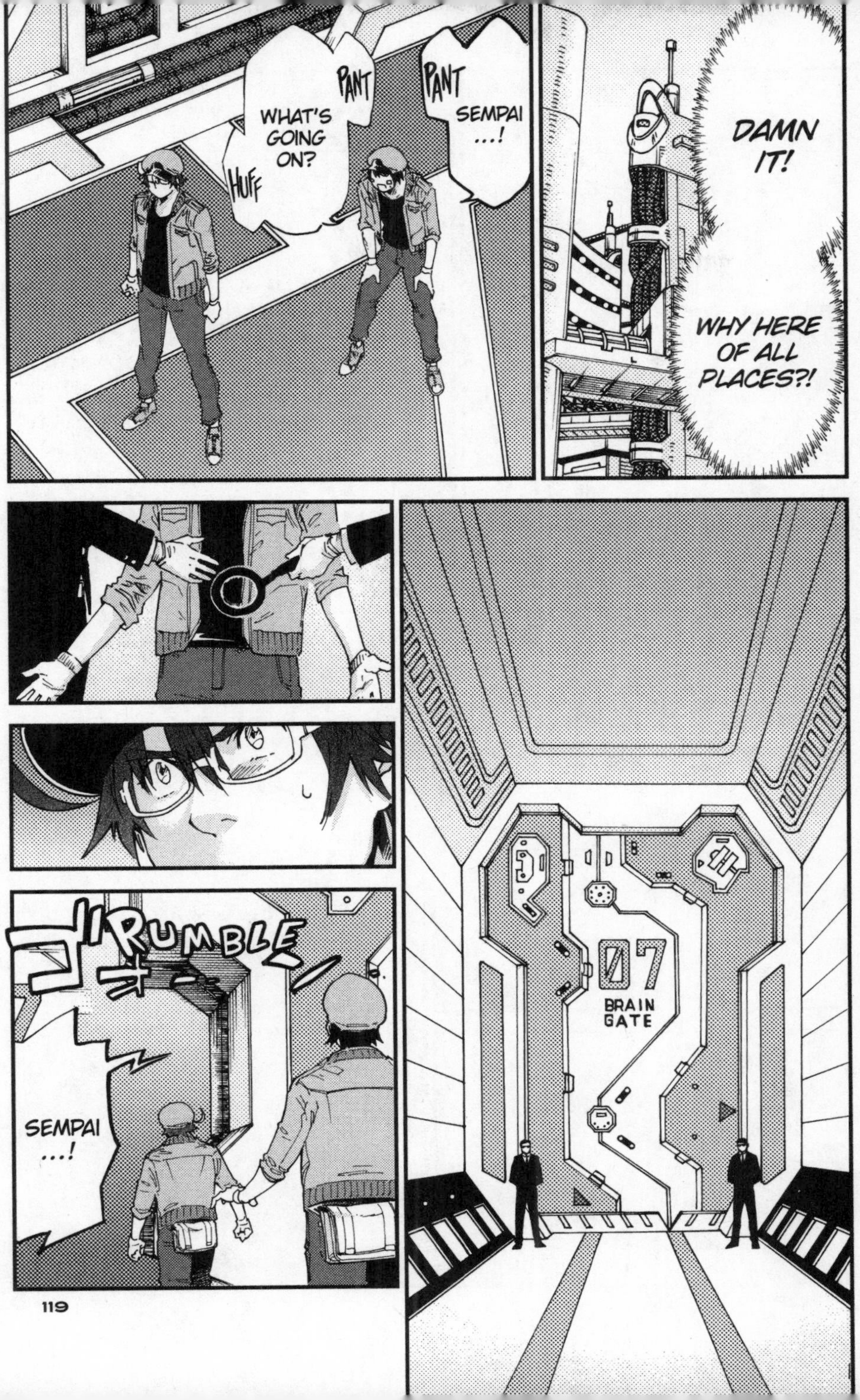
DAMN IT!
WHY HERE OF ALL PLACES?!
PANT
PANT
SEMPAI ...!
WHAT'S GOING ON?
HUFF
07
BRAIN GATE
RUMBLE
SEMPAI ...!

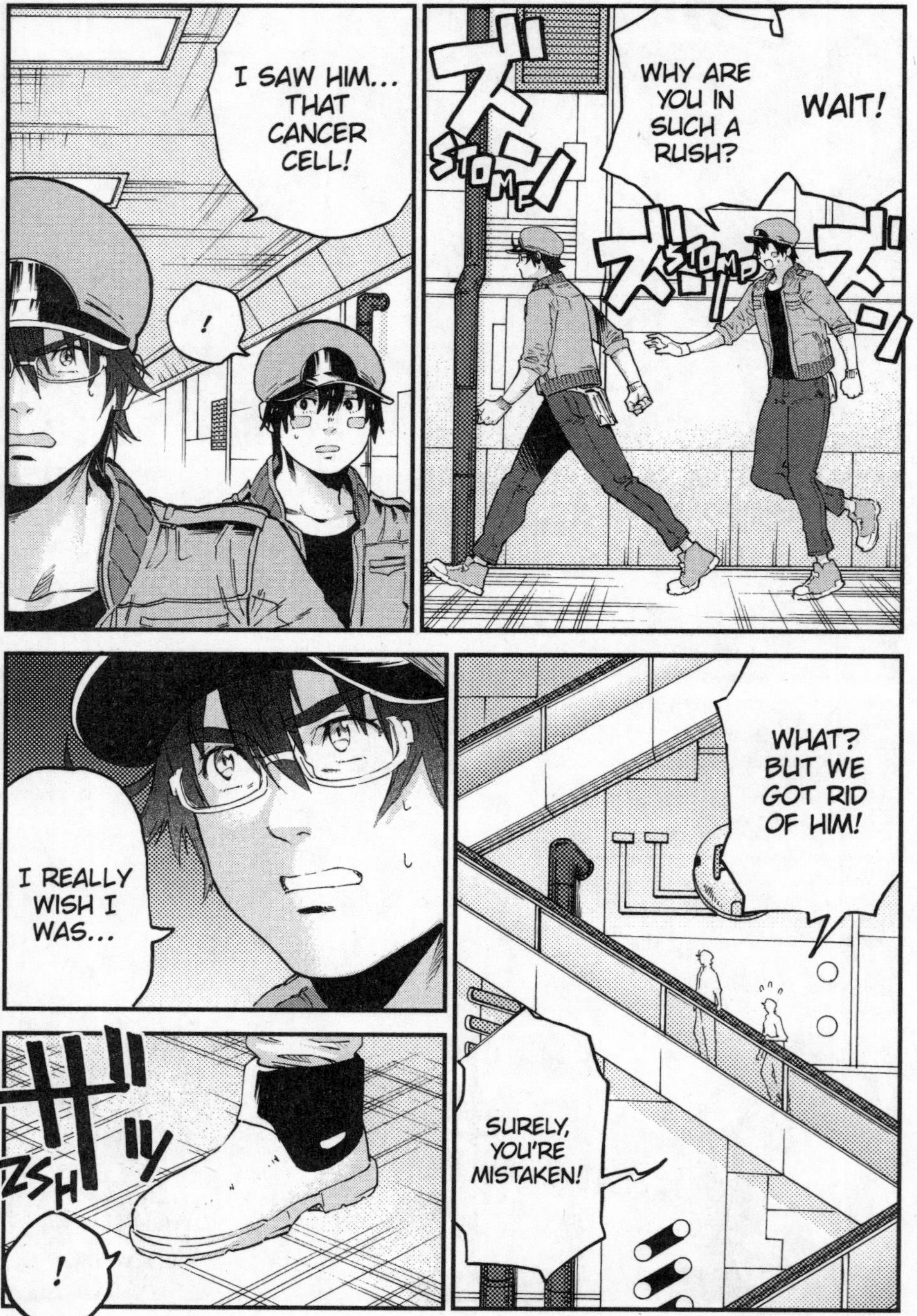
WAIT!
WHY ARE YOU IN SUCH A RUSH?
STOMP
STOMP
I SAW HIM... THAT CANCER CELL!
!
WHAT? BUT WE GOT RID OF HIM!
SURELY, YOU'RE MISTAKEN!
I REALLY WISH I WAS...
ZSH
!

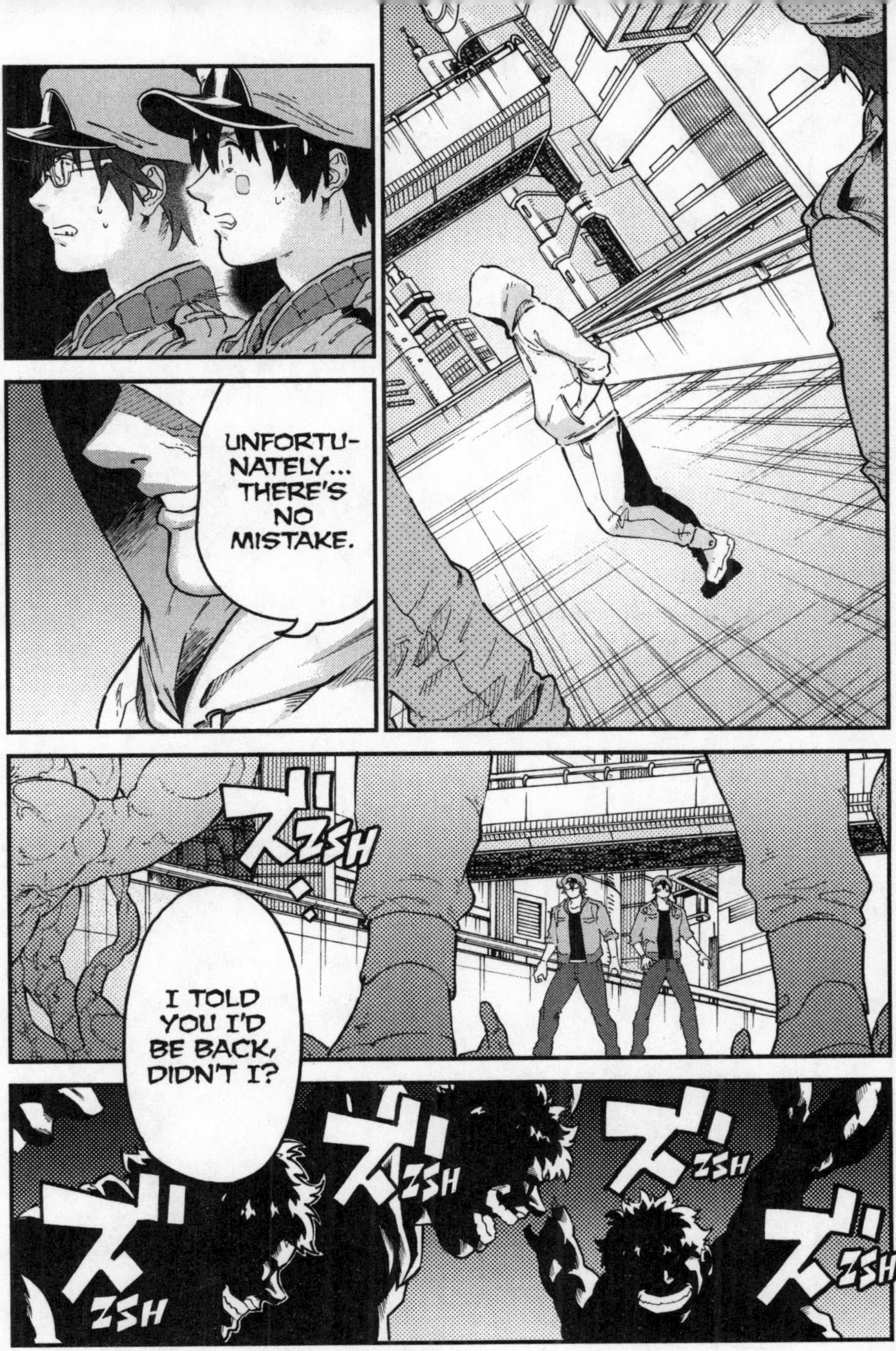
UNFORTU-NATELY... THERE'S NO MISTAKE.
ズ ZSH
I TOLD YOU I'D BE BACK, DIDN'T I?
ズ ZSH
ズ ZSH
ズ ZSH
ズ ZSH

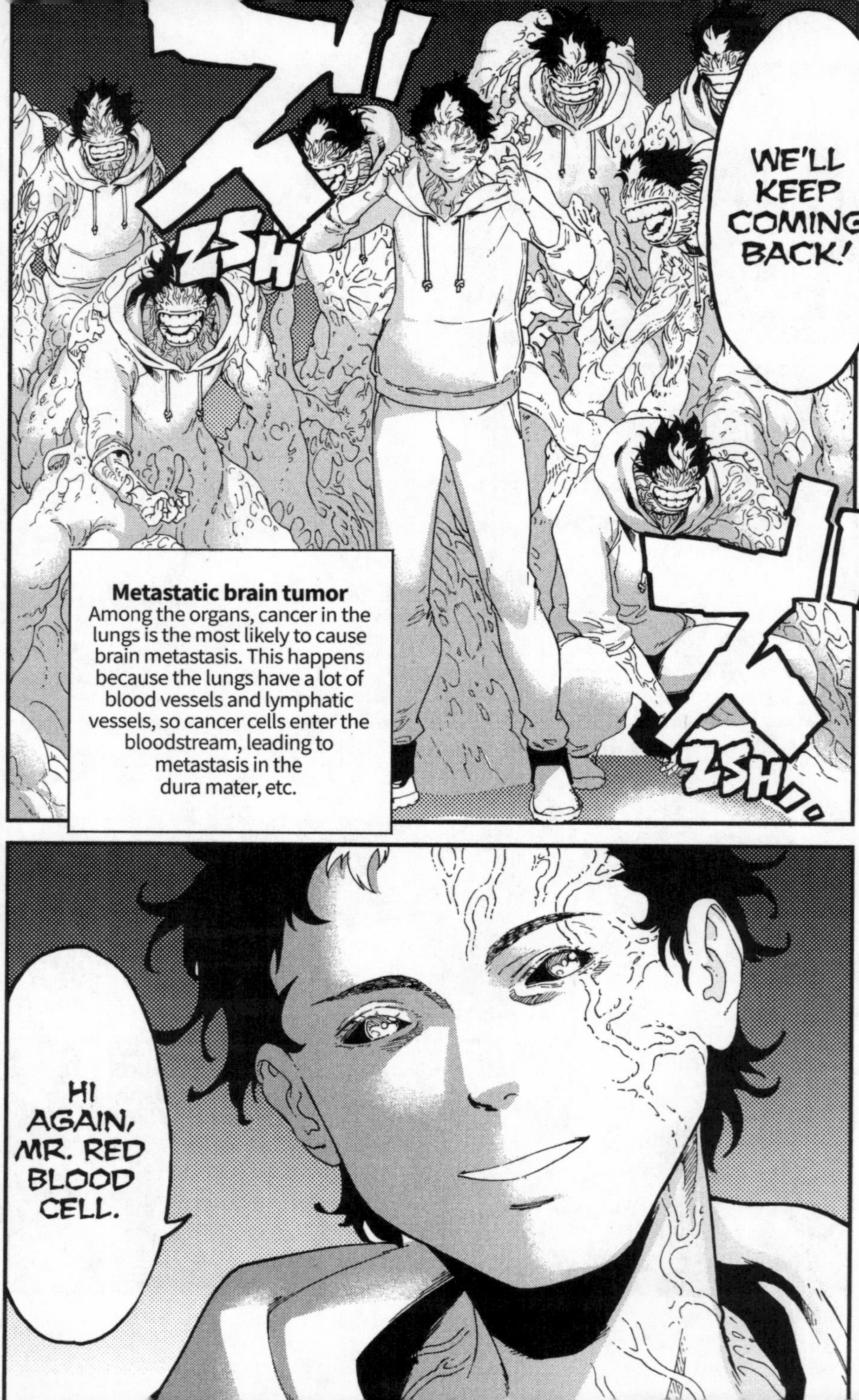
WE'LL KEEP COMING BACK!
ZSH
ZSH..
Metastatic brain tumor
Among the organs, cancer in the lungs is the most likely to cause brain metastasis. This happens because the lungs have a lot of blood vessels and lymphatic vessels, so cancer cells enter the bloodstream, leading to metastasis in the dura mater, etc.
HI AGAIN, MR. RED BLOOD CELL.

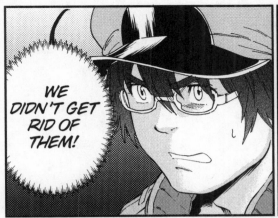

C- CANCER CELL...!
WE DIDN'T GET RID OF THEM!
AND OF ALL PLACES... THEY'RE NOW IN THE BRAIN!
When brain metastasis occurs, the brain swells and pressure in the skull rises, resulting in headaches and nausea. Depending on what part of the brain is affected, symptoms such as paralysis, lightheadedness, loss of speech, and visual field defects can also occur.
COMMAND-ER...!
WE'VE CONFIRMED THE PRESENCE OF CANCER CELLS IN THE BRAIN!
I SEE... THIS TIME, WE WON'T LET HIM DO AS HE PLEASES!

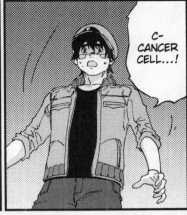

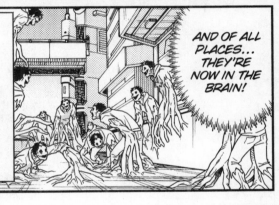

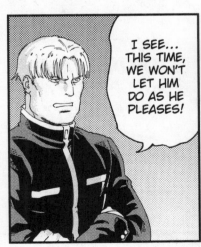

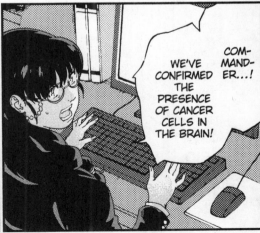

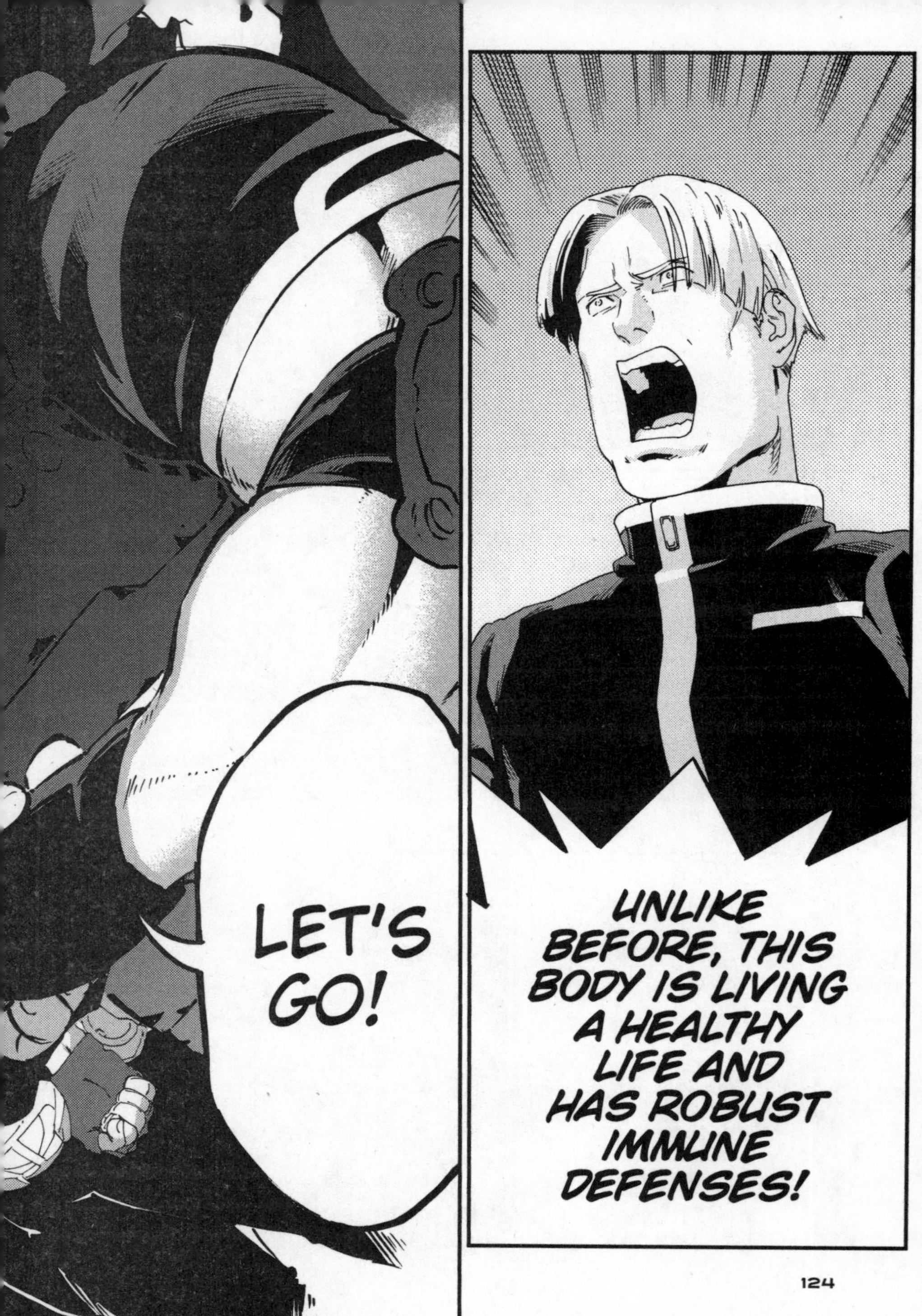
UNLIKE BEFORE, THIS BODY IS LIVING A HEALTHY LIFE AND HAS ROBUST IMMUNE DEFENSES!
LET'S GO!

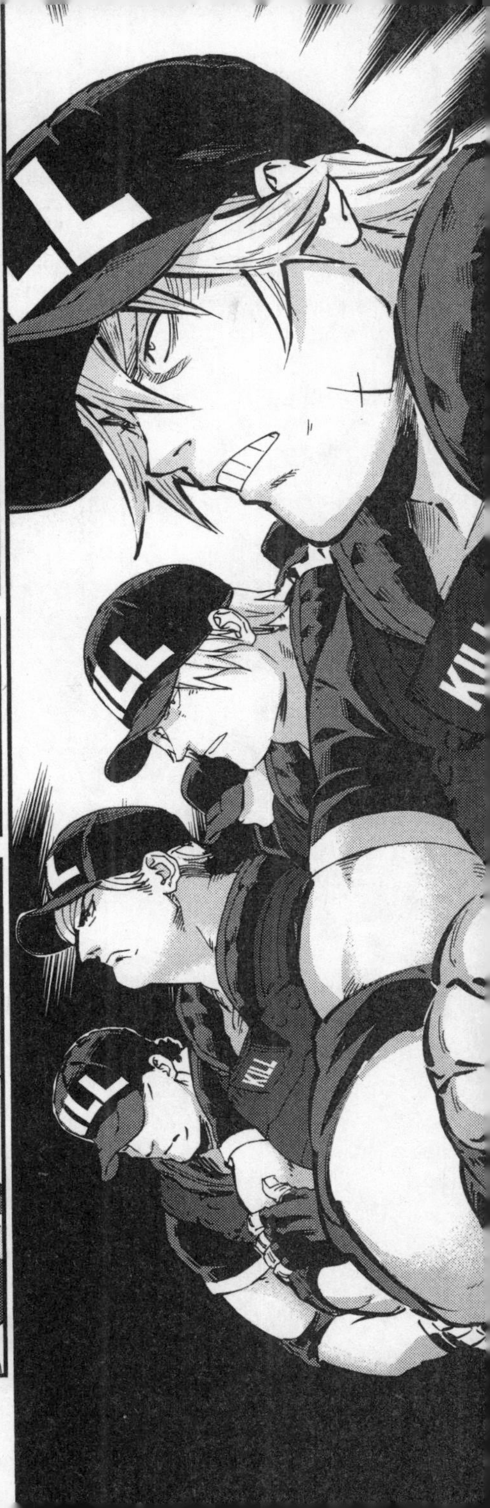

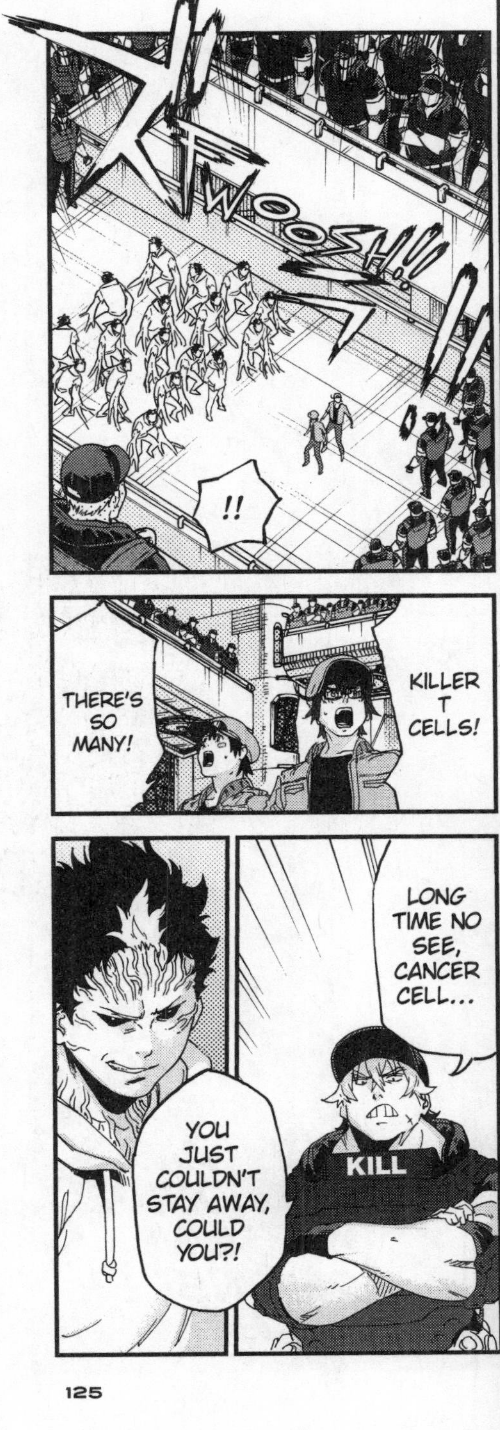
WHOOSH!!
!!
KILLER T CELLS!
THERE'S SO MANY!
LONG TIME NO SEE, CANCER CELL...
YOU JUST COULDN'T STAY AWAY, COULD YOU?!
KILL

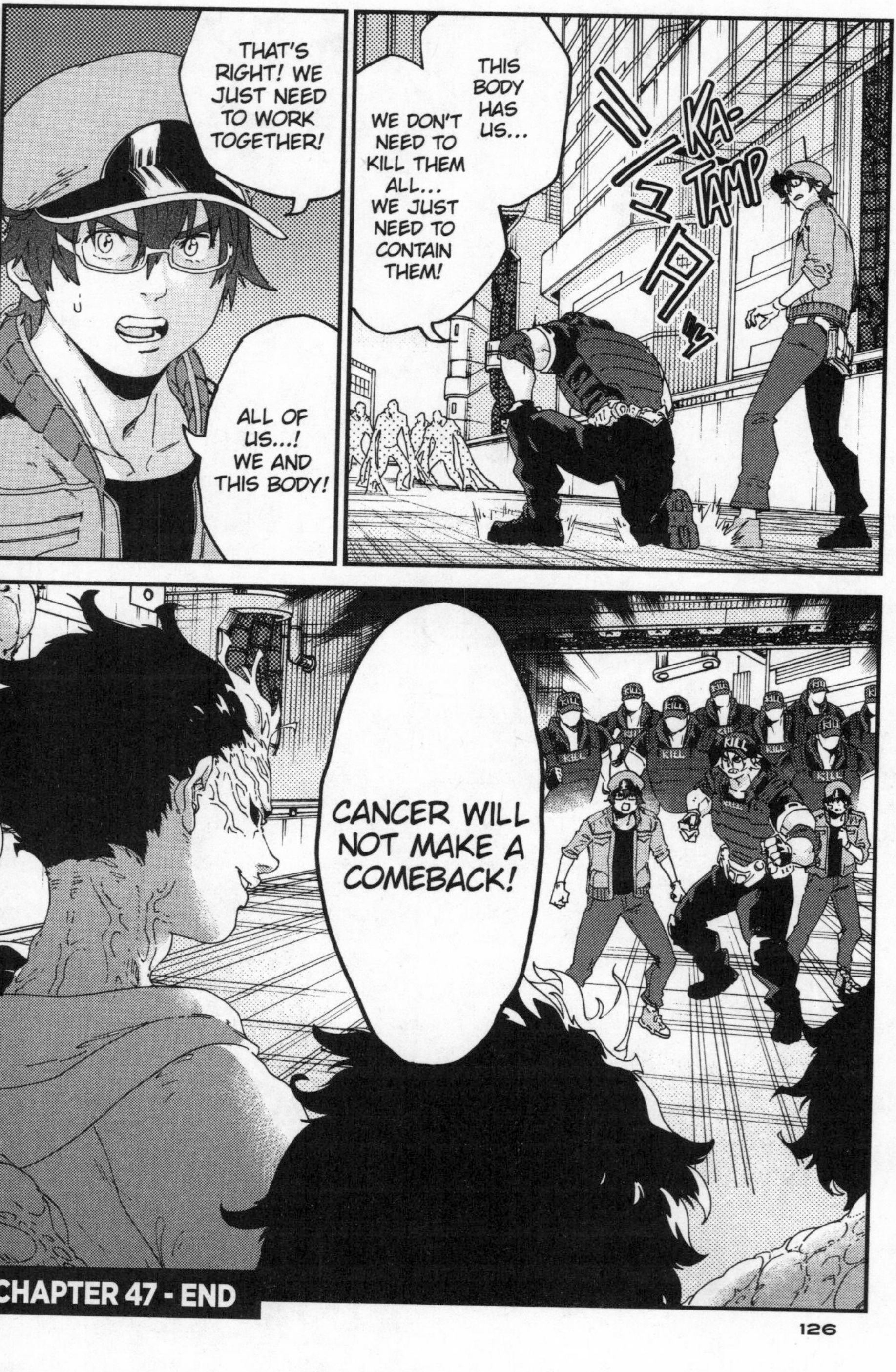
THIS BODY HAS US...
WE DON'T NEED TO KILL THEM ALL... WE JUST NEED TO CONTAIN THEM!
KA-TAMP
THAT'S RIGHT! WE JUST NEED TO WORK TOGETHER!
ALL OF US...! WE AND THIS BODY!
CANCER WILL NOT MAKE A COMEBACK!
CHAPTER 47 - END

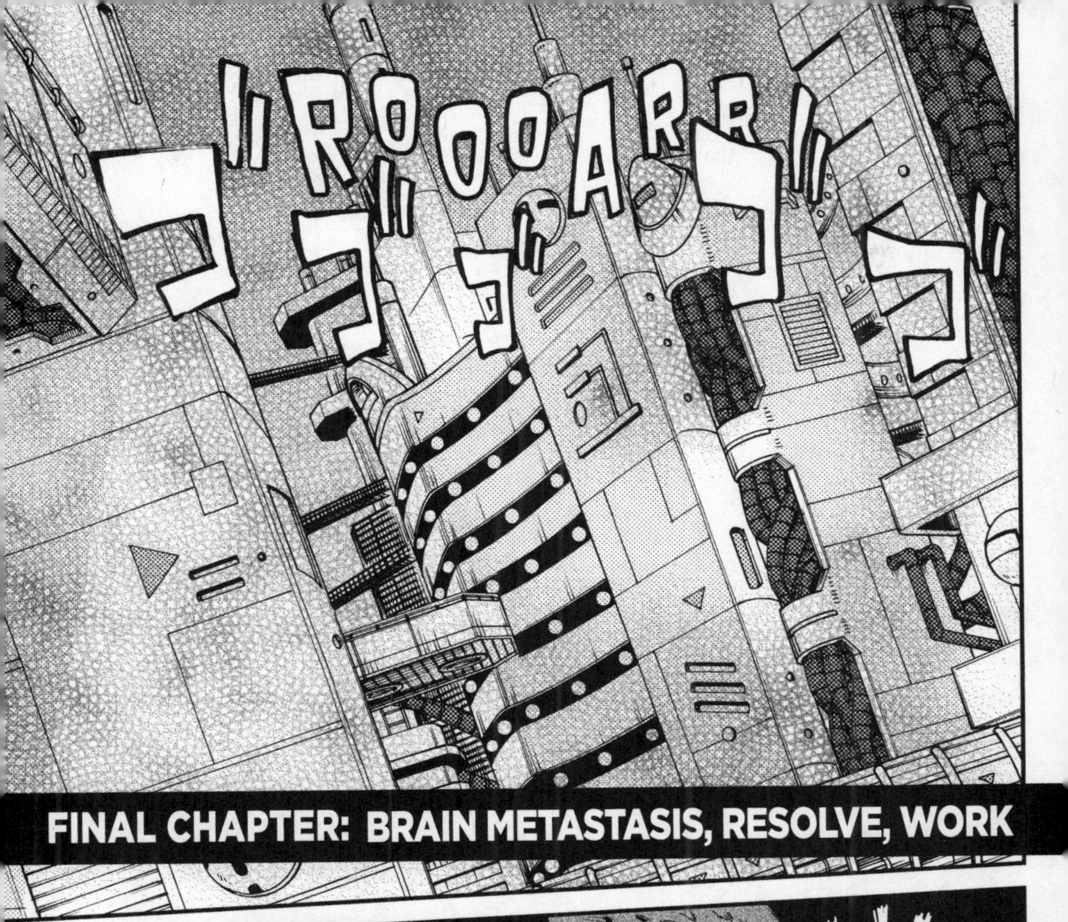
ROOOARR
ゴゴゴゴ

# FINAL CHAPTER: BRAIN METASTASIS, RESOLVE, WORK

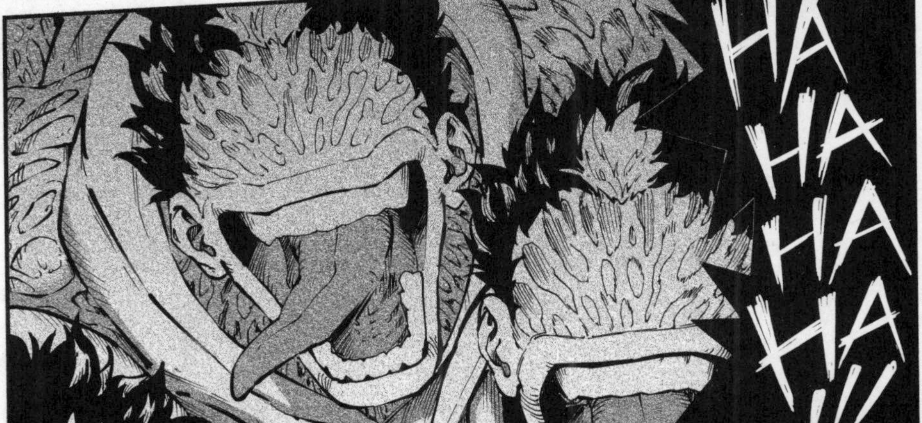
HAHAHAHAHA!!!

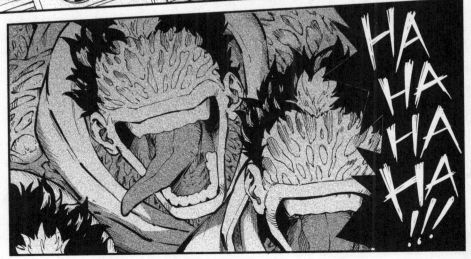

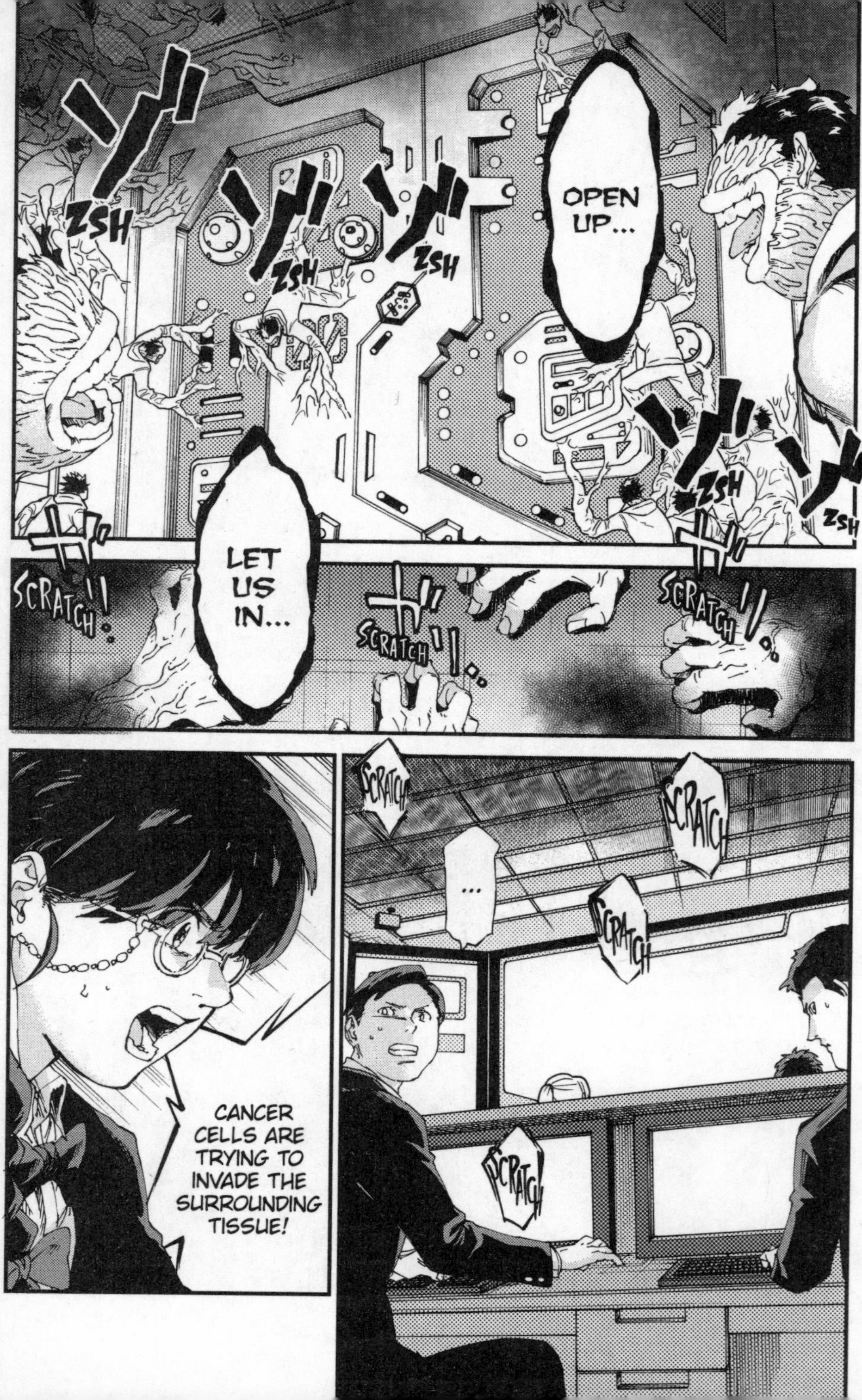
ZSH
ZSH
OPEN UP...
ZSH
ZSH
ZSH
SCRATCH
SCRATCH
LET US IN...
SCRATCH
SCRATCH
SCRATCH
...
SCRATCH
SCRATCH
CANCER CELLS ARE TRYING TO INVADE THE SURROUNDING TISSUE!

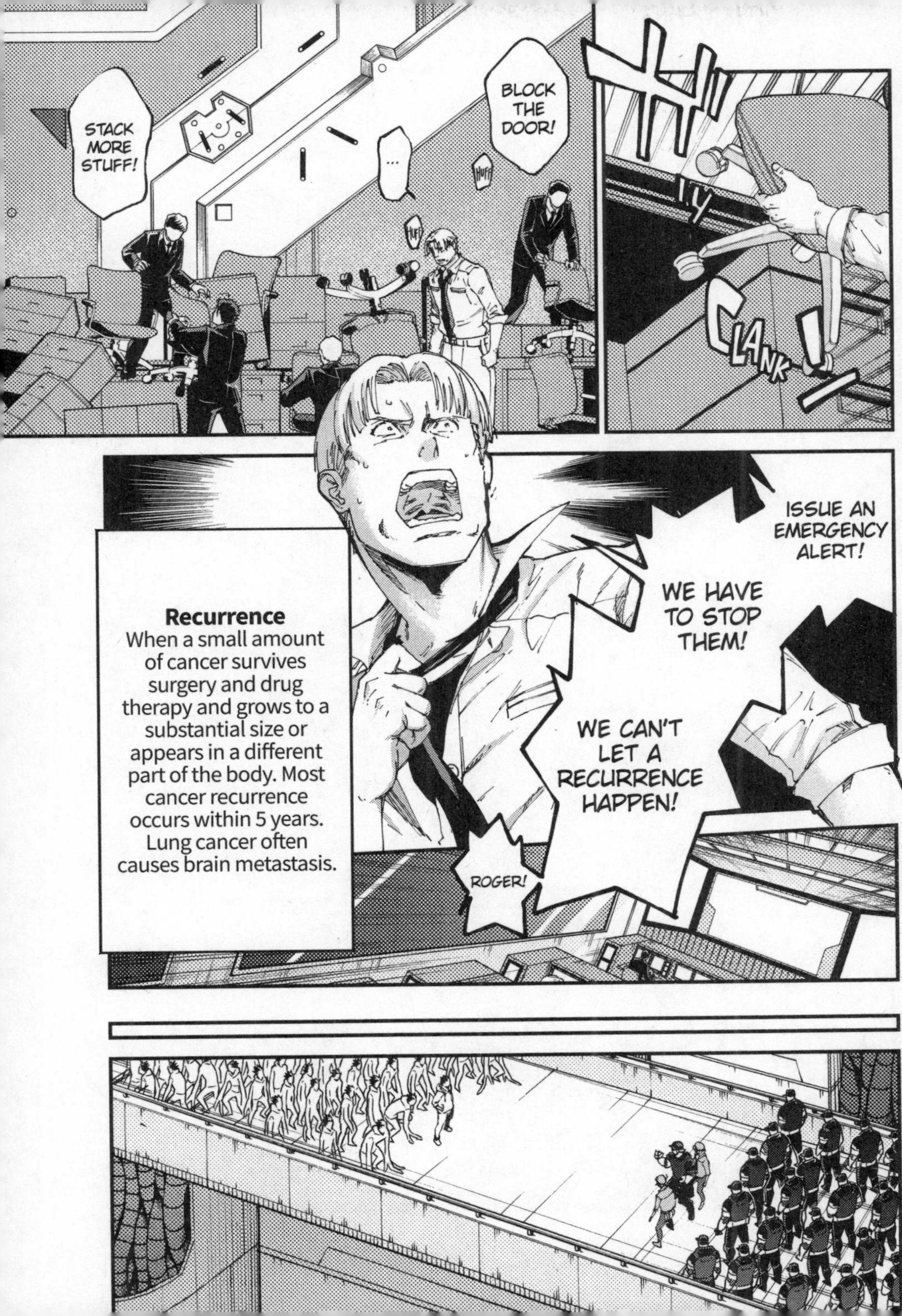
CLANK!
BLOCK THE DOOR!
...
HUFF
HUFF
STACK MORE STUFF!
ISSUE AN EMERGENCY ALERT!
WE HAVE TO STOP THEM!
WE CAN'T LET A RECURRENCE HAPPEN!
Recurrence
When a small amount of cancer survives surgery and drug therapy and grows to a substantial size or appears in a different part of the body. Most cancer recurrence occurs within 5 years. Lung cancer often causes brain metastasis.
ROGER!

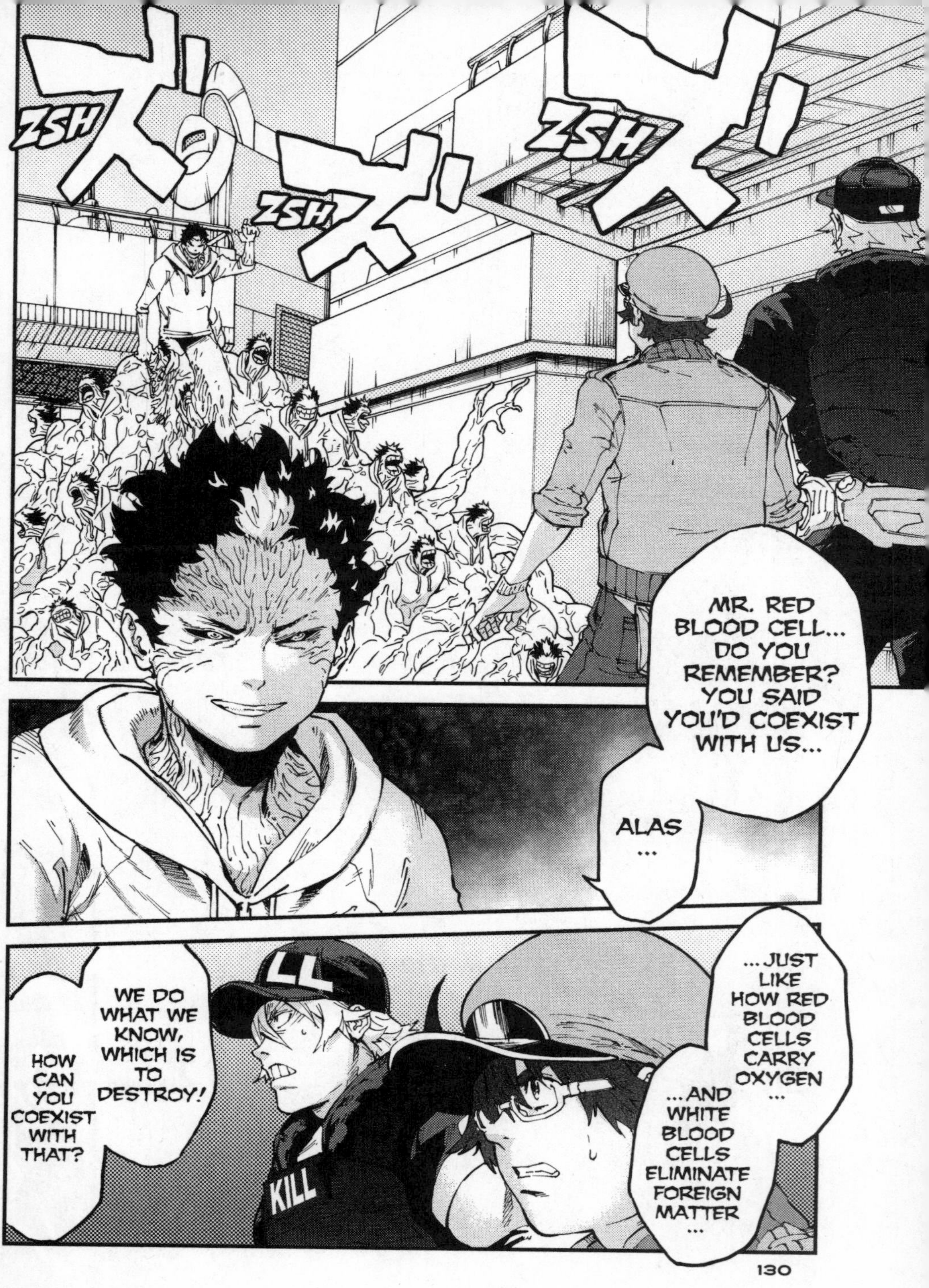

ZSH
ZSH
ZSH
MR. RED BLOOD CELL... DO YOU REMEMBER? YOU SAID YOU'D COEXIST WITH US...
ALAS ...
...JUST LIKE HOW RED BLOOD CELLS CARRY OXYGEN ...
...AND WHITE BLOOD CELLS ELIMINATE FOREIGN MATTER ...
LL
KILL
WE DO WHAT WE KNOW, WHICH IS TO DESTROY!
HOW CAN YOU COEXIST WITH THAT?

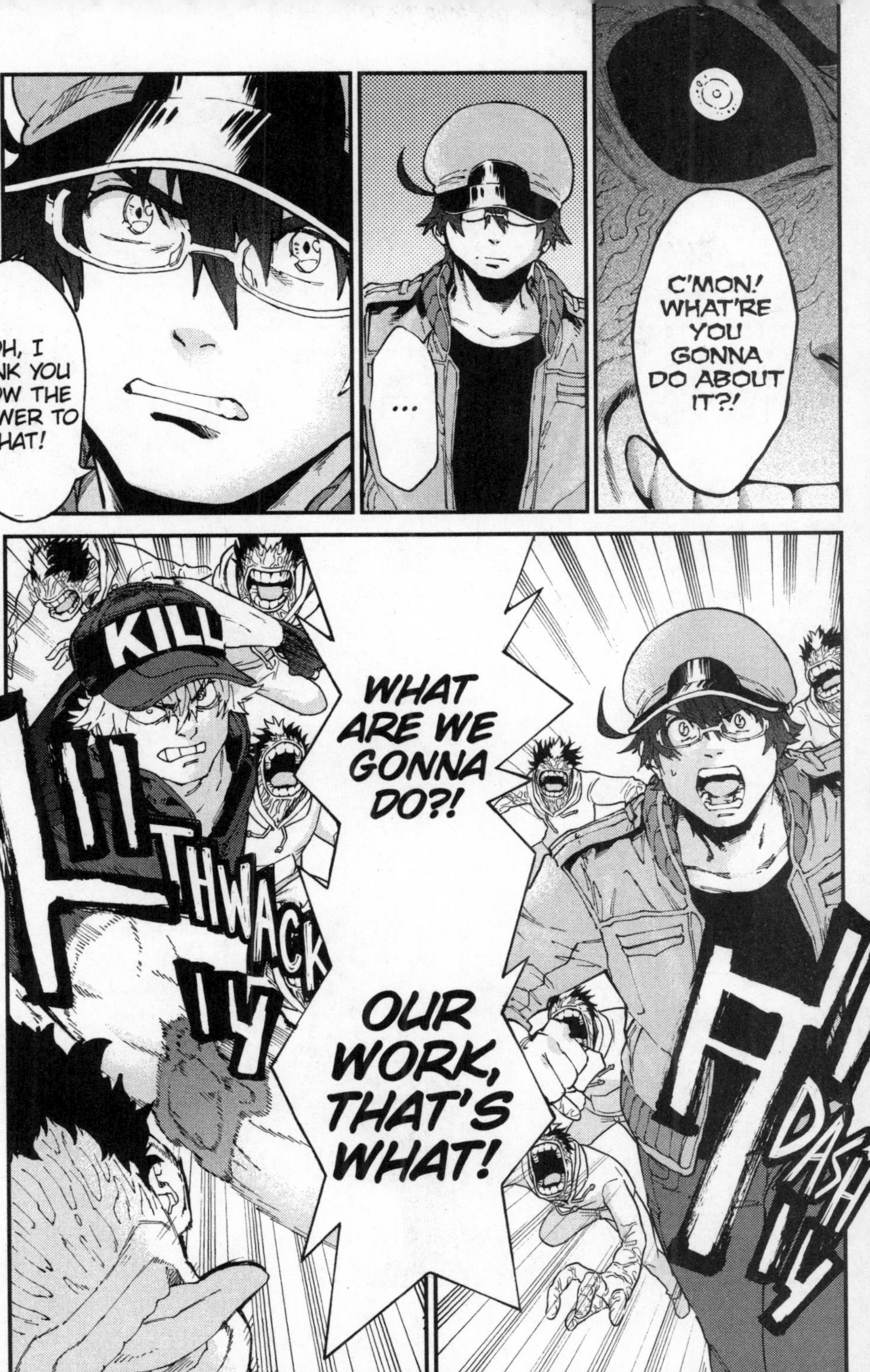
C'MON! WHAT'RE YOU GONNA DO ABOUT IT?!
...
OH, I THINK YOU KNOW THE ANSWER TO THAT!
DASH
WHAT ARE WE GONNA DO?!
OUR WORK, THAT'S WHAT!
THWACK
KILL

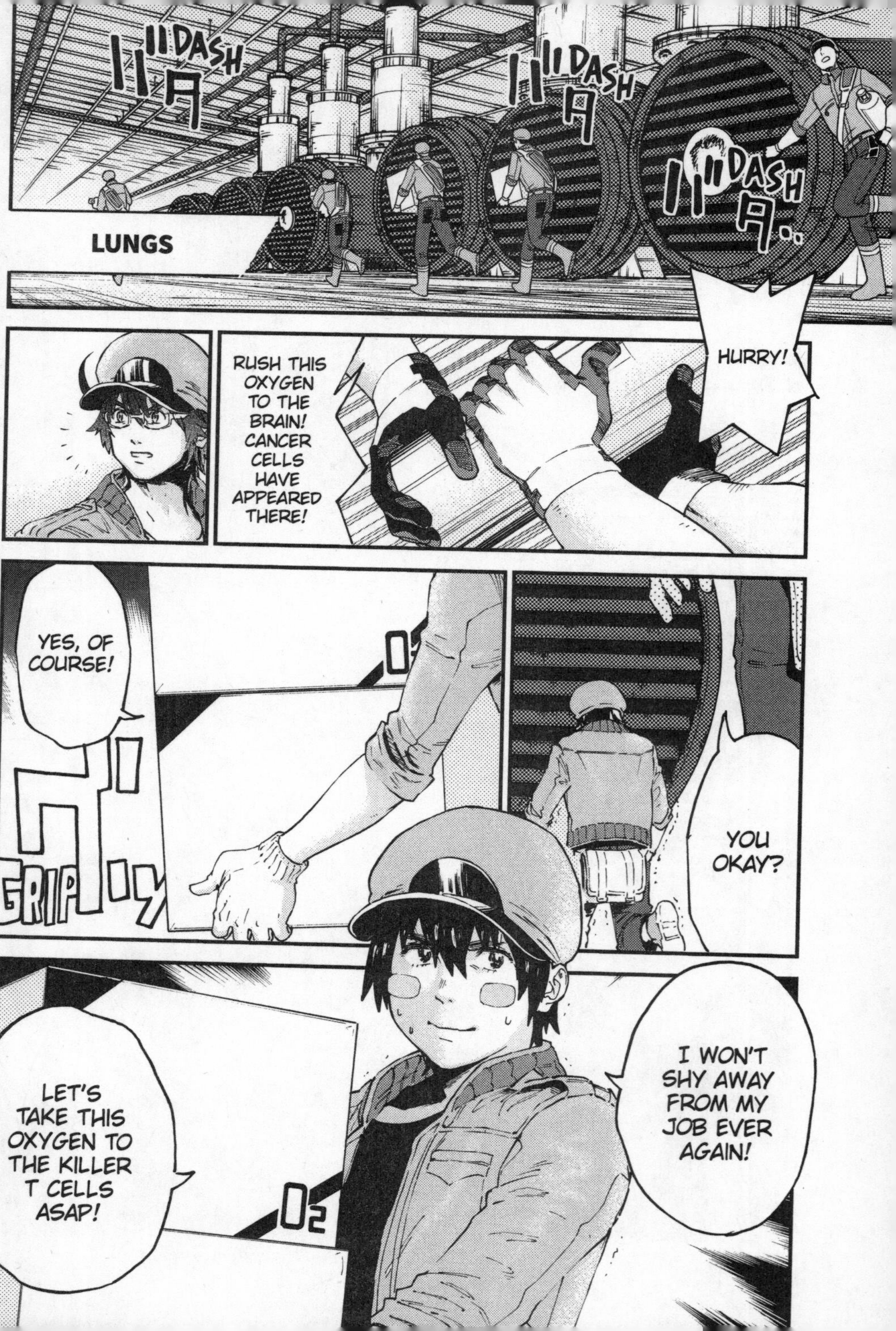
DASH
DASH
DASH
LUNGS
HURRY!
RUSH THIS OXYGEN TO THE BRAIN! CANCER CELLS HAVE APPEARED THERE!
YOU OKAY?
YES, OF COURSE!
GRIP
I WON'T SHY AWAY FROM MY JOB EVER AGAIN!
LET'S TAKE THIS OXYGEN TO THE KILLER T CELLS ASAP!
O2

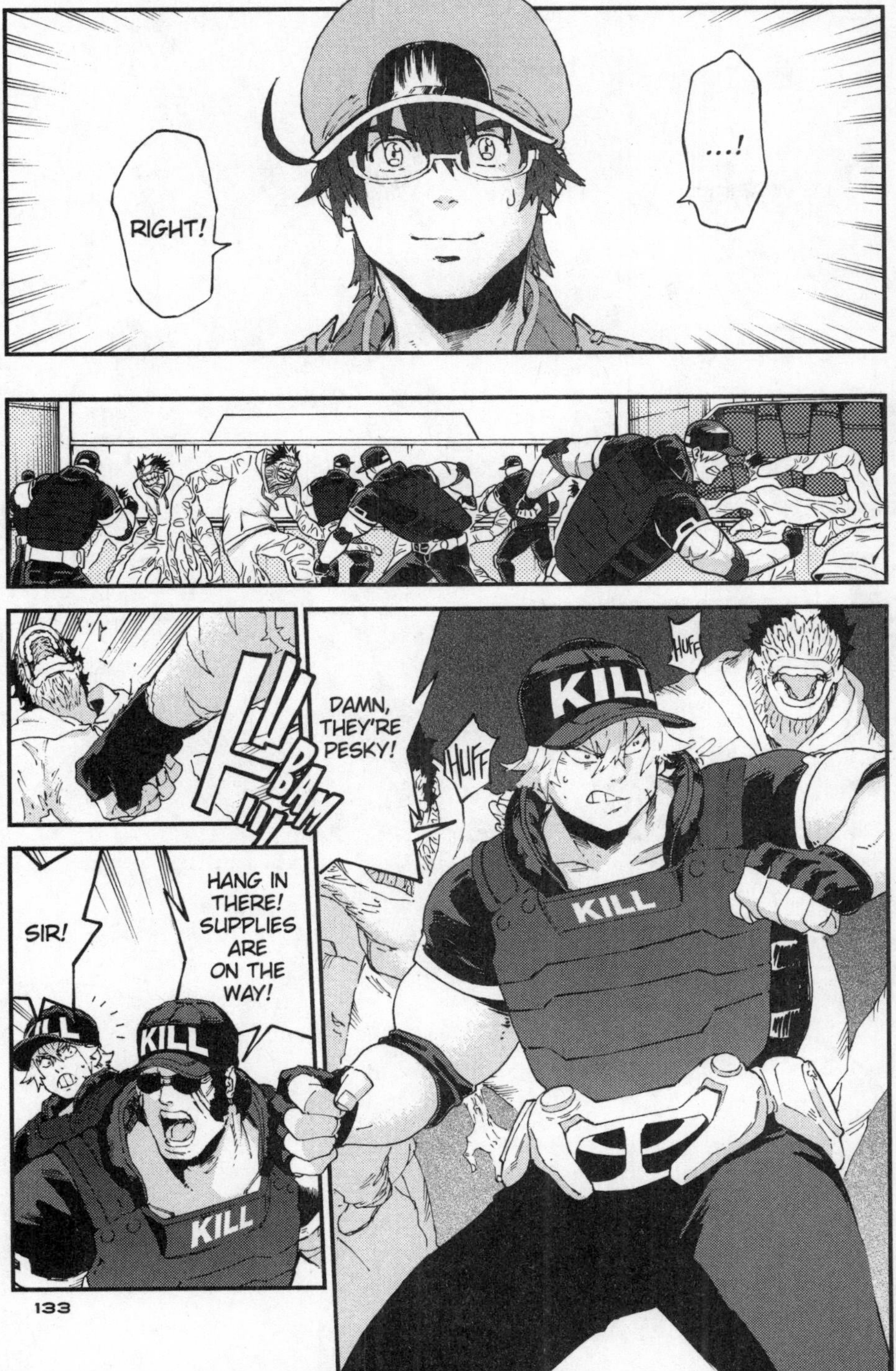

...!
RIGHT!
HUFF
HUFF
DAMN, THEY'RE PESKY!
KILL
BAM
HANG IN THERE! SUPPLIES ARE ON THE WAY!
SIR!
KILL
KILL

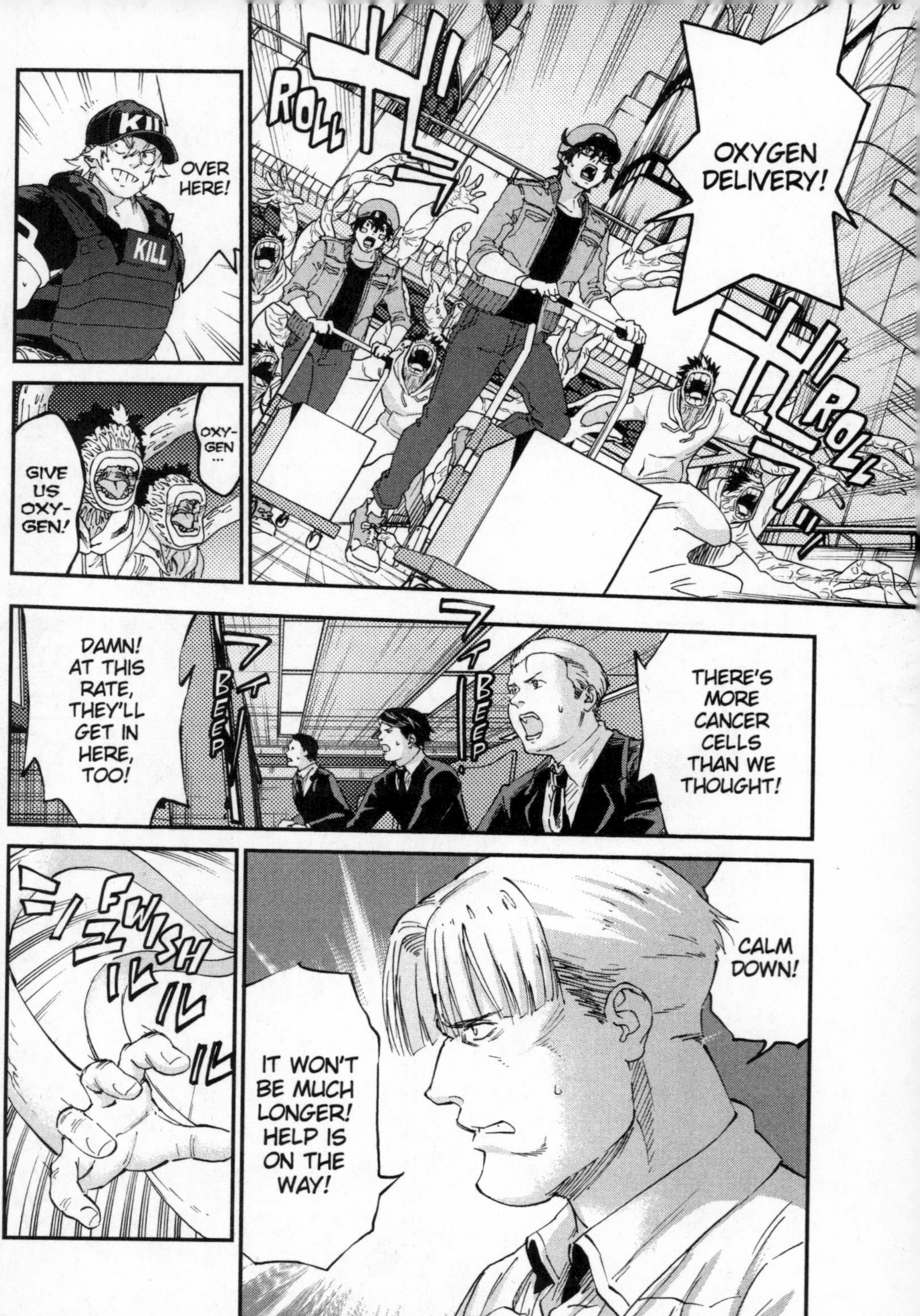
ROLL
OXYGEN DELIVERY!
ROLL
OVER HERE!
OXY-GEN...
GIVE US OXY-GEN!
THERE'S MORE CANCER CELLS THAN WE THOUGHT!
BEEP
BEEP
DAMN! AT THIS RATE, THEY'LL GET IN HERE, TOO!
CALM DOWN!
IT WON'T BE MUCH LONGER! HELP IS ON THE WAY!
FWISH

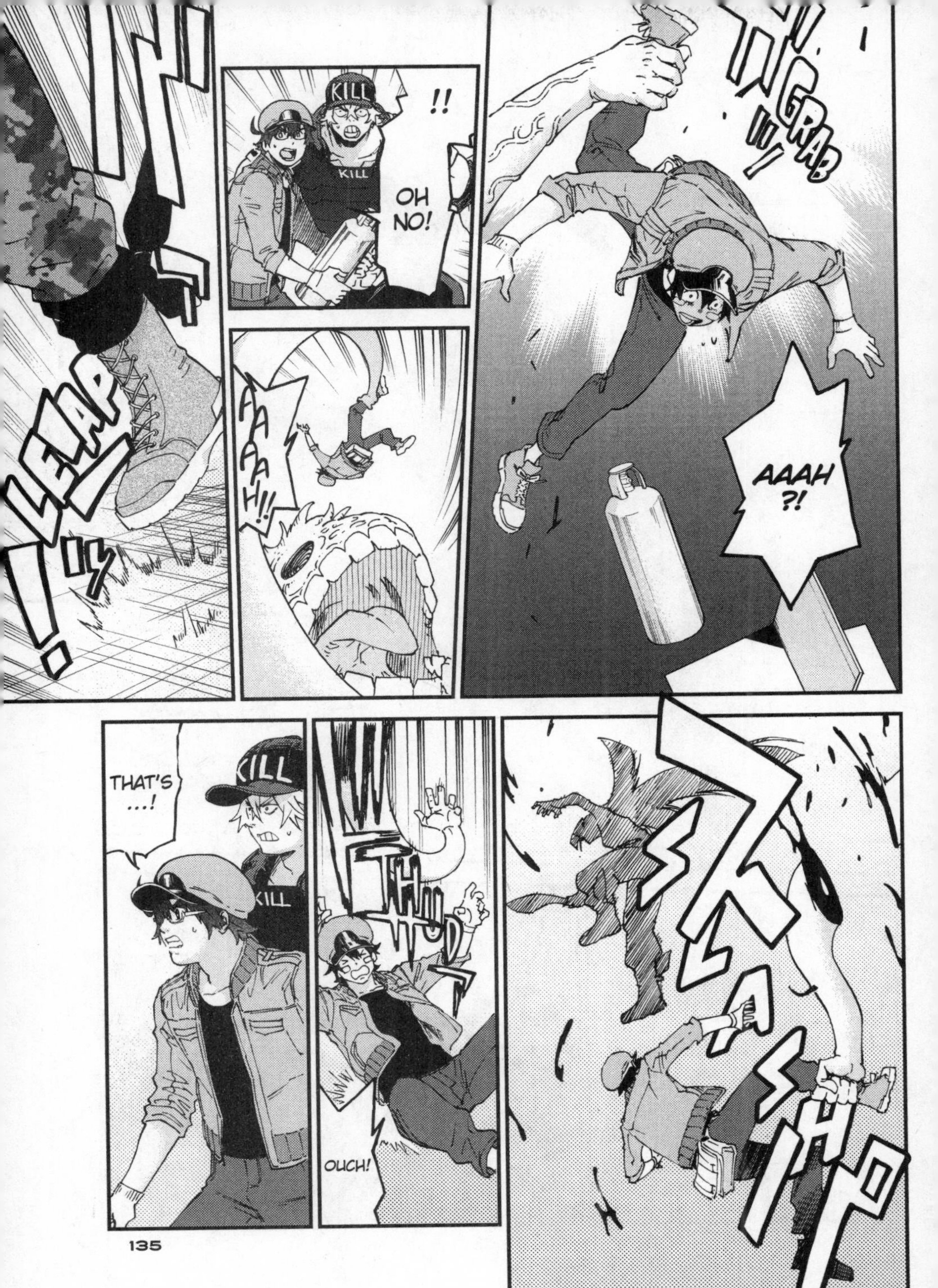
GRAB
AAAH ?!
!!
OH NO!
AAAAH!!
LEAP
!!
THUD
OUCH!
THAT'S ...!

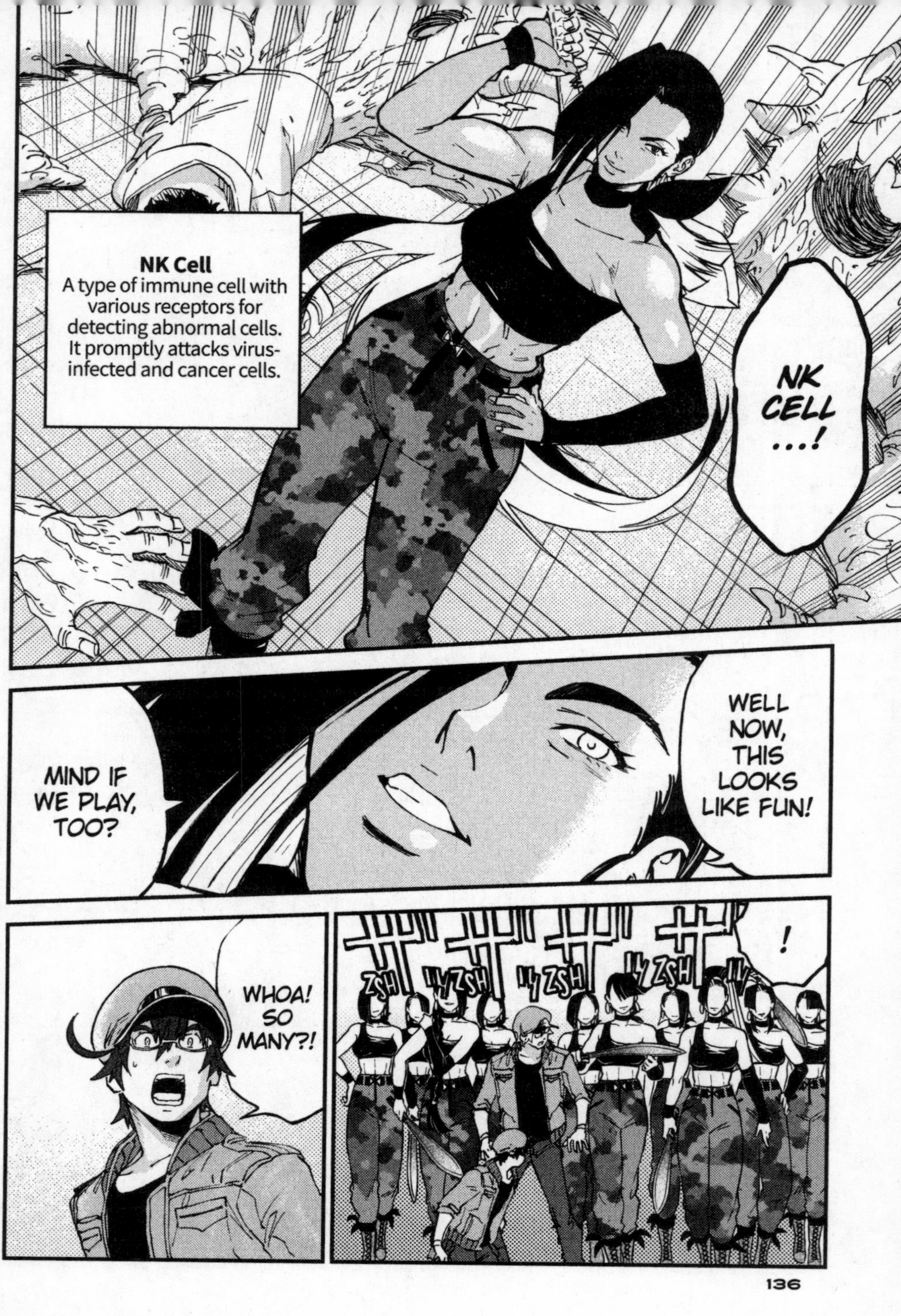
NK CELL ...!
NK Cell
A type of immune cell with various receptors for detecting abnormal cells. It promptly attacks virus-infected and cancer cells.
WELL NOW, THIS LOOKS LIKE FUN!
MIND IF WE PLAY, TOO?
!
ZSH
ZSH
ZSH
ZSH
WHOA! SO MANY?!

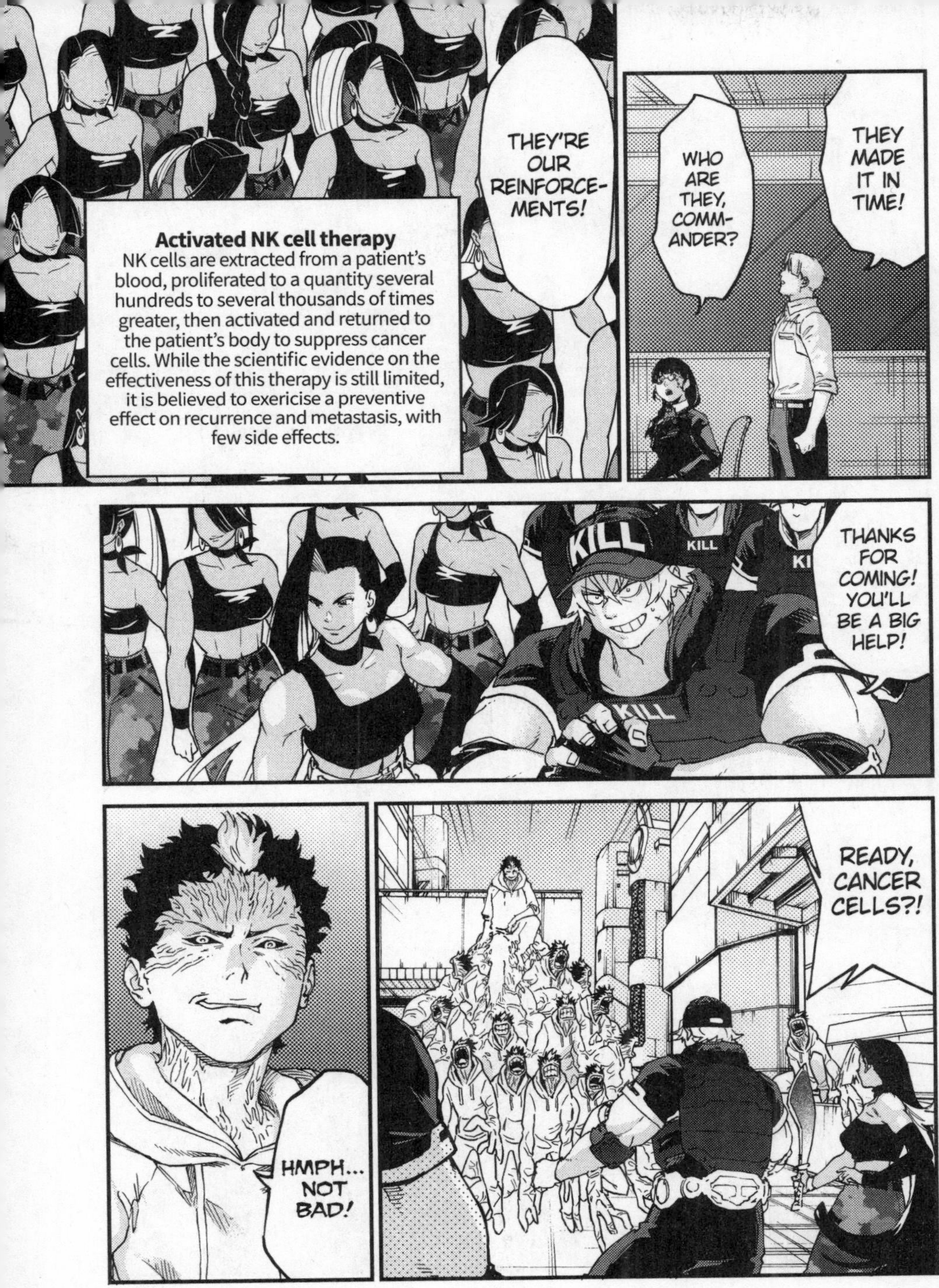
THEY MADE IT IN TIME!
WHO ARE THEY, COMMANDER?
THEY'RE OUR REINFORCEMENTS!
Activated NK cell therapy
NK cells are extracted from a patient's blood, proliferated to a quantity several hundreds to several thousands of times greater, then activated and returned to the patient's body to suppress cancer cells. While the scientific evidence on the effectiveness of this therapy is still limited, it is believed to exericise a preventive effect on recurrence and metastasis, with few side effects.
THANKS FOR COMING! YOU'LL BE A BIG HELP!
KILL
READY, CANCER CELLS?!
HMPH... NOT BAD!

THUD
THUD
THUD
THUD
WE'RE IN THIS, TOO...
IT'S NOT JUST THE IMMUNE CELLS...
THIS IS ABOUT ALL OF US!
WE CELLS ALL WANT THIS BODY...
LIVER
...TO BE HEALTHY...
NEPHRON
...AND...

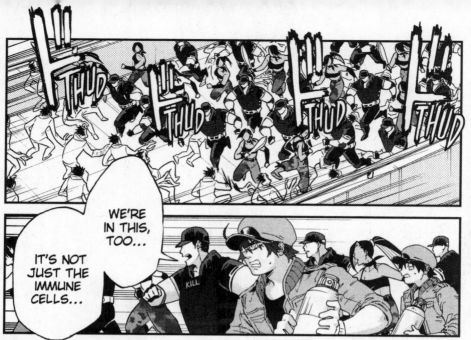

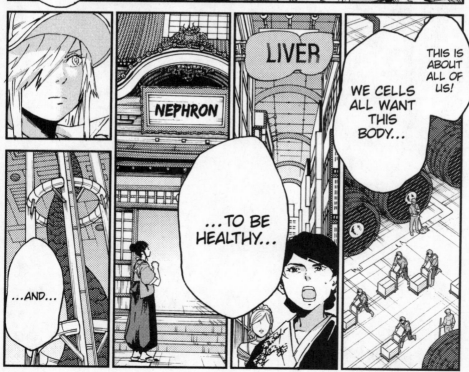

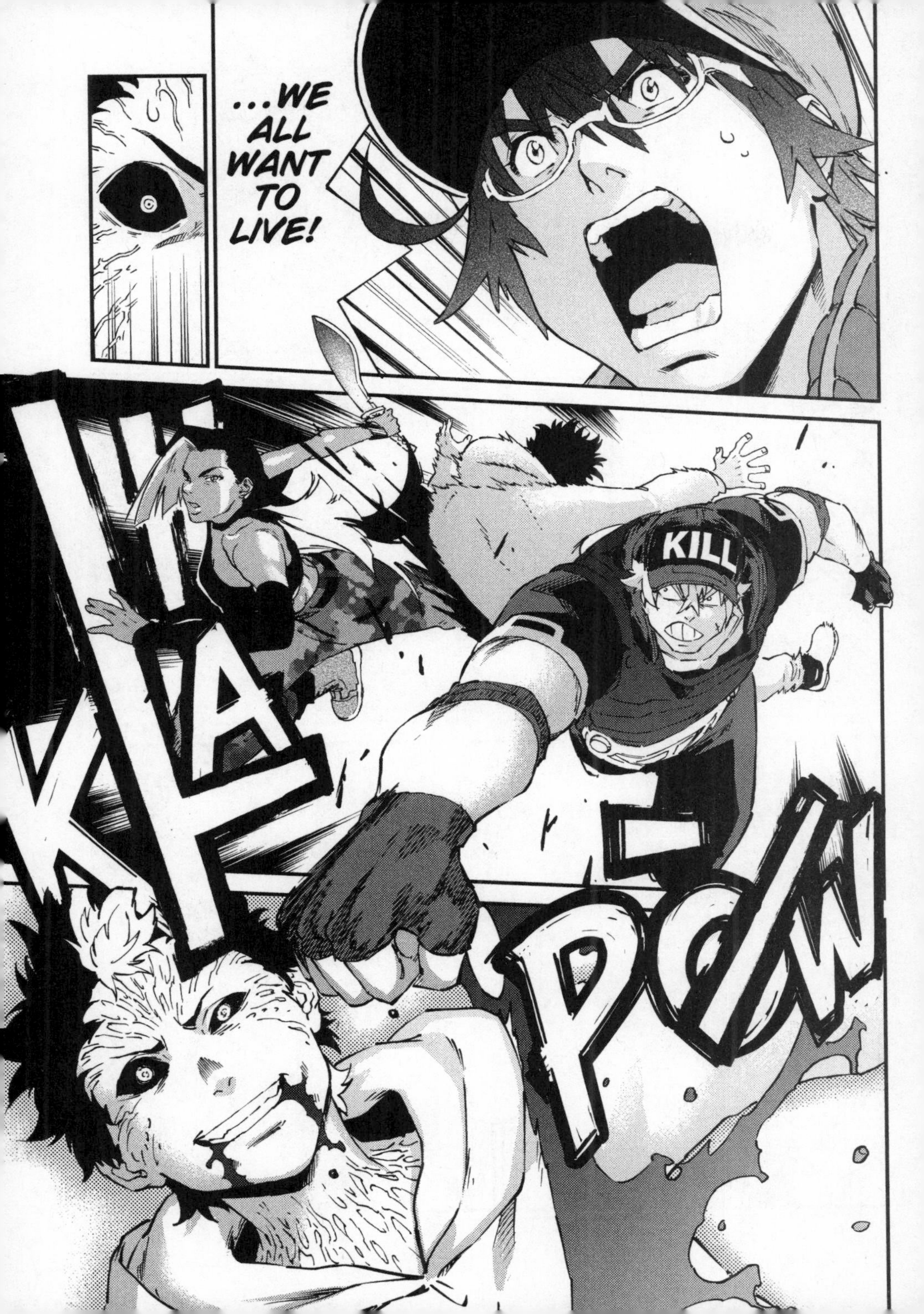
...WE ALL WANT TO LIVE!
KA-
POW
KILL

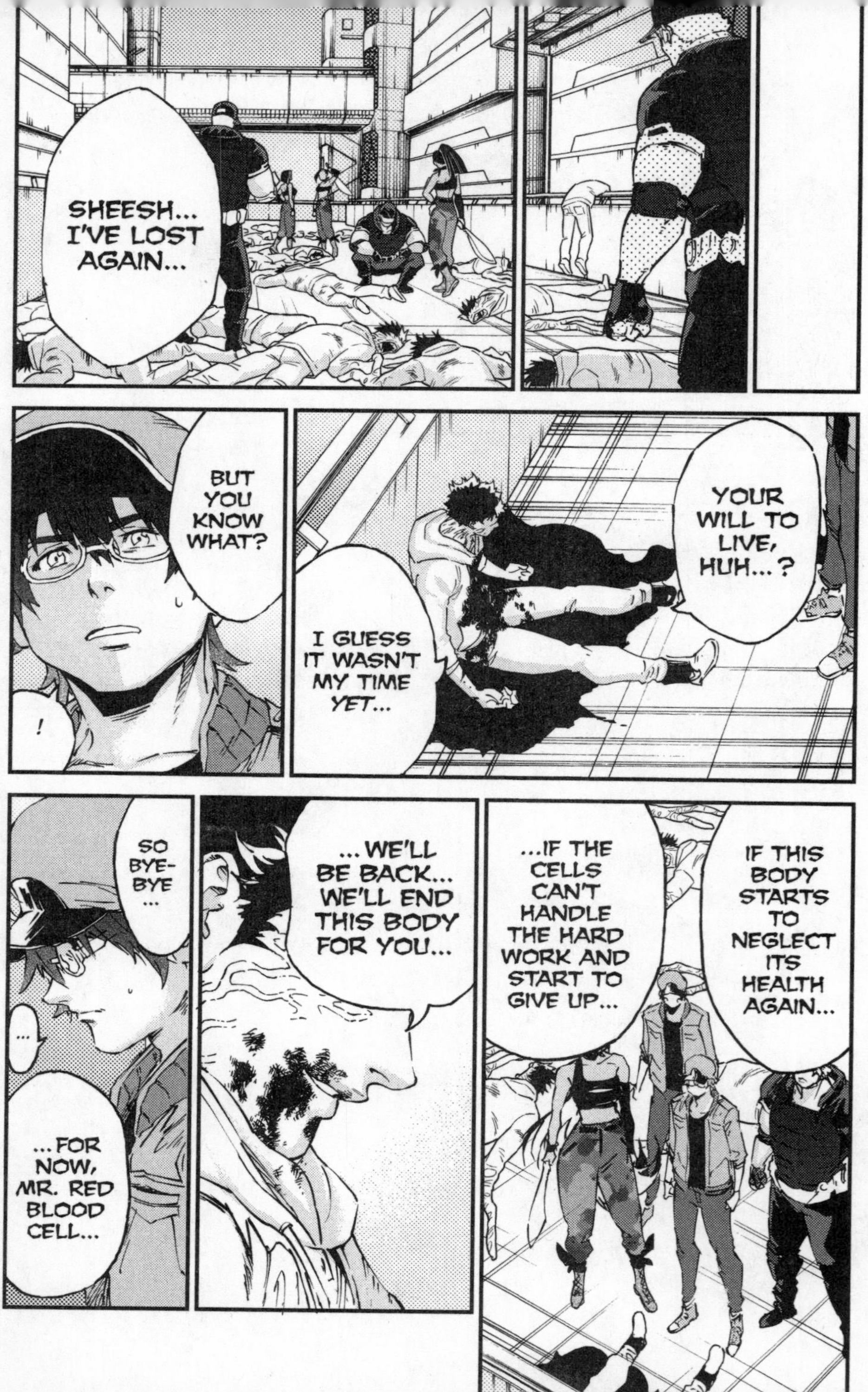
SHEESH... I'VE LOST AGAIN...
YOUR WILL TO LIVE, HUH...?
I GUESS IT WASN'T MY TIME YET...
BUT YOU KNOW WHAT?
!
IF THIS BODY STARTS TO NEGLECT ITS HEALTH AGAIN...
...IF THE CELLS CAN'T HANDLE THE HARD WORK AND START TO GIVE UP...
...WE'LL BE BACK... WE'LL END THIS BODY FOR YOU...
SO BYE-BYE...
...
...FOR NOW, MR. RED BLOOD CELL...

RAH

THE IMMUNE CELLS HAVE WIPED OUT MOST OF THE CANCER CELLS!

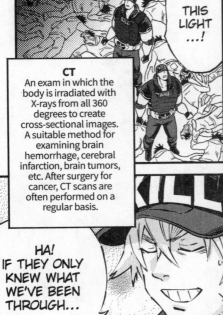

THIS LIGHT...!

**CT**
An exam in which the body is irradiated with X-rays from all 360 degrees to create cross-sectional images. A suitable method for examining brain hemorrhage, cerebral infarction, brain tumors, etc. After surgery for cancer, CT scans are often performed on a regular basis.

HA! IF THEY ONLY KNEW WHAT WE'VE BEEN THROUGH...

FLASH

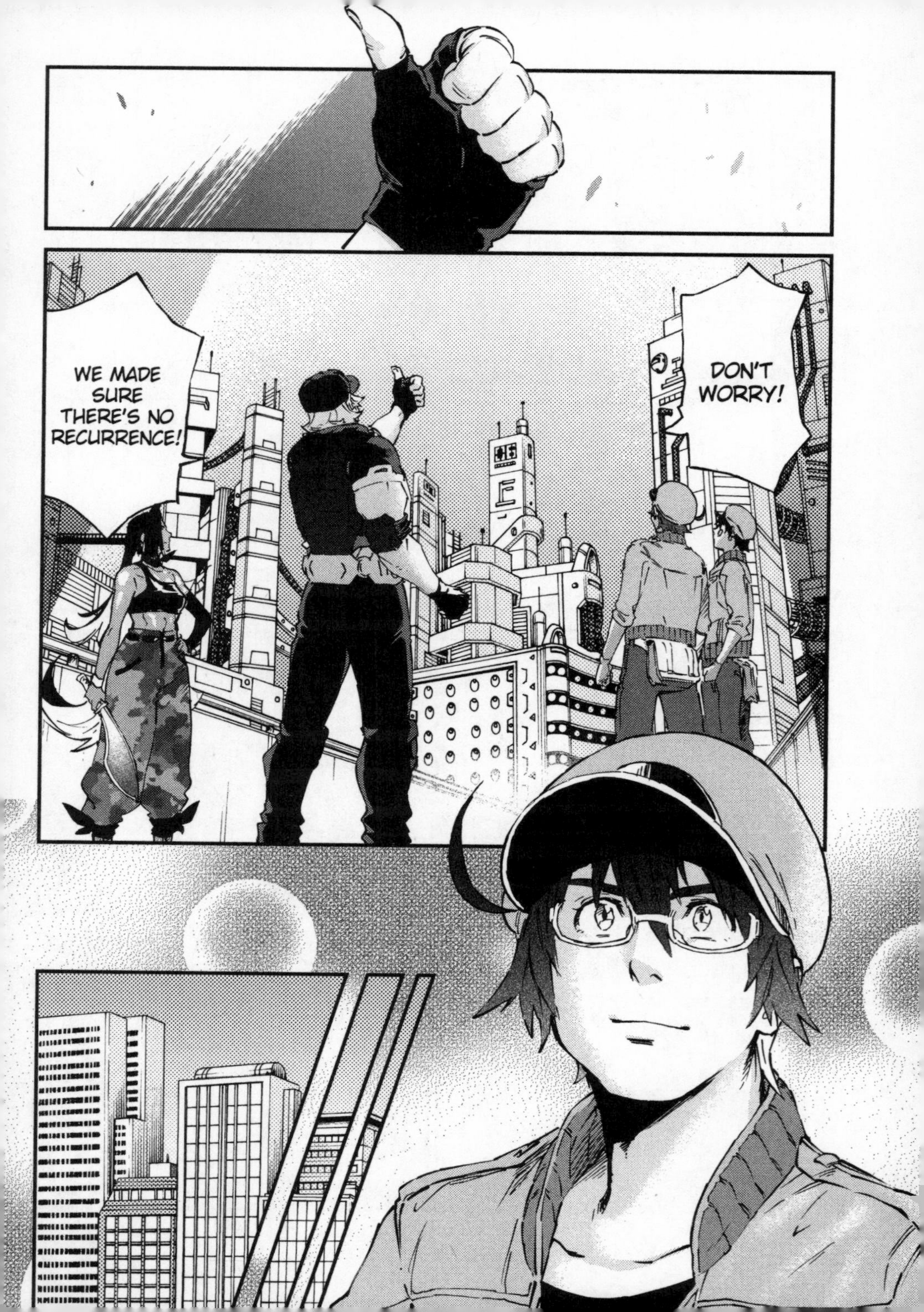
DON'T WORRY!
WE MADE SURE THERE'S NO RECURRENCE!

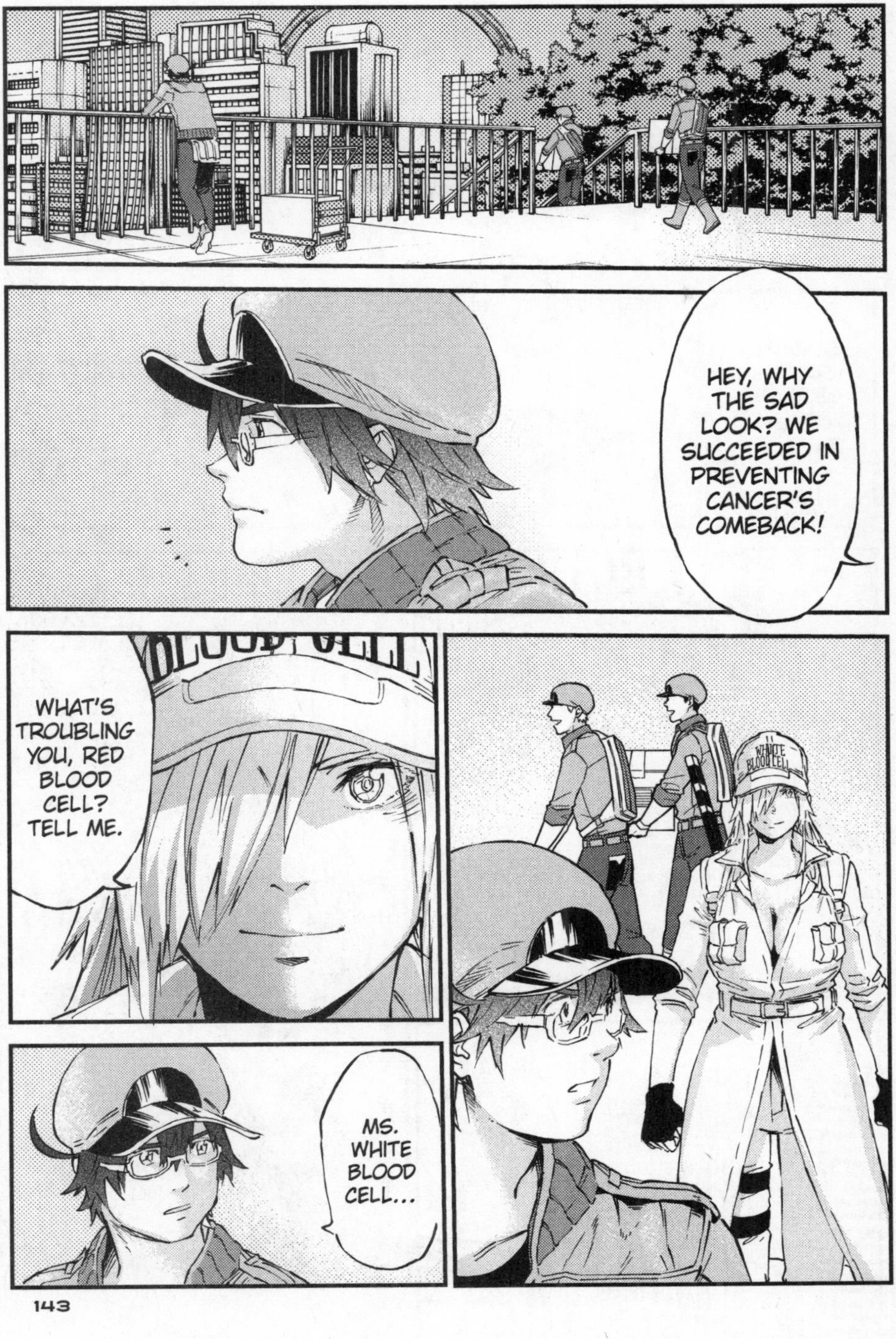
HEY, WHY THE SAD LOOK? WE SUCCEEDED IN PREVENTING CANCER'S COMEBACK!
WHITE BLOOD CELL
BLOOD CELL
WHAT'S TROUBLING YOU, RED BLOOD CELL? TELL ME.
MS. WHITE BLOOD CELL...

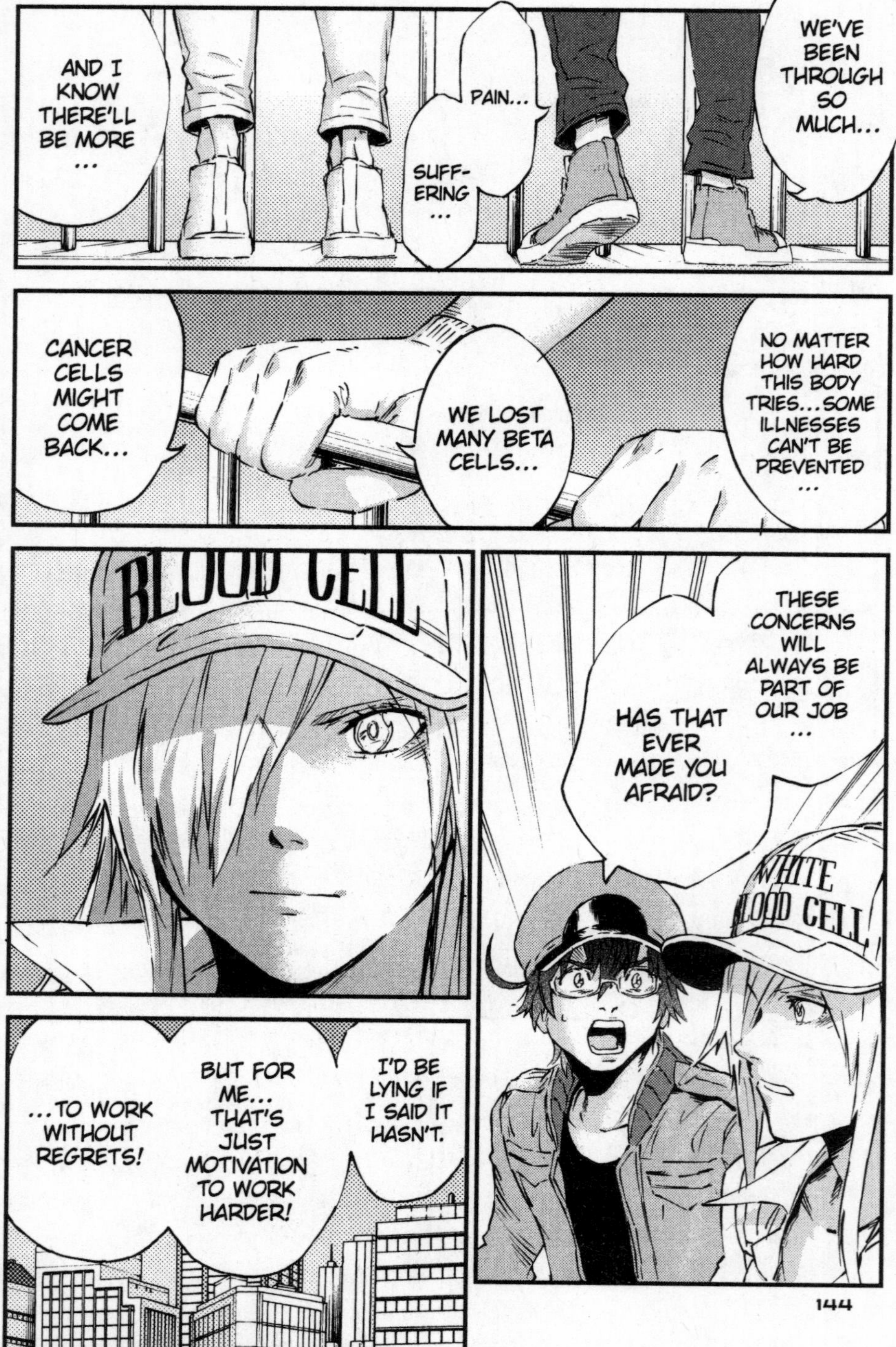
WE'VE BEEN THROUGH SO MUCH...
PAIN...
SUFF-ERING...
AND I KNOW THERE'LL BE MORE...
NO MATTER HOW HARD THIS BODY TRIES...SOME ILLNESSES CAN'T BE PREVENTED...
WE LOST MANY BETA CELLS...
CANCER CELLS MIGHT COME BACK...
THESE CONCERNS WILL ALWAYS BE PART OF OUR JOB...
HAS THAT EVER MADE YOU AFRAID?
BLOOD CELL
I'D BE LYING IF I SAID IT HASN'T.
BUT FOR ME... THAT'S JUST MOTIVATION TO WORK HARDER!
...TO WORK WITHOUT REGRETS!

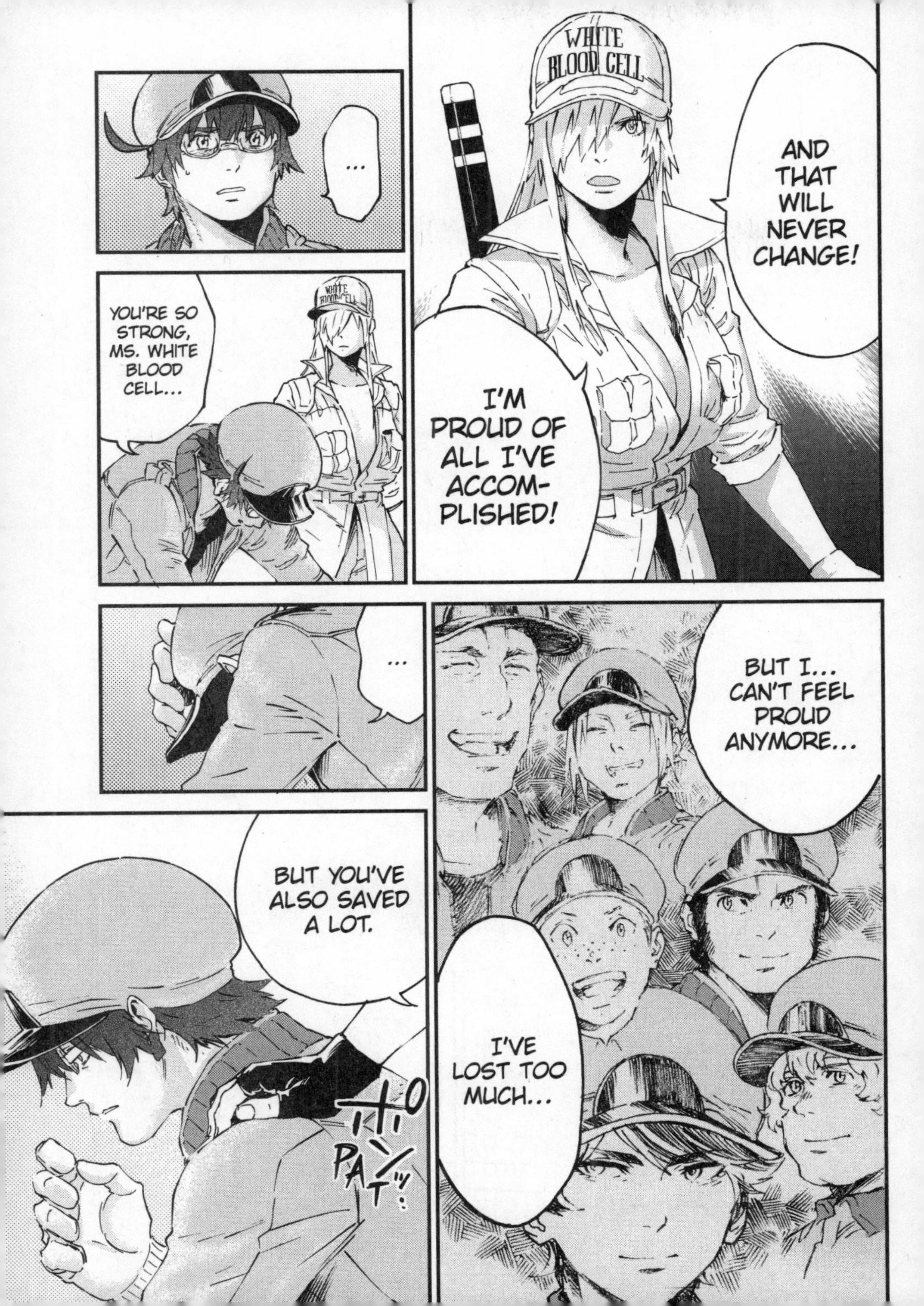
WHITE BLOOD CELL
AND THAT WILL NEVER CHANGE!
I'M PROUD OF ALL I'VE ACCOM-PLISHED!
...
YOU'RE SO STRONG, MS. WHITE BLOOD CELL...
BUT I... CAN'T FEEL PROUD ANYMORE...
I'VE LOST TOO MUCH...
...
BUT YOU'VE ALSO SAVED A LOT.
PAT

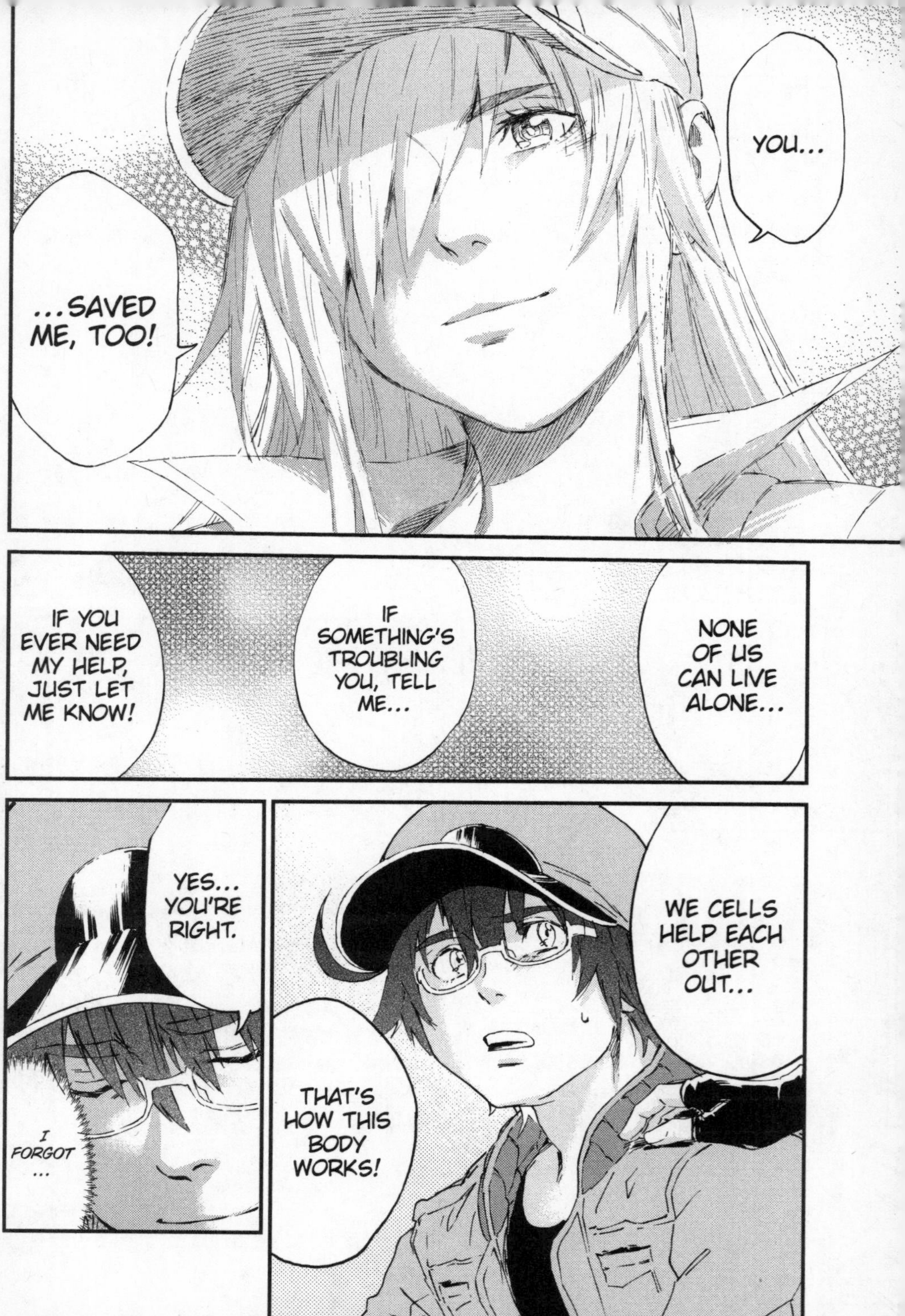
YOU...
...SAVED ME, TOO!
NONE OF US CAN LIVE ALONE...
IF SOMETHING'S TROUBLING YOU, TELL ME...
IF YOU EVER NEED MY HELP, JUST LET ME KNOW!
WE CELLS HELP EACH OTHER OUT...
THAT'S HOW THIS BODY WORKS!
YES... YOU'RE RIGHT.
I FORGOT...

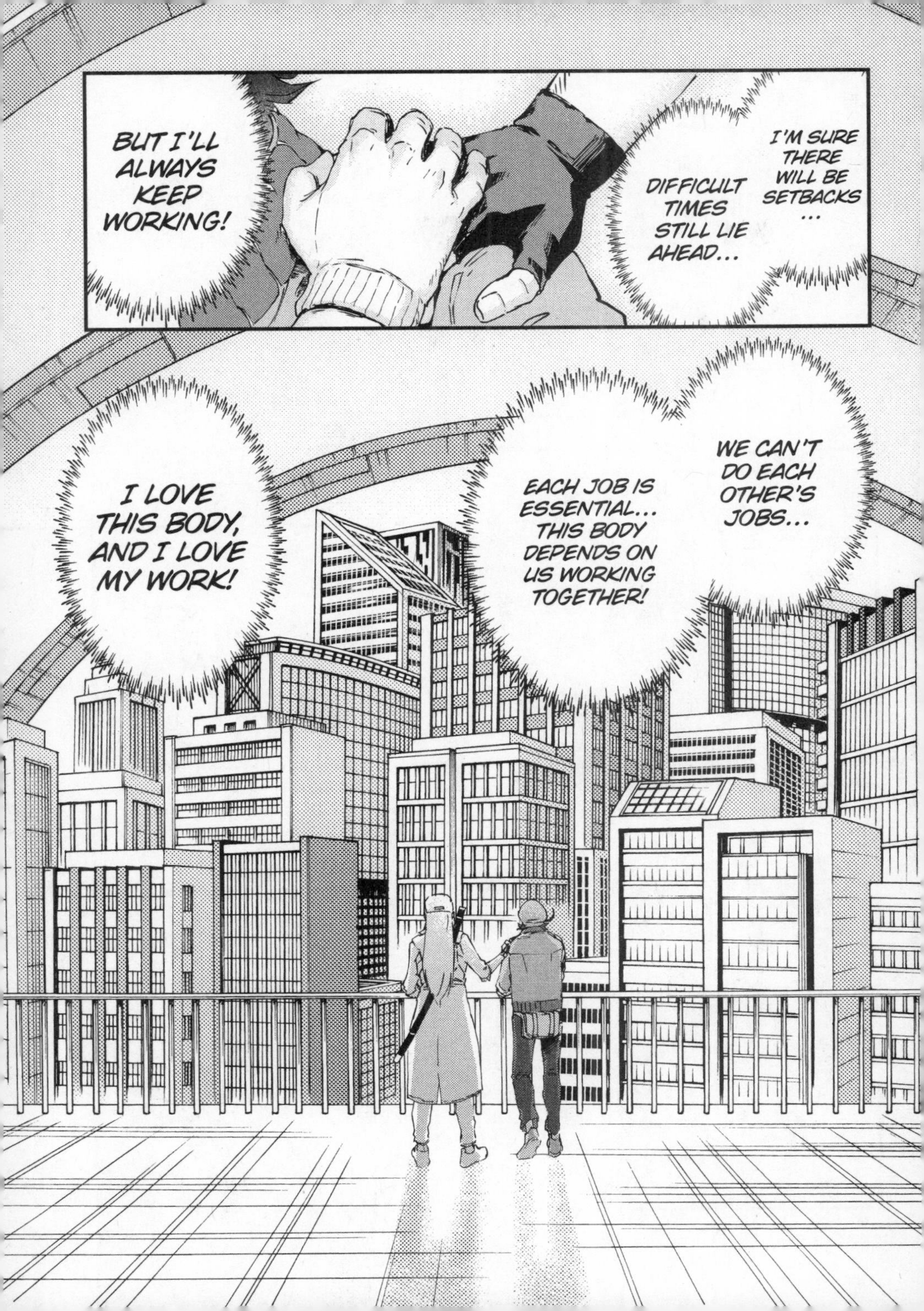
I'M SURE THERE WILL BE SETBACKS...
DIFFICULT TIMES STILL LIE AHEAD...
BUT I'LL ALWAYS KEEP WORKING!
WE CAN'T DO EACH OTHER'S JOBS...
EACH JOB IS ESSENTIAL... THIS BODY DEPENDS ON US WORKING TOGETHER!
I LOVE THIS BODY, AND I LOVE MY WORK!

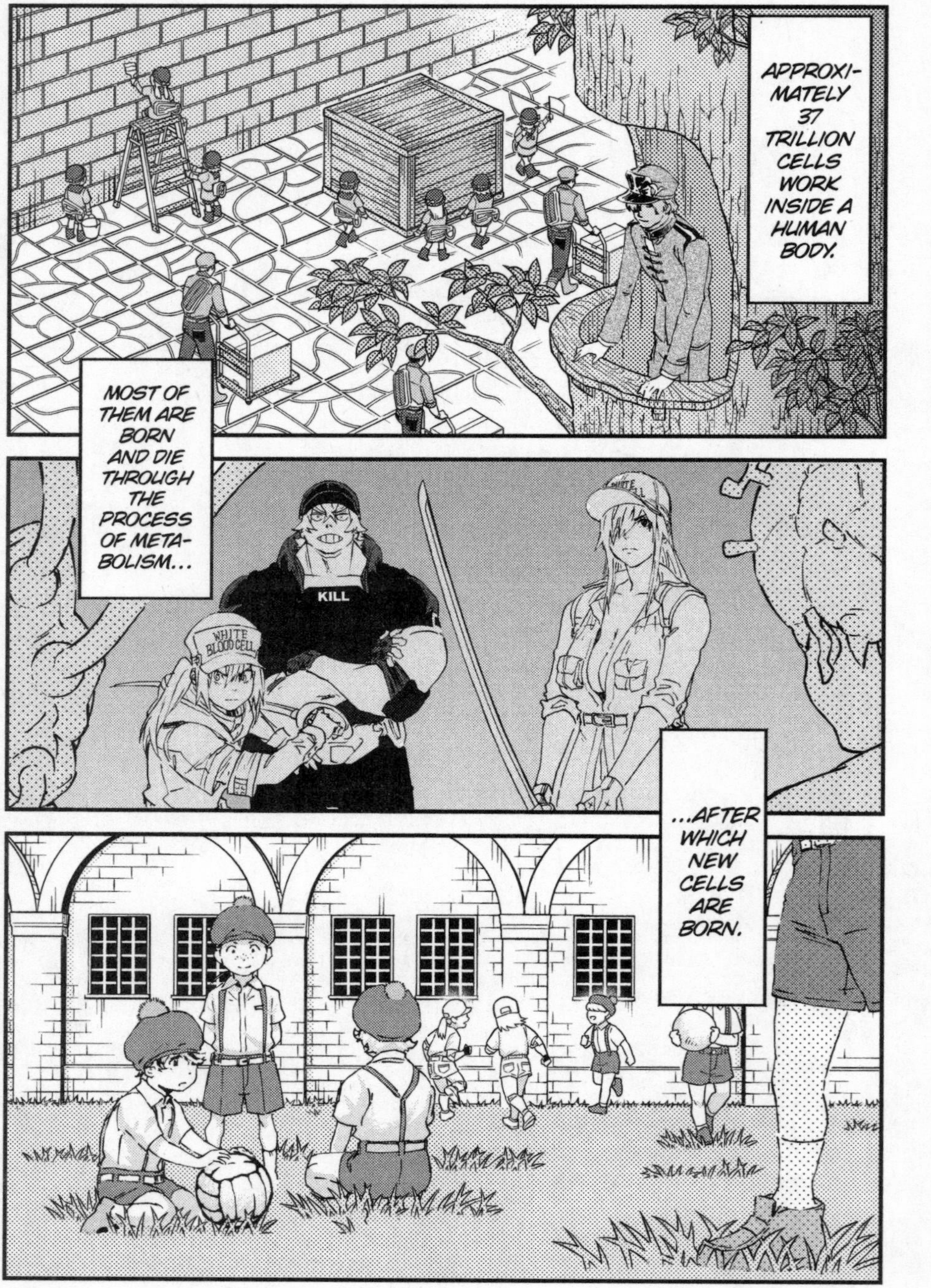
APPROXI-MATELY 37 TRILLION CELLS WORK INSIDE A HUMAN BODY.
MOST OF THEM ARE BORN AND DIE THROUGH THE PROCESS OF META-BOLISM...
KILL
WHITE BLOOD CELL
...AFTER WHICH NEW CELLS ARE BORN.

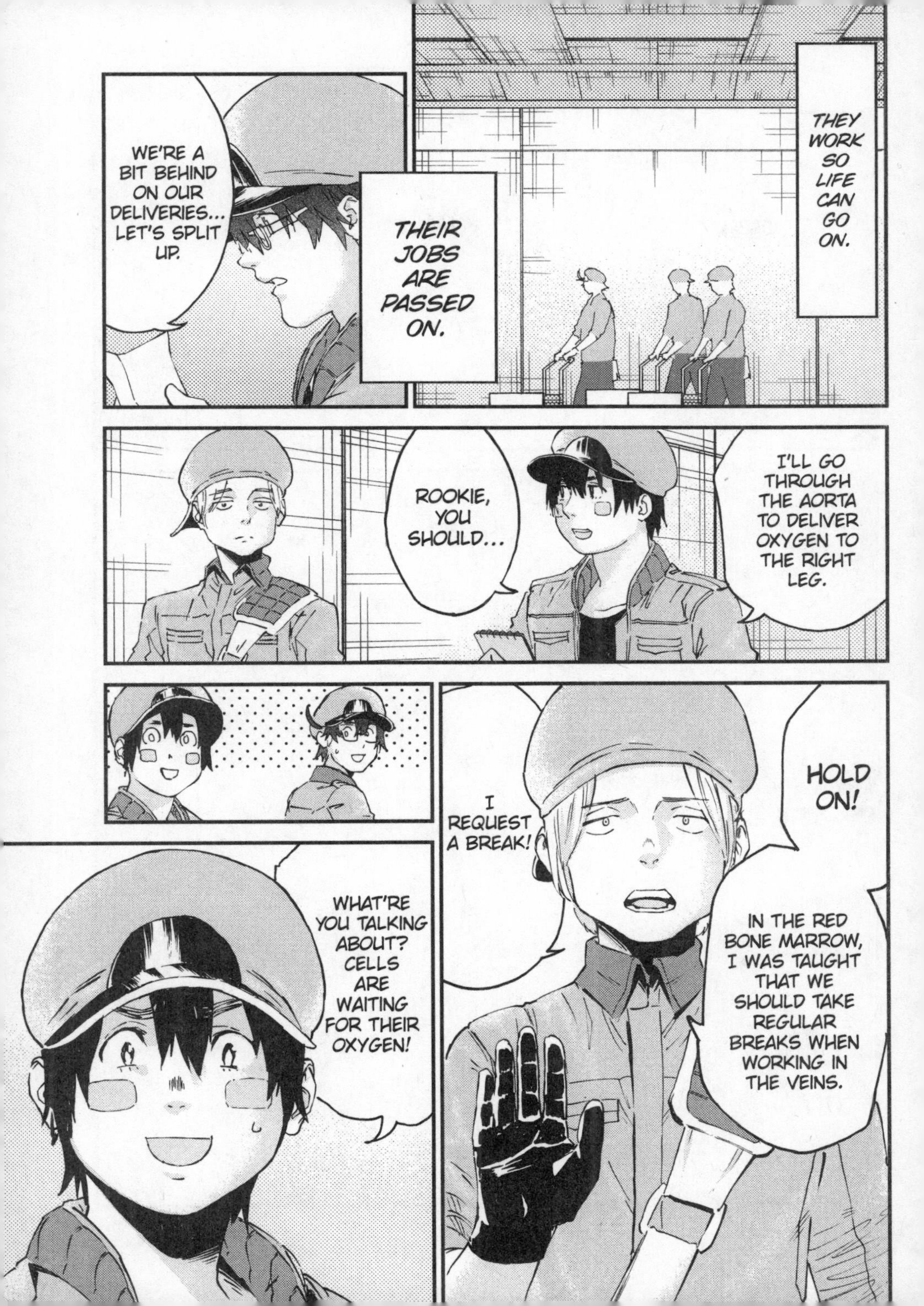
THEY WORK SO LIFE CAN GO ON.
THEIR JOBS ARE PASSED ON.
WE'RE A BIT BEHIND ON OUR DELIVERIES... LET'S SPLIT UP.
I'LL GO THROUGH THE AORTA TO DELIVER OXYGEN TO THE RIGHT LEG.
ROOKIE, YOU SHOULD...
HOLD ON!
I REQUEST A BREAK!
IN THE RED BONE MARROW, I WAS TAUGHT THAT WE SHOULD TAKE REGULAR BREAKS WHEN WORKING IN THE VEINS.
WHAT'RE YOU TALKING ABOUT? CELLS ARE WAITING FOR THEIR OXYGEN!

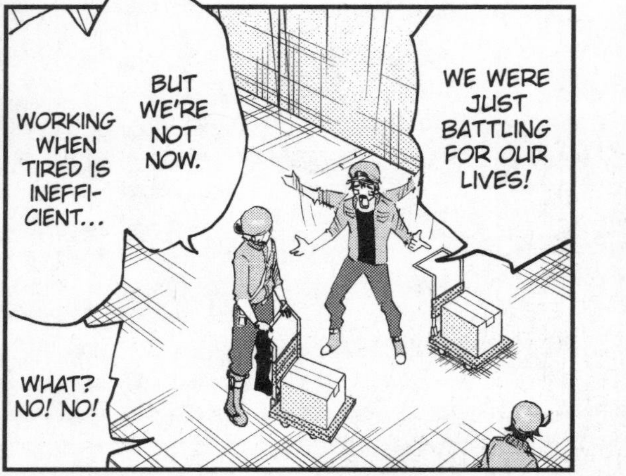
WE WERE JUST BATTLING FOR OUR LIVES!
BUT WE'RE NOT NOW.
WORKING WHEN TIRED IS INEFFICIENT...
WHAT? NO! NO!

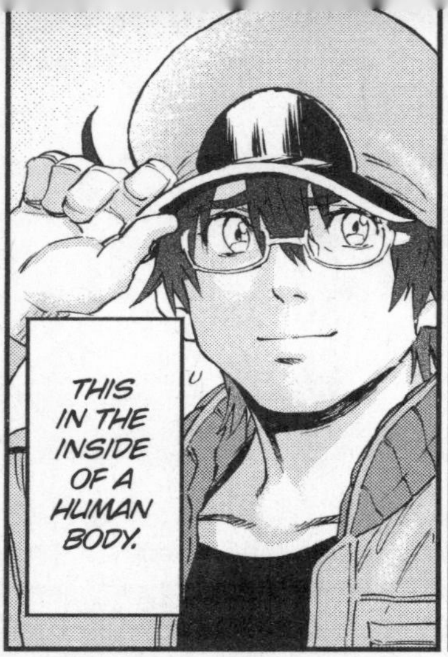
THIS IN THE INSIDE OF A HUMAN BODY.

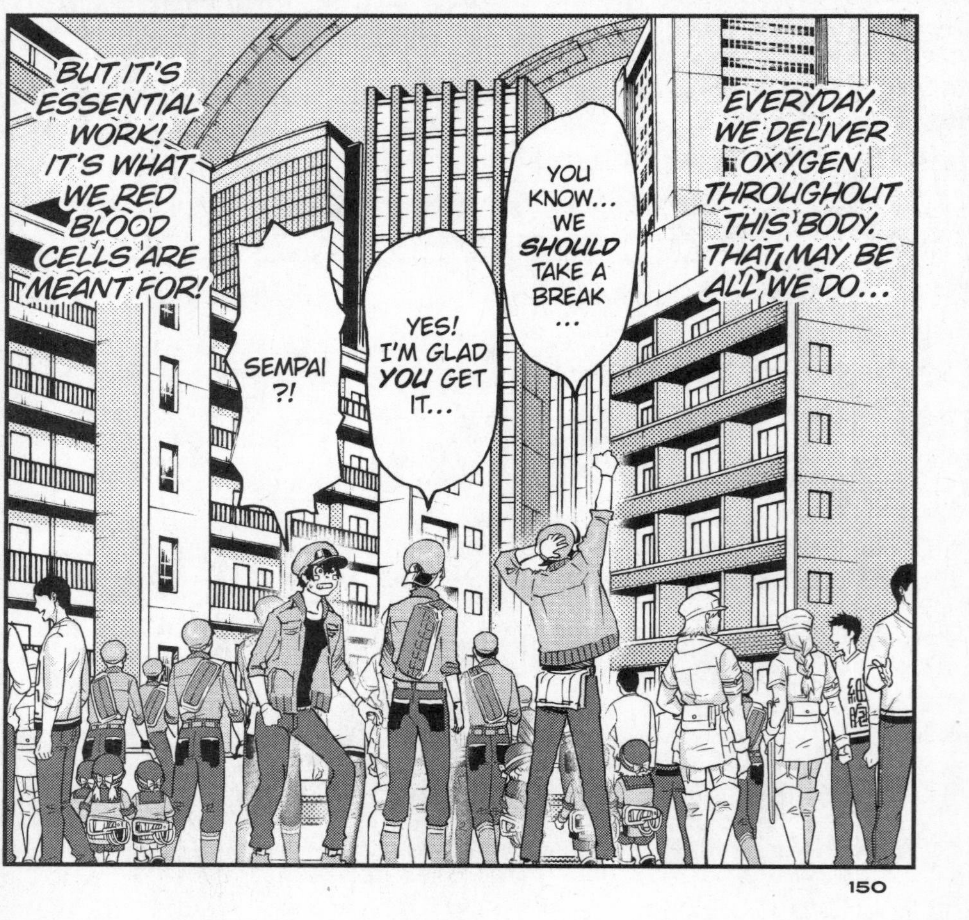
EVERYDAY, WE DELIVER OXYGEN THROUGHOUT THIS BODY. THAT MAY BE ALL WE DO...
YOU KNOW... WE SHOULD TAKE A BREAK...
YES! I'M GLAD YOU GET IT...
SEMPAI ?!
BUT IT'S ESSENTIAL WORK! IT'S WHAT WE RED BLOOD CELLS ARE MEANT FOR!

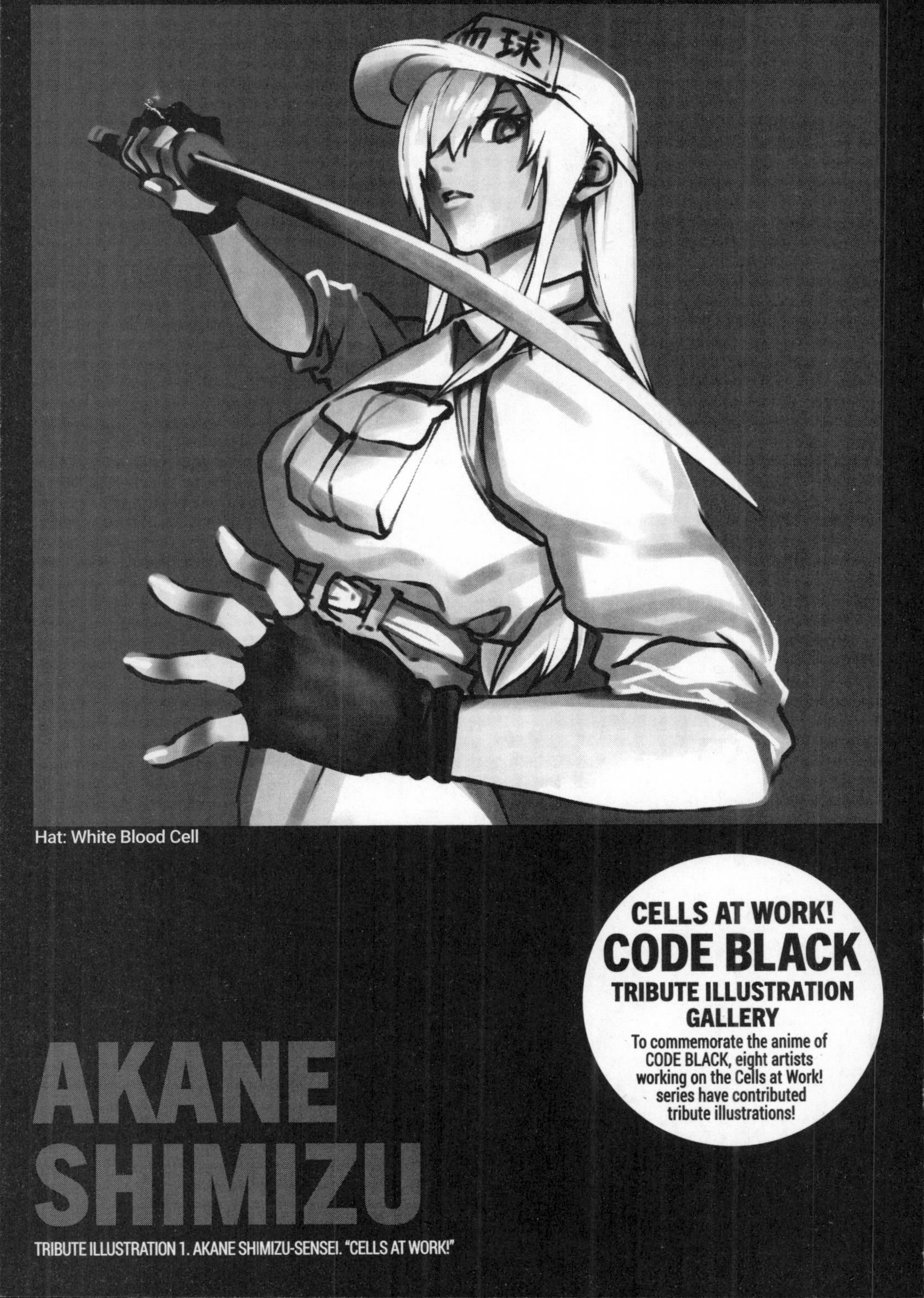

Hat: White Blood Cell

**CELLS AT WORK!**

# CODE BLACK

**TRIBUTE ILLUSTRATION GALLERY**

To commemorate the anime of CODE BLACK, eight artists working on the Cells at Work! series have contributed tribute illustrations!

# AKANE SHIMIZU

TRIBUTE ILLUSTRATION 1. AKANE SHIMIZU-SENSEI. "CELLS AT WORK!"

[redacted]

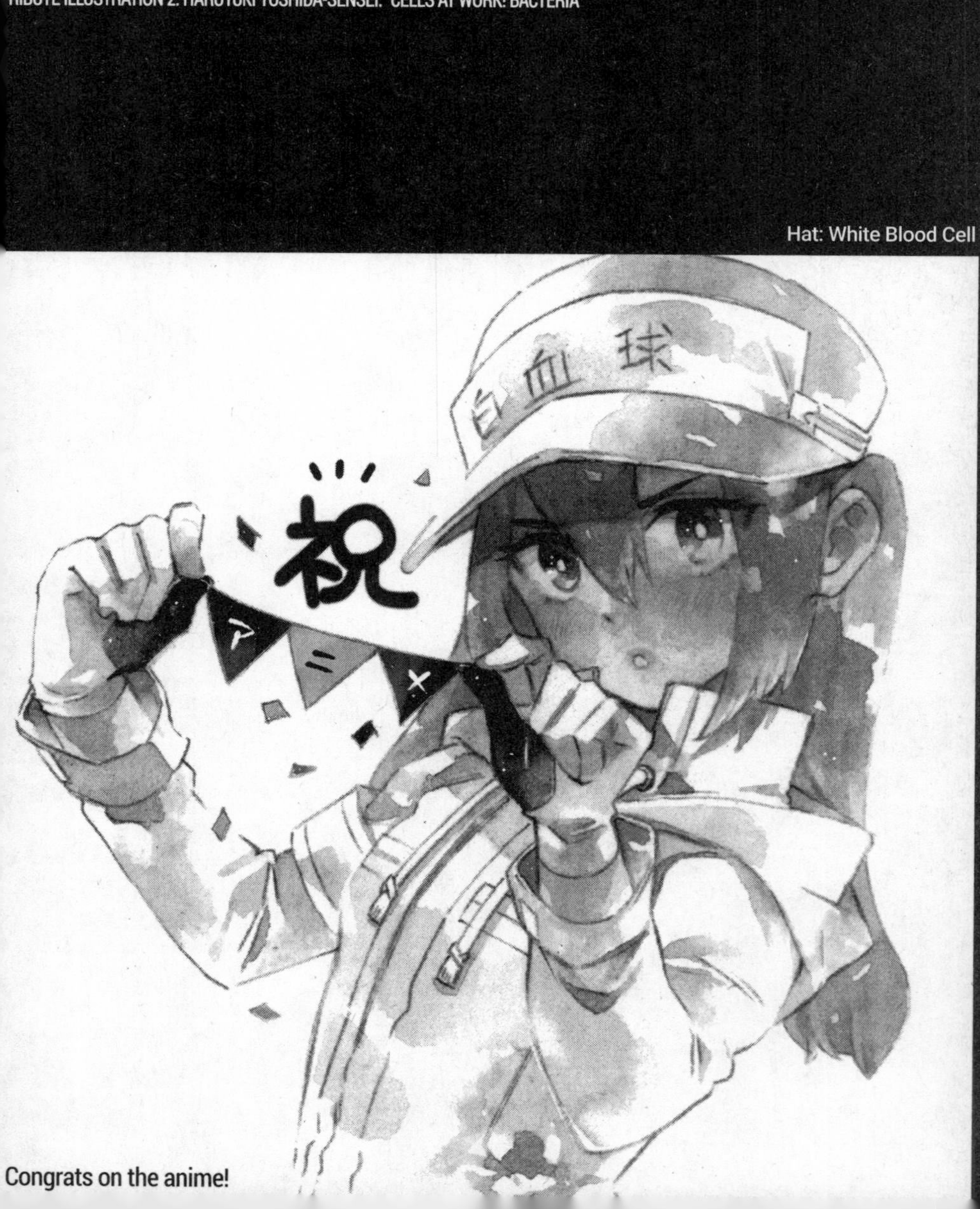
Hat: White Blood Cell
白血球
祝
アニメ
Congrats on the anime!

Congrats on the anime adaptation of CODE BLACK!

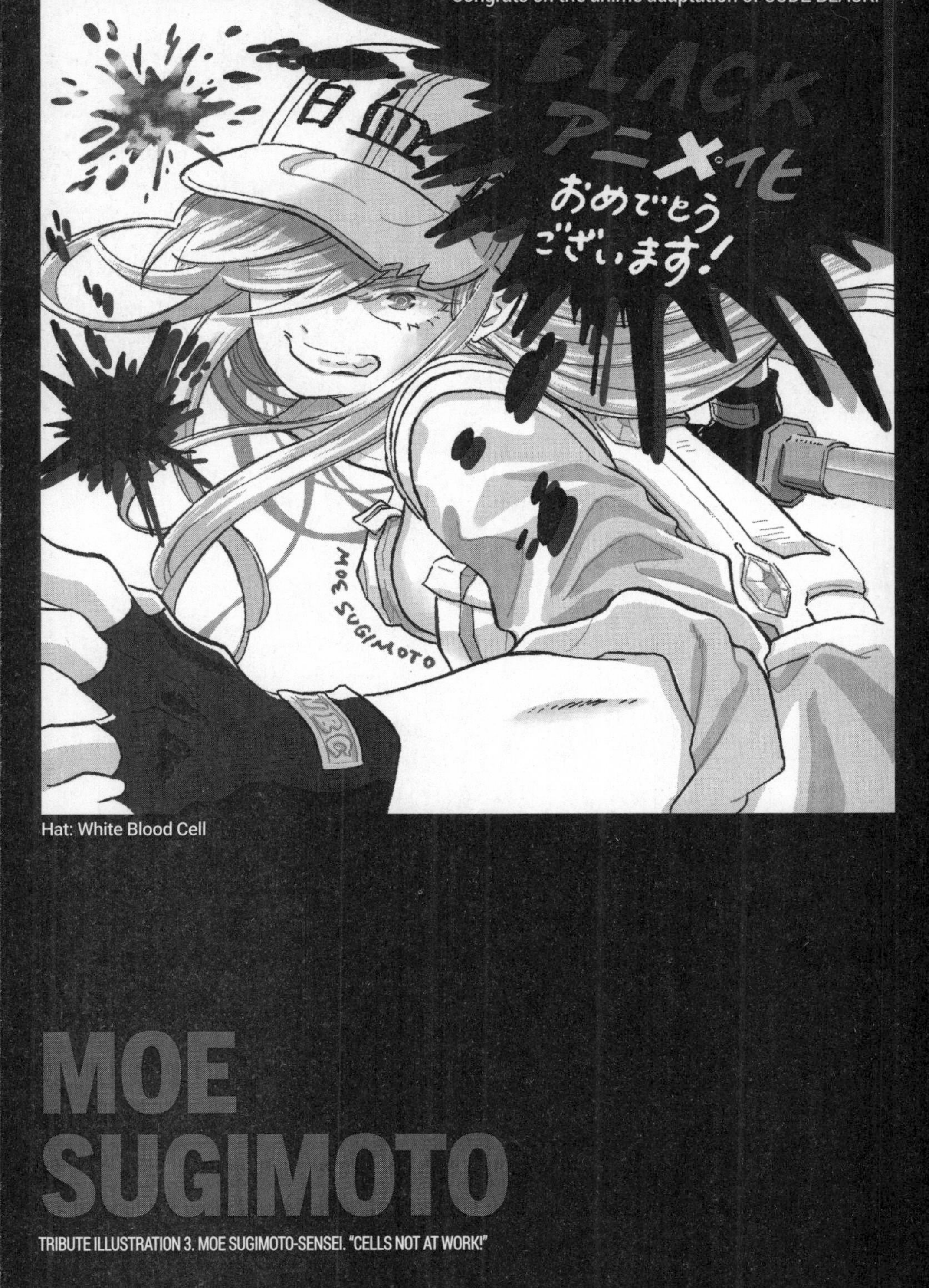
BLACK
アニメ化
おめでとうございます！
白血
MOE SUGIMOTO
WBC
Hat: White Blood Cell

# MOE SUGIMOTO

TRIBUTE ILLUSTRATION 3. MOE SUGIMOTO-SENSEI. "CELLS NOT AT WORK!"

# YASU

TRIBUTE ILLUSTRATION 4. YASU-SENSEI. "PLATELETS AT WORK!"

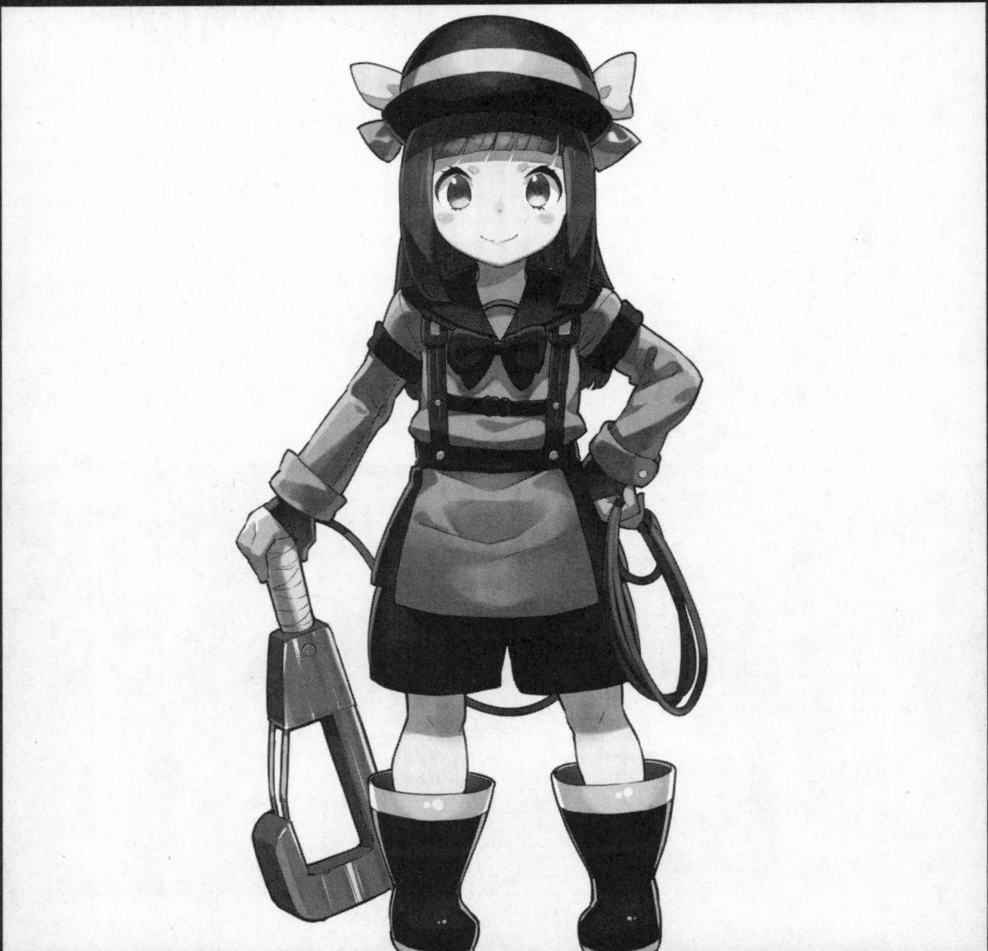

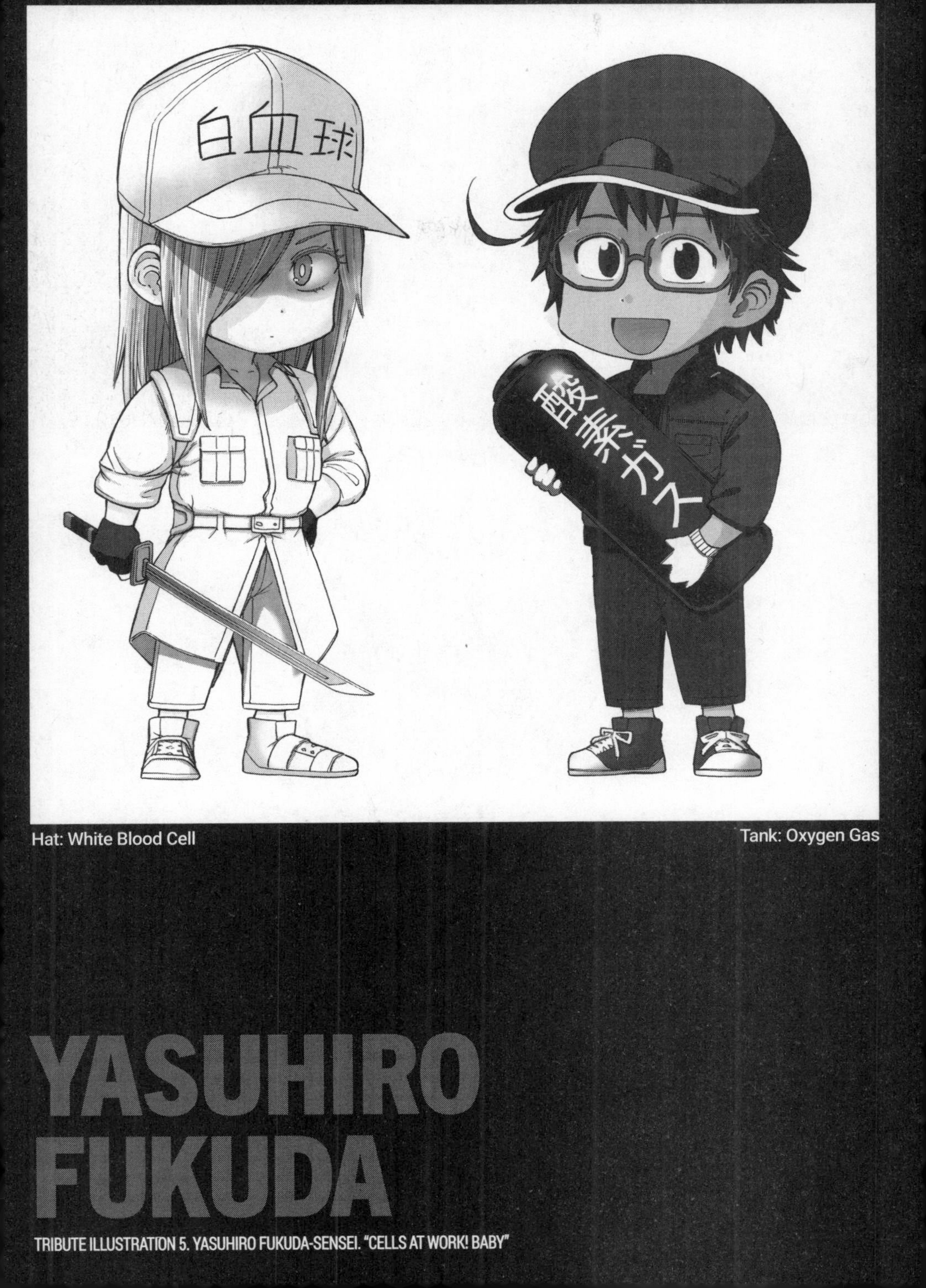
白血球
酸素ガス

Hat: White Blood Cell

Tank: Oxygen Gas

# YASUHIRO FUKUDA

TRIBUTE ILLUSTRATION 5. YASUHIRO FUKUDA-SENSEI. "CELLS AT WORK! BABY"

# AKARI OTOKAWA

TRIBUTE ILLUSTRATION 6. AKARI OTOKAWA-SENSEI. "CELLS AT WORK! LADY"

Cells at Work! CODE BLACK Hat: White Blood Cell Congrats on the anime adaptation!

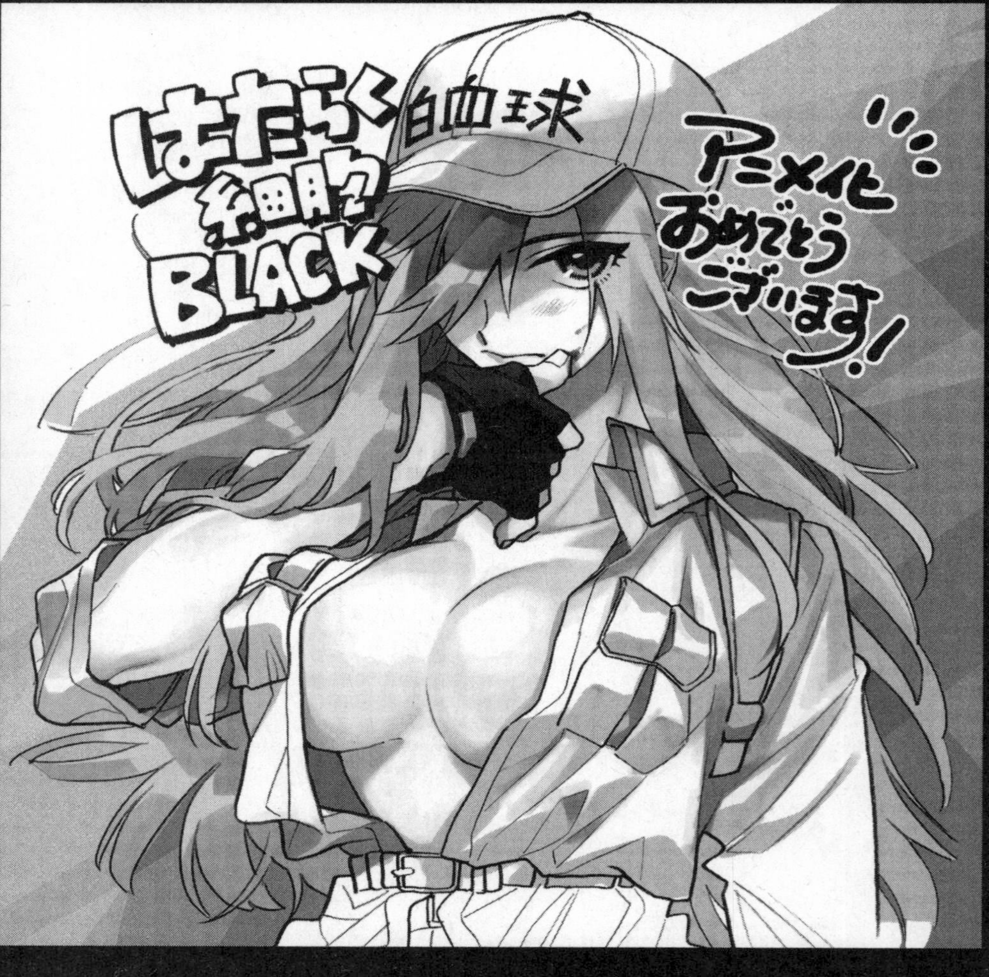
はたらく細胞BLACK
白血球
アニメ化おめでとうございます！

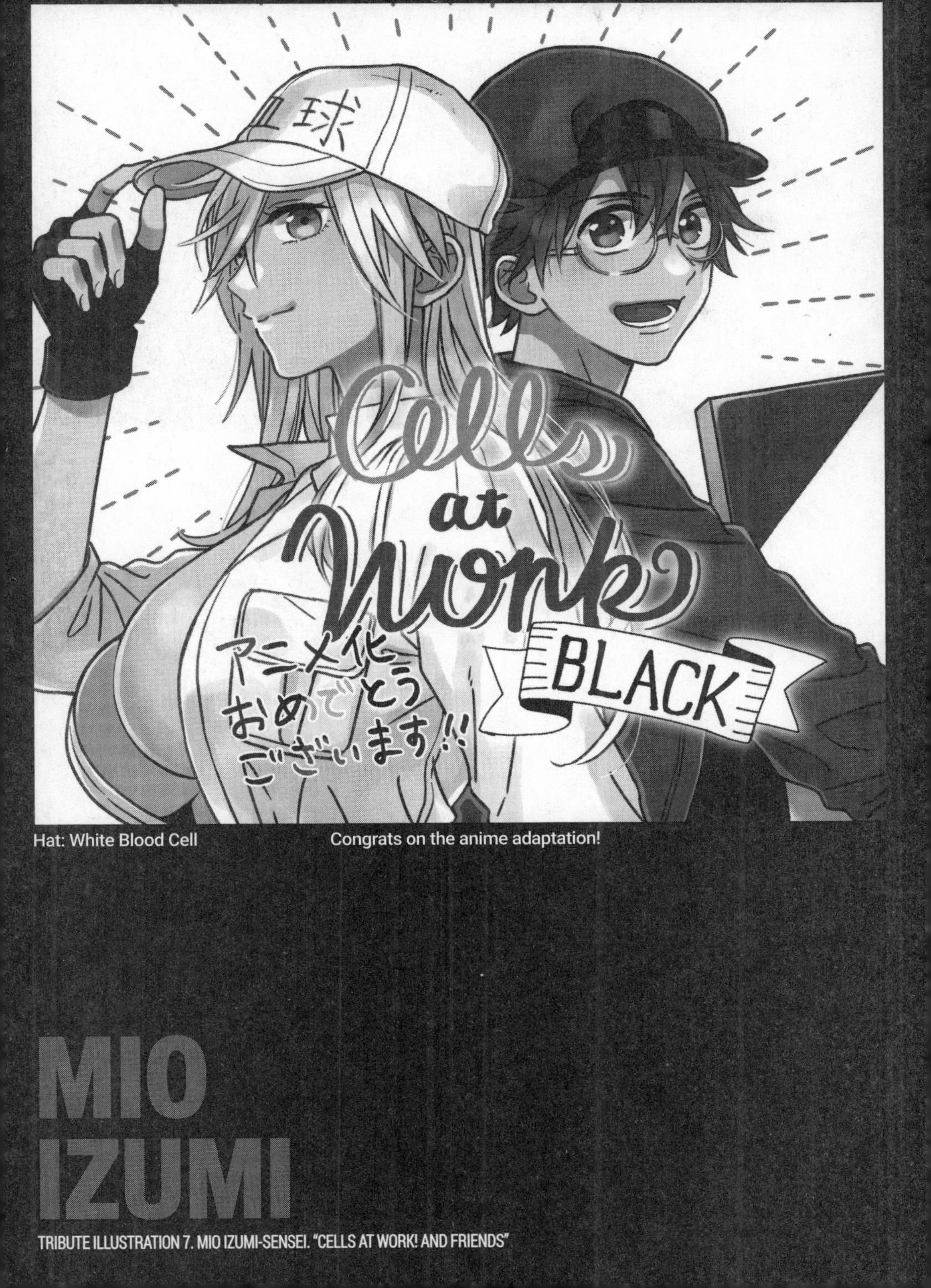
血球
Cells at Work
BLACK
アニメ化
おめでとう
ございます!!

Hat: White Blood Cell

Congrats on the anime adaptation!

# MIO IZUMI

TRIBUTE ILLUSTRATION 7. MIO IZUMI-SENSEI. "CELLS AT WORK! AND FRIENDS"

# TETSUJI KANIE

TRIBUTE ILLUSTRATION 8. TETSUJI KANIE-SENSEI. "CELLS AT WORK! WHITE"

Hat: White Blood Cell

Congrats on the TV anime!

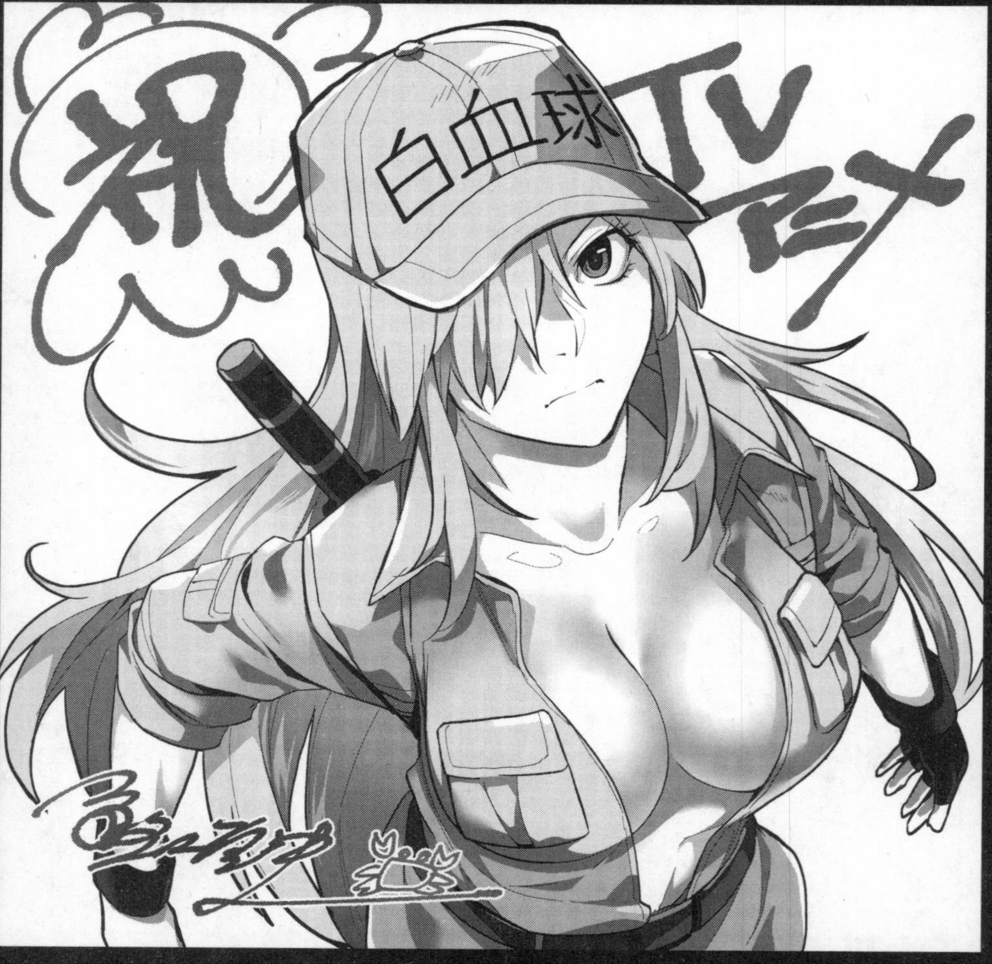

祝
TV
白血球

A Kodansha Comics Trade Paperback Original
*Cells at Work! CODE BLACK 8* copyright © 2021 Shigemitsu Harada/Issey Hatsuyoshiya/Akane Shimizu
English translation copyright © 2022 Shigemitsu Harada/Issey Hatsuyoshiya/Akane Shimizu

Published in the United States by Kodansha Comics, an imprint of Kodansha USA Publishing, LLC, New York.

Publication rights for this English edition arranged through Kodansha Ltd., Tokyo.

First published in Japan in 2021 by Kodansha Ltd., Tokyo as *Hataraku Saibou BLACK, volume 8*.

ISBN 978-1-64651-220-1

Printed in the United States of America.

www.kodansha.us

1st Printing
Translation: Iyasu Adair Nagata
Lettering: E. K. Weaver
Editing: Ryan Holmberg
Kodansha Comics edition cover design by Phil Balsman

Publisher: Kiichiro Sugawara

Director of publishing services: Ben Applegate
Associate director, publishing operations: Stephen Pakula
Publishing services managing editors: Madison Salters, Alanna Ruse
Production managers: Emi Lotto, Angela Zurlo

CPAC